SCRIBBLIN' FOR A LIVIN'

SCRIBBLIN' FOR A LIVIN'

MARK TWAIN'S PIVOTAL PERIOD IN BUFFALO

THOMAS J. REIGSTAD
FOREWORD BY NEIL SCHMITZ

June 21, 2013
For Charlie Clark,
To celebrate Twain's
association with
Buffalo.
All Best Wishes,
Tom Reigstad

Prometheus Books

59 John Glenn Drive
Amherst, New York 14228–2119

Published 2013 by Prometheus Books

Cover image of Mark Twain portrait by Upson and Simson, 1869,
from the Mark Twain Project, University of California, Berkeley

Cover image of C. L. Pond aerial photograph,
courtesy of the Lower Lakes Marine Historical Society

Cover image of *Buffalo Express* from the Buffalo and Erie County Historical Society;
Buffalo State College

Cover design by Jacqueline Nasso Cooke

Inquiries should be addressed to
Prometheus Books
59 John Glenn Drive
Amherst, New York 14228–2119
VOICE: 716–691–0133 • FAX: 716–691–0137
WWW.PROMETHEUSBOOKS.COM

17 16 15 14 13   5 4 3 2 1

Library of Congress Cataloging-in-Publication Data

Reigstad, Thomas J.
    Scribblin' for a livin' : Mark Twain's pivitol period in Buffalo / by Thomas J. Reigstad.
        p. cm.
    Includes bibliographical references and index.
    ISBN 978-1-61614-591-0 (pbk. : alk. paper) • ISBN 978-1-61614-592-7 (ebook)
        1. Twain, Mark, 1835-1910—Homes and haunts—New York (State)—Buffalo.
2. Authors, American—Homes and haunts—New York (State)—Buffalo. 3. Authors, American—19th century—Biography. 4. Buffalo (N.Y.)—Intellectual life—19th century. 5. Buffalo (N.Y.)—Biography. I. Title.

PS1334.R45 2013
818'.409--dc23
    [B]

2012044619

This book is dedicated to the memory of my wife,
Maryanne LePage Reigstad

CONTENTS

Foreword   9
     by Dr. Neil Schmitz

Prologue: I Will Always Confine Myself Strictly to the Truth   15

Acknowledgments   25

Introduction: Offer the New Editor a Chair   29

1. The Boys of the *Express*   35

2. I Would Rather Scribble   57

3. This Caravansery   81

4. My Rascally Pilgrimage   93

5. Aladdin's Palace   111

6. Writing for Enjoyment, as Well as Profit   149

7. Toppling Pyramids   171

Epilogue: This Renewal of the Old Times   189

8   CONTENTS

Appendix 1. "Mark Twain and Niagara"   207

Appendix 2. "In Trouble"   209

Appendix 3. "Mark Twain in a Fix"   211

Appendix 4. Six Illustrations by John Harrison Mills   213

Appendix 5. Police Court Columns   221

Appendix 6. People and Things Columns   231

Appendix 7. "Arthur"   275

Appendix 8. "Innocence at Home; Or Hunting a Hero in Washington"   281

Appendix 9. From Page One, *Buffalo Morning Express*   285

Abbreviations   287

Notes   289

Bibliography   311

Index   319

FOREWORD

Tom Reigstad's prologue takes you on a walk through Forest Lawn Cemetery. The gravesites, the monuments, the family plots, are a "Who's Who of Twain's surprisingly extensive Buffalo social network," as the prologue tells us, and Tom moves respectfully among them—Slee, Wadsworth, Jewett, Gray, to name several—giving you exquisite thumbnail sketches of who they were and how they figured in Mark Twain's Buffalo life. They are the truth of Mark Twain's engaged convivial life in Buffalo; some friends, notably David Gray, became lifetime friends. The accepted literary opinion that Mark Twain's time in Buffalo was miserable, that Buffalo itself—with its hard, cold winter and its gray, snowbound days—weighed upon his spirit, that he was socially isolated (a canard first stated by Albert Bigelow Paine, Mark Twain's Boswell, his official biographer, and generally repeated in canonical Mark Twain biography) is decisively corrected here, at Forest Lawn Cemetery, in Tom's prologue. Yes, illness and death came to the newlywed Clemens/Langdon Buffalo family. There was misery in Buffalo, but Buffalo had nothing to do with it. In Buffalo there was also triumph and glory, Mark Twain entering Aladdin's Palace at 472 Delaware Street (now known as Delaware Avenue); Mark Twain bringing out *Innocents Abroad* and beginning to write *Roughing It*; Mark Twain taking hold of his life and his career, an adult at last, though his wife, Olivia, called him "Child."

Tom Reigstad's research is exhaustive. This is it. There isn't any more to be said about Mark Twain in Buffalo. If you want to think about the subject or write on its issues, this is the book that is open before you. It is so rich in detail and exacting in identification that strange new questions begin to appear.

Everywhere Mark Twain turned in Buffalo, he was talking to someone who was on Jervis Langdon's payroll. How did he start writing *Roughing It* in Buffalo, and why, since the book celebrates the wildcat Confederate scoundrel he, at that point, in Buffalo, forever abjured? Hip Presbyterian and Episcopalian post–Civil War Buffalo was greatly pleased to have this popular literary comedian as neighbor and friend. Mark Twain held forth as the star member of the Nameless Club, St. James Hall, Elmwood Avenue. He shook the hand of old Millard Fillmore, former US president and noble Buffalonian elder. He might have smoked a cigar with Grover Cleveland, ambitious young Buffalo politician. Esther McWilliams, young wife of J. J. McWilliams, a colleague and friend, "sorted and made a list of Mark Twain's dirty clothes, took them back and forth to the laundress, and handled the bill," as Tom tells us. Twain was an installed power at the *Buffalo Express*—co-owner, coeditor, and featured columnist— and he wanted, at first, to redo the *Express* to make it an important newspaper. There were fine minds and good writers at the *Express*, including Josephus Nelson Larned, John Harrison Mills, Earl Berry, and others. Buffalo was there for him, to play with, to play in, to become a man of affairs. He was the young prince in Buffalo. Young Buffalo Presbyterian guys were thrilled to know him. Esther McWilliams did his laundry.

As Tom's research reveals, there were only three holdouts in Buffalo who managed to resist the magnetism of Mark Twain's celebrity, and they make an interesting combination of post–Civil War figures, though of course they did not know each other. One was a wounded Civil War hero; the next, a radical feminist; the third, an African American janitor at the *Express*, each with a justified grievance. George Selkirk, in the field of the major battles at Antietam, Fredericksburg, and Gettysburg, twice wounded and twice decorated, no doubt took a certain measure of his new flamboyant and vociferous partner, resentfully heard that wildcat Confederate drawl. Did he know Mark Twain's Civil War story? He did not. Mark Twain, in the years from 1869 to 1871, did not have a Civil War story he could tell. Mark Twain called Selkirk "Colonel," no doubt with mock respect. When Mark Twain finally sold his interest in the *Express*, he bitterly sold it to Selkirk, suffering a ten-thousand-dollar loss. When Anna Dickinson, a midcentury cultural critic and public speaker, postabolitionist radical feminist, and old and valued friend of Olivia Clemens, visited Olivia in Buffalo, she found Mark Twain to be a "vulgar boor." She, too, heard that drawl. It must have grated on janitor Philip Lee's sensitive ear. And what about Mark Twain's imperious manner? According to legend, Lee played dirty tricks on Mark Twain.

In Buffalo, it might be said, Mark Twain experienced his first unmitigated jubilation: he married the king's daughter. Jervis Langdon, Olivia's father, was the coal king of Buffalo from 1869 to 1871, the years of Mark Twain's residence. But who was Jervis Langdon? He was a magnate. He ran a big energy company, had investments and holdings, one of which was a prime piece of Buffalo's waterfront that Mark Twain held to the end of his life. Langdon was the munificent father of the bride, got Mark Twain his first real job in the serious world of business and politics, bought the mansion at 472 Delaware, and furnished it with drapes and rugs, chairs and tables, so that all Mark Twain had to do was move in and be good.

If he wasn't good, the servants, all of them in the employ of Jervis Langdon, would no doubt report the relapse. When Mark Twain was still an aspirant for Olivia's hand, Langdon made inquiries and got a number of negative letters. Mark Twain was the prince, but under observation, on probation in Buffalo; he was going to church, going to dinner with Langdon's principal Buffalo agents, behaving responsibly, defending Langdon's coal monopoly at the *Express*.

Tom's genius at close identification in biography (everyone Mark Twain meets is working for Langdon) lets another omnipresent Langdon appear, the father whose generosity imprisons. In his private correspondence, Mark Twain describes his father-in-law as a hard, tightfisted capitalist, a killer in all his transactions, one who closely supervised his investments. In public, Mark Twain was properly filial. In Tom's book, we can see that Mark Twain was Jervis Langdon's creature in Buffalo, a conservative Republican, a Presbyterian, a postabolitionist.

Each chapter in Tom Reigstad's book has its compelling story, a new angle or aspect to ponder, a vivid scene to suppose. The first six weeks Mark Twain was in Buffalo, he was on fire. He did local journalism enthusiastically, wrote funny Niagara Falls sketches, wrote a chat column called People and Things, even as he was at work on the final production of *Innocents Abroad*. He was staying at Mrs. J. C. Randall's boardinghouse on East Swan Street. Tom gives us an exemplary morning: Mark Twain rising, doing his ablutions, getting dressed, going down to the breakfast table where his fellow boarders (all named and identified) greet him. As it happens, some of his fellow boarders are on the payroll of Mr. Jervis Langdon. Mark Twain is happily going to work at the *Express* just down the street.

Scribblin' for a Livin' is a movie that needs to be made. The events just described are part of a vignette scene. The big scene is in chapter 5, "Aladdin's Palace," Mark Twain's surprised arrival at 472 Delaware Street, this climax, this culmination.

The doors are thrown open. It is all gold and silver inside. Jervis Langdon gives Mark Twain a handsome wooden box containing the deed to the mansion. This is the gleaming, glistening truth of Buffalo's meaning in Mark Twain's life, going into that mansion. This fabulous moment in Mark Twain's life takes place in Buffalo. Tom gives it its appropriate statement.

We begin the story of this climactic moment, more or less, at the railroad station, a dark night, snow falling. Tom writes, "Charles Underhill heard the train's horn, then saw a rare sight: a single heavyweight custom-built, well-polished, sixty-five-foot-long palace car with an observation platform pulled by a locomotive chugging smoothly into Buffalo's Exchange Street Station." It is Jervis Langdon's private rail car. We get to look inside at its three luxurious staterooms, at the paneled and painted walls, and we're standing on thick expensive carpet. Next we're in a sleigh, wrapped in fur, snowflakes in the wintry air, belled horses jingling, and we're crossing Lafayette Square. After the reception ceremony, beautifully reported, Tom takes us on a tour of the mansion, remarking on the woodwork, the fireplaces, the furniture. It is property—solid, expensive, Langdon property. The lease, Tom tells us, is in Olivia's name.

In 1869, Mark Twain composed a chat column in the *Express*, People and Things, and here it is in the appendixes. You might think the column dated, antique, and quickly scan the entries. However, I find People and Things charming, entertaining. It is like listening to Miles Davis tootle on his trumpet. Mark Twain is playing the news of the day, almost like a standup comedian using a newspaper, and he often gets a kind of urban poetry going, as in this sequence from September 8, 1869:

- Sojourner Truth is probably dead by this time. Charlotte Cushman also.
- Rev. Father Boehm is the oldest Methodist minister in the world. His age is 95, and he still preaches, sometimes.
- A southern paper advises Mrs. Harriet Beecher Stowe to go to the "Erring Woman's Home" in Chicago.
- What was it Archimedes said about the lever? These things escape one's memory from lack of repetition.
- We are to have the Dr. Livingston excitement all over, once more. He is not found again.
- Harriet Martineau, the ancient and reliable, comes to Mrs. Stowe's rescue on the Byron matter.
- Engine 103 drew the special Chicago Express from Syracuse to Rochester Friday evening in eighty-five minutes! Distance, *eighty-five miles*.

Cut this up, reconfigure it, you've got Language Poetry, a Charles Bernstein poem. Diverse news items are dealt one after the other. You get the sense of being in the stream of Mark Twain's cultural consciousness, these disparate stories, sorted and registered. In among them, as we see in the book's appendixes, he does a bit of humor, sets out a tall tale or a hoax. He'll write, "There is a veteran in Ohio 107 years old, who does not go tramping around, or chopping four cords of wood a day, or turning handsprings for exercise. And strange to say, he has not voted for more than half the Presidents, either. Moreover, instead of having a tenacious memory and an unimpaired intellect, he is a driveling old idiot." On he goes elsewhere to remark, "Chicago snubs the century plant." No explanation. And later, this deeply horrifying report: "There is a man in Ohio who has written three thousand communications to the newspapers, not one of which has ever been published." Here's a deadpan one liner: "Brigham Young's mother-in-law is dead."

Nothing Mark Twain wrote in Buffalo is in the canon. He became a young husband and a young father in Buffalo. He was busy. He finished *Innocents Abroad* and began *Roughing It* in Buffalo. Tom Reigstad's *Scribblin' for a Livin'* is in the canon, an instant classic, tersely told, factually correct. It speaks to a number of critical conversations going on in Mark Twain studies, particularly those pondering the question of Mark Twain's midcentury conversion, his going

Republican, going abolitionist. What exactly did it involve? In the *Express*, Mark Twain would mock the turbulence of Southern journalism, attack the incidents of lynching, yet there was, we learn in Tom's book, friction with Philip Lee, the black janitor at the *Express*. *Roughing It*, Mark Twain's racist Wild West book, is begun in high-minded Presbyterian churchgoing Buffalo. You could say of *Roughing It*, a rowdy insolent book, that it is a defiance of Jervis Langdon's Buffalo. *Scribblin' for a Livin'* lets you suppose this, but its resolute scholarship also shows how scattered and fragmentary the provenance is for *Roughing It*. Mark Twain had a different travel narrative in the works, European, a dialogue with a traveling reporter, which failed because the reporter, an Elmira College professor, was too slow in his reporting, not ever at newspaper speed. As a show-business performer, a comic lecturer, Mark Twain was already using his Wild West material. *Roughing It* is not the result of formalist decisions, of a deep well-considered intention to defy Jervis Langdon's Buffalo. If you're writing a scholarly paper on *Roughing It* and wondering about its conception, be advised, Tom Reigstad closely watches *Roughing It* emerge in chapter 7 of *Scribblin' for a Livin'*. Mark Twain has a baby in Buffalo and he begins, in cool Protestant Buffalo, to write his wildcat rebel book. This is all figured out and solved in Tom's definitive account of Mark Twain's life in Buffalo.

—Dr. Neil Schmitz

PROLOGUE

I WILL ALWAYS CONFINE MYSELF STRICTLY TO THE TRUTH

Today there are precious few tangible reminders in Buffalo, New York, of Mark Twain's association with that city. The most famous legacy is his handwritten manuscript of *Adventures of Huckleberry Finn* owned by the Buffalo and Erie County Public Library. The Central Library in downtown Buffalo also features an attractive Mark Twain Room with two furnishings from Twain's Buffalo home. His boardinghouse and wedding-gift mansion have long since been demolished, although the mansion's carriage house survives. Several fireplace mantelpieces from Twain's Buffalo dwelling exist, but only two are accessible to the public. Other stray fragments of the house are scattered around Western New York—a pair of shutters here, a length of decorative wooden-rope molding there, and even a backyard barbecue fireplace in the suburban town of Tonawanda, built from bricks rescued when Twain's mansion was being torn down. There is a street, also in the town of Tonawanda, called Twain Court, a building named Clemens Hall on the north campus of the University at Buffalo housing the English Department on its third floor, a historic marker on the city's west side stating that on that site Twain visited William Fargo in his mansion (a claim I have not yet confirmed), and a plaque in honor of Twain embedded in a sidewalk along Elmwood Avenue as part of a "Cultural Walk of Fame" that also pays tribute to over thirty other Buffalonians, including actress Amanda Blake and singer Rick "Super Freak" James. There is a rumor that somewhere on the east side of Buffalo, in the old brewery district off Ellicott Street, there was once a street known as Twain Alley, but that legend, too, remains unverified.

Perhaps a better way to capture the spirit of Twain's presence in Buffalo is to stroll through Forest Lawn Cemetery, 263 acres of serene, park-like green space that preceded Frederick Law Olmsted's Delaware Park, which lies along the cemetery's northern border.[1] In the mid-1890s, during a brief stopover in Buffalo, Twain took a quick carriage tour through the winding lanes of Forest Lawn. Today the list of those whose remains are in the cemetery reads like a who's who of Twain's surprisingly extensive Buffalo social network. Not far from the graceful arched entrance at West Delevan and Delaware Avenues, the same entrance accessed by Twain in 1895, amid a group of mature pine trees, sits a ball monument for the Berry family and the marker for Earl D. Berry, a cub reporter whom Twain trusted to carry out his myriad of editorial innovations at the *Buffalo Morning Express*. Just thirty yards away are the gravesites of Mary A. Ripley and James N. Johnston, two members of the Nameless Club, a vibrant literary club to which Twain belonged when he lived in Buffalo. Approximately twenty additional Nameless Club members who spent pleasant evenings with Twain sharing their writings and reading poetry can be found throughout the cemetery. Not far from Berry is the marker for James Howells, a contractor and Delaware Street neighbor with whom Twain was acquainted. Nearby, too, is the spot where Thomas Kennett is buried. Kennett reportedly bragged about having "done" Twain in, selling him his one-third share of the *Express* in 1869 at $10,000 above its market value. Ironically, Kennett later lost his fortune and died penniless. He and his wife occupy unmarked graves in Forest Lawn. A walk westward into the cemetery atop a rolling grassy slope is the Graves monument and an individual stone for Augusta Moore Graves, who, as a talented young sculptor, was commissioned to create a bust of baby Langdon Clemens from his death mask in 1872. Twenty yards to the rear, on the same incline, is Rev. Grosvenor W. Heacock, a spiritual advisor to Twain and his wife, Olivia. Heacock, of Lafayette Presbyterian Church, was their favorite preacher in Buffalo. Still on the same hill, directly behind Graves, is an obelisk (one of 710 in the cemetery) memorializing Andrew Simson and Jefferson Upson, brothers-in-law at whose Main Street studio Twain posed for a photograph shortly after arriving in Buffalo. Toward the south center of Forest Lawn is the Frederick A.

Cook Chapel Crematorium, where the remains of George Brewster Mathews are kept in an urn behind locked glass doors. As a young clerk in 1869, he lived in the same boardinghouse as Mark Twain and occupied a seat directly across the dining table from him. Mathews grew up to become one of the wealthiest men in Buffalo.

In the northwest sector of Forest Lawn, amid the older, original eighty acres bought for Forest Lawn in the 1840s, within a grassy fenced-in square graced by walnut and oak trees, is the plot of former US president Millard Fillmore. Fillmore was a distinguished elder citizen of Buffalo whom Twain encountered at least twice during his stay in the city. Just south of Fillmore's plot is that of Dr. Cornelius Cox Wyckoff, a physician and recent widower when he was Twain's next-door neighbor on Delaware Street. Continuing south through the cemetery toward today's Delaware Avenue, one finds on an elevated ridge that is the highest spot in Forest Lawn the burial sites of Joseph Nelson Larned and his wife, Frances. Larned co-owned and coedited the *Buffalo Express* with Twain. He and his wife remained lifelong friends of Twain and Olivia. Directly behind the Larned section in this area of prominent Buffalonians, near the lake and mausoleum, sits the gravesite of Victor Tiphaine, whose Main Street saloon Twain frequented. Tiphaine's tavern must have done quite well, since an expensive, large, monumental vase is part of his family's site. Along the western edge of the cemetery are the impressive markers for Dennis Bowen and Sherman S. Rogers, whose law firm handled the paperwork when Twain purchased one-third ownership of the *Express* for $25,000 in August of 1869. A stone's throw away, perched on a well-landscaped knoll among maple and fir trees that provide a stirring view across Delaware Avenue's *S* curve to the eastern, forested side of Delaware Park and its lake, Twain's other *Express* co-owner, Col. George H. Selkirk, is buried next to his wife, Emily. The couple socialized with Twain and Olivia, and Selkirk kept in touch with Twain for years concerning *Express* business matters.

At the top of a hill that offers a grand view westward overlooking Delaware Park's Hoyt Lake is the solid, square tombstone of Dr. Andrew R. Wright, a physician who delivered Twain's premature son, Langdon, in Buffalo and looked after the sickly baby and Twain's equally ailing wife for weeks after the birth. The inscription on Wright's stone reads "The Beloved Physician." Another influential local Presbyterian cleric and his wife, Rev. John C. Lord and Mary Elizabeth Johnson Lord (Twain was very fond of both of them), can be found in this area of the cemetery where other former Buffalo "movers and shakers" rest. The Lords' section boasts a tall monument and a cenotaph. Continuing along the elevated rim, offering the vista of Delaware Park, one sees the Gray family lot, where Twain's Buffalo soul mate, fellow journalist, and friend for life, David Gray, is interred. Gray's wife, Martha, whom Twain and Olivia adored and called "Miss Mattie," is buried beside her husband.

In section H of Forest Lawn is another family lot, owned by Charles Munson Underhill, a clerk with the Buffalo office of J. Langdon and Company, the coal firm owned by Twain's wealthy father-in-law from Elmira, New York. Underhill, his wife, Anna, and their son, Irving (all buried there), remained close to Twain his entire life. In the same family lot are markers for Underhill's dear brother-in-law, John D. F. Slee, and his wife, Emma. Slee was in charge of the Buffalo coal office for J. Langdon and Co. and helped Twain with personal and financial affairs. He and his wife were trusted lifelong companions of Twain and Olivia, too. In the same northern region of Forest Lawn are the monument and marker for wealthy Buffalo businessman John J. Albright and his wife, Harriet, a first cousin of Twain's wife. A few steps farther toward the northwestern corner of Forest Lawn are the resting places of William G. Fargo, cofounder of Wells-Fargo Express and president of the Buffalo Club when Twain was admitted in 1871, and tycoon and philanthropist William Pryor Letchworth, another fellow Nameless Club member. Occupying an adjoining corner of property in the northwest region of the cemetery is the Welch lot, where Jane Meade Welch rests. As a teenager she charmed Twain by sprinkling the dusty dirt road in front of his Delaware Street home with a watering can. Welch, her mother, and her grandmother, all interred in the lot, were Delaware Street neighbors of Twain, and he paid them a cordial visit after the watering-can episode. Just across a road from the Welch lot, attorney George Wadsworth and his wife, Emily Marshall Wadsworth, are buried. Emily Wadsworth paid social calls at Twain's 472 Delaware Street home. Along the northernmost border of Forest Lawn Cemetery, in the old section overlooking Crystal Lake, is a mausoleum with the remains of Andrew Langdon, a wealthy Buffalo businessman and another first cousin of Twain's wife. In this sector of the cemetery, facing the slowly meandering Scajaquada Creek, is the McWilliams monument, with tombstones for John J. McWilliams and his wife, Esther. McWilliams, bookkeeper for the Buffalo branch office of Langdon's coal company, and his wife lived in the same boardinghouse as Twain during his weeks as a bachelor in Buffalo. They provided companionship for Twain and stayed friends for years afterward.

This roll call of names, ghosts from Mark Twain's Buffalo past, adds up to a sizable social register of family and friends who touched Twain's life in Buffalo. Many of the associations that Twain established in Buffalo continued to be part of his social circle for decades. Curiously, nearly one hundred years' worth of biographies and critical studies of Twain typically cite only four or five of these individuals. Almost all the names are routinely ignored. I noticed this gap as a graduate student at the University of Missouri while writing a paper in Leon T. Dickinson's seminar on Twain. I grew up in Buffalo and had a dim awareness of Twain's brush with the city. When delving into Twain's Buffalo period for my course at Missouri, I realized that books and journal articles consistently wrote off the Buffalo era, describing it as insignificant to Twain's literary development, as dominated by personal tragedies, and as a period of sparse social contacts and bleak weather. It seems as though Twain's first literary executor, Albert Bigelow Paine, first set the somewhat low bar in his 1912 biography. According to Paine, Twain and his wife were socially isolated: "Almost the only intimate friends they had in Buffalo were the family of David Gray, the poet–editor of the *Courier*. . . . They did not mingle much or long with the social life of Buffalo."[2] Paine further maintains that Twain's writing at the *Buffalo Express* was inconsequential, not equal to the caliber of his recently released *The Innocents Abroad*, and, in fact, was a kind of artistic backslide toward his earlier writing apprenticeship: "As a whole, the literary result of Mark Twain's Buffalo period does not reach the high standard of *The Innocents Abroad*. It was a retrogression—in some measure a return to his earlier form."[3] A final sample of Paine's penchant for categorical statements paints Twain's Buffalo experience with a broad, damning brush: "On the whole the Buffalo residence was mainly a gloomy one."[4] Paine's authority has been accepted for the most part as gospel ever since.

As I continued to investigate this corner of Twain studies in the ensuing years, especially by consulting local archival material and interviewing Western New Yorkers who were descendants of Twain's Buffalo acquaintances, the long-held low opinion of Buffalo puzzled me. Contrary to prevailing beliefs, I kept unearthing name after name of people with whom Twain worked and socialized in Buffalo. And examining his *Express* writings suggested to me that, at the least, he was maintaining successful composing formulas from *The Innocents Abroad*. Nevertheless, the drumbeat of slighting Buffalo, initiated by Paine, rolled on. In 1943, Delancey Ferguson perpetuated the "friendless" theory ("Nor had Buffalo furnished much in the way of congenial society"),[5] and introduced a new spin toward disrespecting Twain's Buffalo stay—that is, its weather: "The bleak, sunless Buffalo winter dragged on, and all the high hopes with which Mark had embarked on his undertaking in the *Express* faded out in the universal grayness."[6] Unfortunately, the few existing photos of Twain's Delaware Street house do not support a bright, sunny, welcoming climate. All of the photos are in black and white and invariably show a stark landscape with either a snowy front yard or barren tree limbs. *The Mark Twain Handbook*, published fourteen years after Ferguson's book, also commented on Buffalo as a place lacking social companionship for Twain and Olivia, with an entry on Buffalo as "uncongenial and gloomy; somehow they had never really managed to feel themselves a part of the community."[7] In 1969 Arthur L. Scott mirrored Paine's earlier criticism of the amateur quality of Twain's *Express* stories: "His writings for the *Express* . . . are of little interest."[8] A 1966 study, however, seemed to cast the low opinion of Twain's life in Buffalo in permanent cement. Justin Kaplan's Pulitzer Prize–winning biography *Mr. Clemens and Mark Twain* reiterated the one-two punch of dull society and bad weather as two reasons for Twain's ultimate discontent with the city: "At best Buffalo had been a city of only mild social diversions for Clemens."[9] Then a few pages later Kaplan calls Twain's Buffalo a "city of cold winds and hard luck."[10] Since that time, into the 1990s, Twain scholars have not departed from the dominant critics' party line, variously referring to Buffalo as a city with a long winter, as a city for which Twain had no affection, as a tough city to settle into socially, and as a city of clouds. This attitude toward Twain's Buffalo period persists into the twenty-first century. Fred Kaplan's 2003 biography once again blames Buffalo weather as a major cause of Twain's dissatisfaction with living there: "Sickness had helped make Twain sick of Buffalo. So too had the freezing winter weather."[11] As recently as 2010, Jerome Loving proclaimed Paine-like in his Twain biography that "Buffalo had never pleased him."[12]

This book is not meant as a defense of Buffalo. As a native of the city, I enjoy experiencing all four seasons but find winters challenging. The winter winds, gray skies, and heavy snowfalls probably contribute to cases of seasonal affective disorder. I am well aware of Buffalo's collective but undeserved inferiority complex and have found it curious that, in a sense, it carries over to Twain scholarship. Just as my probing discovered that Twain had a richer social network and more significant literary output than commonly believed, I could not find compelling evidence that Twain hated winters so much that the snow drove him from Buffalo. If anything, Twain seemed favorably disposed to Buffalo's climate, even embracing its notorious winters. I aim to tell the story of Twain's multifaceted affiliation with Buffalo in a full, well-documented fashion based on years of examining records and interviewing key sources. My findings contradict some of the prevailing myths about Twain's Buffalo period.

If you believe in kismet or karma, perhaps I was predestined to explore Twain's Buffalo period. On the day I was born, November 29, 1947, in Sisters Hospital on Main Street in Buffalo, New York, the area was hit by one of the worst November snowstorms in history. In some towns south of the city, thirty-four inches of snow piled up. And fierce squalls sweeping in off Lake Erie created high snowdrifts, icy highways, and poor visibility throughout the city. On that very day, the *Buffalo Evening News* published a lengthy feature story in its Saturday magazine page about Mark Twain in Buffalo, complete with photos and illustrations.[13] The local-interest feature story was timed to appear the day before Twain's own birth date, November 30. I came across this coincidence of the *Buffalo Evening News* article printed on the day of my birth many years later, of course.

This path of coincidental Twain encounters continued with my first full-time job out of undergraduate school at the *Buffalo Courier-Express*, a daily newspaper whose forerunner was Twain's *Express*. From time to time, the *Courier-Express* proudly trumpeted its ties to Twain. For example, full-page ads in two October 1977 editions displayed pen-and-ink drawings of Twain and a steamboat with the headline "A Tradition of Editorial Excellence," and the accompanying text that emphasized the newspaper's historical link to Twain read as follows: "Good writing in The Courier-Express began with Samuel Clemens, better known to the world as Mark Twain. . . . As an editor of the Morning Express a tradition of editorial excellence was begun that continues in The Courier-Express today!" I worked at the *Courier-Express* off and on for thirteen years as a features writer and copy editor right up to the last night it existed, September 19, 1982. During that time I had the privilege of writing and editing Sunday magazine feature stories for the *Courier-Express* about Twain's Buffalo years. In the mid-1990s I was associate editor of *Bills Insider*, the official magazine of the NFL's Buffalo Bills. The publication's offices were at 472 Delaware Avenue, the site of Twain's former home. Although the house had long since been demolished, some of our editorial work was conducted in the original carriage house, which survived. Over the years, I have also contributed Twain-related stories to *Buffalo Business First*, a weekly that for several years also operated at Twain's old Delaware Avenue address. And for three years I was a part-time copy editor at the *Niagara Falls Gazette*, a position that presented opportunities for me to explore and publish stories about Twain's strong connections to Niagara Falls.

For twenty-six years I was an English professor at SUNY College at Buffalo and was fortunate to be able to schedule class meetings on the last day of the semester in the library director's conference room. A handsome marble fireplace mantelpiece saved from Twain's Buffalo house is mounted on a wall in the conference room. I often suggested that students rest an elbow on the mantel, as Twain may have done, in order to soak up (in Blarney Stone fashion) his writer's luck. I have been well positioned to contact local kin (children, grandchildren, and great-nephews) of people who knew Twain when he lived in Buffalo, to collect relevant and illuminating family lore, and to talk to Buffalonians intimately familiar with the house in which Twain lived prior to its demolition in 1963. Archival material available in Western New York historical-research facilities has afforded me some rare, never-before-revealed insights into Twain's social, work, and domestic habits during his Buffalo period. I have even found original *Buffalo Express* stories never before reprinted in book form. I will never forget small "Eureka!" moments that are so rewarding to persistent researchers. One such moment was at Elmira College, when I pinned down the accurate address of Twain's Buffalo boardinghouse, which for decades had been listed wrongly in publications as the McWilliams home on Oak Street. Or sitting at the microfilm machine in the wee hours in the *Niagara Gazette*'s cramped library space when I came across an original 1869 letter to the editor responding to Twain's *Express* story on Niagara Falls, a letter perhaps authored by Twain and, at the least, definitely influenced by him and an *Express* colleague. Then, recently, when I was following up a hunch at the Niagara Falls Local History Department on the second floor of the Niagara Falls Public Library, I flipped through several pages of an old hotel register and found Twain's signature, thus confirming the correct dates of Twain's first visit to Niagara Falls. Small but sweet victories for a researcher.

I have been encouraged by my wife, friends, and colleagues to tell Twain's story. Sabbaticals granted by SUNY College at Buffalo and a researcher-in-residence award at Elmira College's Center for Mark Twain Studies have helped enable me to do the necessary reading and research along the way. Although Twain kept notebooks all his life, none are known to exist for the months he lived in Buffalo. Furthermore, several letters between Twain and Olivia of that time period are lost. Therefore, picking up tidbits from a wide variety of sources and trying to assemble a complete puzzle picturing the richness of Twain's Buffalo experience has been my mission for many years. In introducing himself to *Buffalo Express* readers, Twain promised facetiously to stick "strictly to the truth, except when it is attended with inconvenience."[14] Whether guided by fate, or not, I have attempted to present a truthful account and to do justice to Mark Twain's encounter with my native city of Buffalo, New York. In doing so, larger bodies of primary-source material, specifically that which is presented in the appendixes, maintain the spelling, grammar, terminology, and idiosyncrasies (such as open quotation marks that are missing their corresponding closing quotation marks) used in the original documents at the time of their publication.

ACKNOWLEDGMENTS

My brave and beautiful wife, Maryanne, and our wonderful sons, Luke and Leif, have lived with the topic of Twain and Buffalo for as long as we have been together and I thank them for their constant support. They have put up with books and papers scattered around every available surface in the family room and attic, have traveled with me to Twain conferences in Elmira, and have provided invaluable feedback on drafts. I have been blessed to be surrounded by three gifted and loving editors and writers. Luke and Maryanne also helped with photography. Breast cancer claimed our beloved Maryanne before she read the last chapters, but her everlasting love remains my moral compass and guiding star.

My parents instilled in me a love of reading at an early age and made sure I read versions of *Tom Sawyer* and *Huckleberry Finn* while still in Cub Scouts. Whatever good is in me as a man and as a writer comes from them.

In working on a long-term project like this one, some friends and supporters have passed on. I treasure and will never forget their kindnesses and encouragement. My mentor and pal at SUNY College at Buffalo, John Dwyer, was always interested in my work. Irene Jennings Liguori, a valued colleague at the *Buffalo Courier-Express* and at the college, was a dedicated Twain aficionada and Twain-museum visionary. Herbert A. Wisbey Jr., Twain scholar at Elmira College, invited me to publish, and he shared his extensive knowledge. Martha Hamlin Visser't Hooft, granddaughter of David Gray, was generous with her time and shared her enthusiasm about Twain. I owe a great debt to Martin Fried and Charles S. Underhill. Professor Fried was a neighbor who guided my early work on Gray and Twain, published pioneer studies on Twain's Buffalo tenure, and gave me his painstakingly assembled reprints of Twain's original *Buffalo Express* contributions. Mr. Underhill, whose father and grandfather knew Twain in Buffalo, was a passionate Twain scholar whose correspondence, conversation, and friendship never failed to energize my Twain studies. Stuart Cary Welch Jr., great-nephew of Twain's young Buffalo neighbor Jane Meade Welch, was generous with family anecdotes and was enthusiastic about my project. Charlotte Albright shared family information that helped shed light on her grandmother, Harriet Langdon Albright, a Buffalonian and cousin of Twain's wife. George F. Goodyear helped me with family history on 472 Delaware Avenue; Jervis Langdon Jr. nudged me toward investigating the J. Langdon and Company's Buffalo office. James D. DiLapo Sr., who owned the Twain house on Delaware Avenue and the restaurant that was built on that site, was very generous with insights about the interior of the house and barn and was very interested in my research. Richard M. Thurston, a neighbor, had the foresight to rescue a marble mantelpiece from Twain's Buffalo home before it was torn down, and he donated the mantelpiece to my college. He also gave me three bricks he had salvaged from Twain's home. Charles A. Brady, legendary English professor at Canisius College, and his wife, Eileen, neighbors of mine, were enthusiastic about my project, provided local Twain stories and friendship, and helped steer my research in the right direction. Darryl Baskin, as director of the Elmira College Center for Mark Twain Studies, kindly granted me a productive Quarry Farm fellowship. Tom Tenney, longtime editor of the *Mark Twain Journal*, was a friend who provided scholarly advice and encouragement. I miss these friends and supporters and wish they could have seen the fruition of my effort.

I am grateful to SUNY College at Buffalo. I received sabbaticals and worked with valued colleagues, particularly Charles Bachman, Tom Giambrone, Dave Karnath, Carole Knuth (scholar, healer, and trusted friend), Frank Kowsky (whose knowledge of nineteenth-century Buffalo history is boundless), Dave Lampe, Dave Landrey, Joe Marren, Mike Parks, Nancy Paschke, Ralph Wahlstrom, and Craig Werner. College photographers Phil Gerace, Steve Mangione, and Bruce Fox were always helpful. I relied heavily on the excellent staff at Butler Library, especially director Maryruth Glogowski, and the library's long line of distinguished college archivists over the years—Sr. Martin

Joseph Jones, Mary Delmont, Al Reiss, Daniel D. DiLandro, and archives assistant Peggy Hatfield. My undergraduate and graduate students in Twain seminars at SUNY College at Buffalo and, recently, at Canisius College invigorated me with their curiosity and intellect. Michele Eodice, Wynnie Fisher, Jeffrey A. Jablonski, and David Shapiro-Zysk were among the best of them.

The staff at the Buffalo and Erie County Historical Society library—Mary Bell, Pat Virgil, Venessa Hughes, and Cynthia Van Ness—provided me with a second home. The Rare Book Room and Grosvenor Room librarians at the Buffalo and Erie County Library provided invaluable help, too. Amy Pickard, Peter Scheck, Charles Alaimo, and Anne Conable deserve my special thanks. William H. Loos, former curator of the Rare Book Room, has been a valued friend for more than thirty years. He first endured my reporter's questions about the *Huck Finn* manuscript in 1978. Later on we paced off the number of steps it took Twain to walk from his boardinghouse to the *Express* office. Over lunches and at meetings and conferences, Bill has offered many tidbits on Twain that I never would have found on my own.

Many other Buffalonians have helped me in a variety of ways. Ted and N. Averie Montagu (Mr. DiLapo's granddaughter); Roger Putnam, Dr. Theodore I. Putnam, and John G. Putnam Jr.—descendants of sculptor Augusta Graves; Mrs. Carl N. Reed, whose husband was a grandson of John J. McWilliams; Jack Mesmer of the Lower Lakes Marine Historical Society; John H. Conlin, former editor of *Western New York Heritage* magazine; Patrick Kavanagh, historian extraordinaire of Forest Lawn Cemetery; Maureen O'Connell; Martin Wacledo, for insights into Buffalo's architectural history; Charles "Jack" Hahn; and Vic Doyno, a kind and generous Twain scholar who taught me as an undergraduate how to write essays in response to literature.

Robert H. Hirst, director of the Mark Twain Project (MTP), has been a good friend and enormously informative and generous with his collection at Berkeley. Vic Fischer, also of the MTP, has devoted much time to my questions, too. And Neda Salem, an assistant at the MTP, was always prompt and helpful in handling inquiries. The MTP is a treasure trove of material that the staff makes easily accessible.

The Center for Mark Twain Studies at Elmira College welcomed me as a researcher and conference speaker. I extend special gratitude to Gretchen

Sharlow, Mark Woodhouse, and Barbara Sneddecor, as well as to the friendly Quarry Farm caretakers when I stayed there, Gayle and Jon Earley.

The Niagara Falls Local History Department, located at the Niagara Falls, New York, Public Library's main building, has been an important resource for me. Linda Reinumagi has been especially accommodating.

I have always come away invigorated by talking with Maggie Vaughn, poet laureate of Tennessee, about Twain, and by reading her Quarry Farm poetry.

I have been privileged to work with talented local journalists who, as colleagues and as friends, nurtured my interest in Twain and often opened space in their newspaper pages for my stories: Jack Connors, my buddy at the *Buffalo Courier-Express*, the *Niagara Gazette*, and *Buffalo Business First*; and Jeff Wright, Gary Burns, and Donna Collins at the *Niagara Gazette* and *Business First*. My hat goes off to Sean Kirst, a former colleague at the *Niagara Gazette*, whose writing on Twain's Fredonia connection is seminal.

My inner circle of longtime friends, particularly Mick Cochrane, Ron Eaton, and Don McAndrew, has helped keep me honest, entertained, and engaged in the life of the mind. My oldest friend, Dave Leibelshon, braved snow drifts at Forest Lawn Cemetery to help me locate and photograph David Gray's gravesite. Dave and I have followed an endless quest for the mythic companion to Twain's term *penny-a-liner*. Kami Day was outstanding as a copy editor and manuscript typist, and my longtime colleague Amy Kline deserves my gratitude for her meticulous typing assistance.

Our cats, Ethel and Lucy, have kept me from being an isolated, lonely writer hanging out in the attic. Lucy, by napping on my lap and resting her chin on the keyboard, has sometimes forced me to type with one finger instead of two. Any spelling errors are hers.

I greatly appreciate Neil Schmitz of the University at Buffalo for his encouraging words and for writing the foreword to this book.

Finally, many thanks to the staff at Prometheus Books, particularly to the editor-in-chief, Steven L. Mitchell, and my copy editor, Mariel Bard, for their kindnesses, boundless patience, support, and invitation to transform the idea of this book into a reality.

INTRODUCTION

OFFER THE NEW EDITOR A CHAIR

I t is slightly after 7:30 a.m. in the business district of Buffalo, New York. A blanket of grayish cloud cover drifting in from the west off Lake Erie and the ever-present waterfront breeze on this mid-August morning in 1869 start the day off at a comfortably cool sixty degrees.

An energetic thirty-three-year-old bachelor of average height and slight build, with a hawkish nose and russet hair, bounces out the door of his East Swan Street boardinghouse. He lights his first cigar of the day. The man is dressed in white-collar-worker's clothing: brown derby, brown suit and vest, white shirt with a starched collar and cuffs, and a brown necktie.

With his belly full from his landlady's breakfast of fresh biscuits and coffee, he is eager to begin his first day on the job.

From the sidewalk the young man surveys his new territory. On the blocks of Swan Street, looking east away from Main Street, stand brick boardinghouses like his own—former mansions divided into one- and two-room apartments—a handful of office buildings, and a few splendid private homes.

He turns his gaze toward Main Street and sees his new workplace. It is a four-story building across the street, just one block away.

Already, the hubbub of commerce is warming up. Wagons are hitching up in front of shops to unload goods. Merchants are arranging displays of their wares near the curbs. Two-wheel hand-delivery carts, with long wooden handles, at rest on the walkways await their first mission of the day.

The young man hopscotches across Swan on patches of the dirt street still damp from dew to avoid getting his shoes and trousers dusty from the dry spots. He has read how the Common Council recently failed to hire a street sprinkler to patrol Swan. It was too late in the season for such an additional municipal expense.

After striding across to the even-numbered side of East Swan, he glances back over his shoulder at the tall, stone, sturdily built St. John's Episcopal Church, with its graceful buttresses, next door to his boardinghouse.

The young man approaches the intersection of Swan and Washington. The corner building on the block he is headed for is William E. Storey's Liquors and Bitters (their window sign reads, "Fresh lager on tap").

He stops to double-check the time kept by his pocket watch against the huge round clock mounted above the entrance to Church and Sons jewelers across the street at 17 East Swan Street. Ralph Church has just pulled up the shades to reveal window shelves jammed with gold watches and mantel clocks.

He lingers in front of Long and Carpenter's Oysters, 16 East Swan Street, to breathe in familiar fragrances of the sea and then navigates the sidewalk through kegs and crates of canned sardines, lobsters, and foreign fruits.

In no time at all, he is there. Number 14 East Swan Street, a modest structure in a block lined with similar three- to four-story buildings. Before entering, he checks out the view directly across the street from his new work address. Two businesses occupy 13 and 15 East Swan. Howard and Bunting manufactures picture frames and proudly shows off frames, mirrors, paintings, and samples of rosewood and gilt moldings in its windows. Post and Viergiver (they advertise "Glazing done to order" in the Buffalo City Directory) specializes in art supplies, glass, window sashes, turpentine, and varnishes.

The young man seems satisfied with his tidy sphere of home and work, tied together handily within a 175-yard walk each way.

He wheels around, hops up the two steps from the sidewalk, and disappears inside 14 East Swan.

He is immediately struck by the strong but agreeable odor of printer's ink wafting up from the printing presses in the basement. He peeks in at the business office on the ground floor, scales the stairs past the second-floor printing-job office, and reaches the third floor. He stands in the doorway, waiting for someone to notice him.

After the stranger is ignored for an annoying few seconds, one of the gaggle of lolling reporters and political hangers-on in the smoke-filled editorial room lazily looks up and asks, "Is there anyone you would like to see?"

Without missing a beat, the young man replies, "Well, yes, I would like to *see* someone offer the new editor a chair!"

Mark Twain has officially arrived at the *Buffalo Morning Express*.[1]

In some respects, Samuel Langhorne Clemens's (Mark Twain's) path to Buffalo began two years earlier, in September of 1867, in a stateroom on board the steamer *Quaker City* in the Bay of Smyrna, Turkey. It is here that Charley Langdon of Elmira, New York, showed his fellow passenger an ivory miniature of his older sister, Olivia.[2] Twain was hooked.

Twain, already a celebrity, was nearing the end of a celebrated voyage that began in June and was to end in November of 1867. Previously, he had held jobs as a printer, a steamboat pilot, a miner, and a newspaper reporter. He had become a popular humorist due to his widely read *Jumping Frog of Calaveras County and Other Sketches* (1867) and his successful lectures. He joined the famous excursion to Europe, the Holy Land, and Egypt and was paid by the *Daily Alta California* to submit fifty letters describing his trip. When the cruise ended, he set to work transforming the letters into a book and winning the affections of Olivia Langdon. Twain spent much of 1868 in Washington, DC, writing and revising the book, which would become *The Innocents Abroad*, and in Elmira, wooing Olivia. They announced their engagement in February of 1869.

During the first half of 1869, Twain visited Elmira often, lectured frequently, fine-tuned *The Innocents Abroad* manuscript, and explored job opportunities at several newspapers. Mindful of his upcoming marriage, Twain felt obliged to secure a stable position. He sought an opening that offered a business partnership and a key journalistic role. He considered the *New York Tribune*, the *Cleveland Herald*, and the *Post* and the *Courant* in Hartford, Connecticut. A conjoining of fateful elements brought Twain to the *Buffalo Morning Express*.

Early in the summer of 1869, Thomas A. Kennett, whom Twain mistakenly remembers as Mr. Kinney in his *Autobiography*,[3] decided to sell his one-third share of the *Express*. Jervis Langdon, Olivia's father, learned of this newspaper opening from one of the employees of the Buffalo branch office of his hugely successful coal business, which was headquartered in Elmira. Twain was in limbo; Hartford had balked at taking him on, and Cleveland's partnership seemed too expensive. Langdon nudged Twain to invest in the *Express*.

Langdon wanted to set up his future son-in-law in Buffalo. His cadre of trusted managers at the Buffalo coal office would be available to cater to Twain's needs—and to keep an eye on the self-proclaimed "Wild Man of the Pacific Slope"[4] during his last months of bachelorhood. And, once married, Langdon's daughter and son-in-law would live only 190 miles away—just a five-hour train ride—from Elmira. The price tag was attractive as well. Kennett was asking $25,000, whereas the *Cleveland Herald* share would cost more than twice as much. Finally, Langdon was sagely aware of the advantage of having a prominently placed journalist who could be counted on as sympathetic to the controversial issue of the coal monopoly in Buffalo.

Jervis Langdon acted quickly. He offered Twain half the asking price to buy into the *Buffalo Express*. By July 14, Twain was in Buffalo. He investigated the *Express* and the city and liked what he saw. He stayed at Buffalo's finest hotel, the Tifft House, and thought that "the private residences of Buffalo are the finest in the country."[5] Twain shuttled in and out of Buffalo, once with Jervis Langdon, over the next two weeks to examine the financial records of the *Express*. By the end of the first week of August, he had a room in the East Swan Street boardinghouse. One week later, he was a co-owner and coeditor of the *Buffalo Express*.

Mark Twain's Buffalo period, from mid-August 1869 to mid-March 1871, was marked by stunning extremes. The eighteen-month Buffalo experience was rewarding yet trying. Professionally, he produced much lackluster writing that failed to push his creative envelope. On the other hand, he composed some distinctive stories for the *Express*. His work habits were erratic. A long stretch of inactivity was often followed by weeks of writing at a feverish, breakneck pace.

In Buffalo, Twain held down a responsible job and launched a stable domestic life. But his commitment to a career in journalism wavered, and a relentless string of deaths and illness shook his idyllic, tranquil home life.

Twain's personality and behavior exhibited drastic contrasts, too. He displayed an abrasive side that repelled some people. Yet he managed to mingle easily with influential Buffalonians and to forge lifelong friendships.

Image I.1. The Tifft House on Main Street was Buffalo's finest hotel. Twain stayed there in July of 1869 and reported on Prince Arthur's luncheon there a few weeks later. (Photograph courtesy of the Buffalo State College Archives, *Courier-Express* Collection.)

Twain's Buffalo experience was pivotal. He came to Buffalo as an unmarried man staking his career hopes on the grind of daily newspaper work. He departed Buffalo as a husband and father, intent on the lofty vocation of literary artist. After the *Buffalo Morning Express*, Mark Twain abandoned full-time journalism for good.

Of all the highs and lows in Buffalo, the bestseller status of *The Innocents Abroad* brought constant joy to him. He exploited his editor's chair to publicize the new book. It is ironic that Twain later borrowed a metaphor from *The Innocents Abroad* to refer to the decline of his Buffalo fortunes. With his wordplay regarding the pyramids, he defined the roller-coaster nature of his ride through Buffalo.

Twain came to Buffalo with the proof pages of *The Innocents Abroad* fresh in mind. Toward the end of his 651-page book, when describing his encounter with the great pyramids of Egypt, Twain addresses his struggle to reconcile the continual push and pull of dream and reality, illusion and disillusionment, high expectations and disappointments that life serves up:

> At the distance of a few miles the Pyramids rising above the palms, looked very clean-cut, very grand and imposing, and very soft and filmy, as well. They swam in a rich haze that took from them all suggestions of unfeeling stone, and made them seem only the airy nothings of a dream—structures which might blossom into tiers of vague arches, or ornate colonnades, may be, and change and change again, into all graceful forms of architecture, while we looked, and then melt deliciously away and blend with the tremulous atmosphere. . . . A laborious walk in the flaming sun brought us to the foot of the great Pyramid of Cheops. It was a fairy vision no longer. It was a corrugated, unsightly mountain of stone.[6]

Twain's Buffalo experience, too, began amid a dreamy innocence. His life with Olivia in Buffalo started as a "fairyland."[7] But as tragedy and disenchantment disturbed the dream, Twain's attitude soured. He revived the pyramids conceit to explain his despair once the Buffalo utopia crumbled. Just four months before uprooting his ailing family from Buffalo, he wrote: "Work is piling on me in toppling pyramids."[8]

But the pyramids must have still represented an alluringly mysterious unknown, a dreamlike, creative force in the mind of the young editor who optimistically stepped out of his boardinghouse that August morning of 1869. Mark Twain was soon to be the toast of the town, the guest of honor at a welcome party hosted by his fellow Buffalo journalists. The city of Buffalo was at his feet.

1

THE BOYS OF THE *EXPRESS*

In August of 1869, Mark Twain began his new job at the *Buffalo Morning Express* on the busiest weekend of the summer. As befitted a boomtown with a population well over one hundred thousand and growing fast,[1] the city was buzzing with a full calendar of events that competed with Twain's journalistic debut. Horse races advertising a $30,000 purse drew huge crowds to the Driving Park. New municipal open-sided horse-drawn streetcars were bursting with ninety passengers each. The Academy of Music boasted sold-out performances of Lydia Thompson's Blondes Burlesque Troupe production of *Sinbad the Pirate*, which opened on Monday night, August 16.[2] A standing-room-only throng at the opera house waited three hours for the featured sparring exhibition between Ned "The Irish Giant" O'Baldwin and Mike McCoole to finally begin. The Niagara Regatta delighted swarms of waterfront onlookers with a Saturday afternoon of yacht races and single-scull, double-scull, or four-oared outrigged boat competitions. All of this took place despite unseasonably cool weather. Longtime Buffalonians complained of sixty- to seventy-degree days all summer that had brought fall fruit (black raspberries, apples, and pears) to market stands earlier than usual.

Amid this frenzied summer weekend, Twain was welcomed into the Buffalo journalistic fraternity. On Saturday afternoon of August 14, newspapermen representing papers like the *Courier*, the *Commercial Advertiser*, the *Christian Advocate*, the *Commercial Report and Market Review*, the *Demokrat*, the *Freie Presse*, the *Evening Post*, and Twain's own *Express* gathered at Elam R. Jewett's grand estate.

Jewett, founder of the first envelope factory west of New York City and former owner and publisher of the *Buffalo Commercial Advertiser*, had for years hosted the annual dinner meeting of the Western New York Press Club. This year's special guest was Mark Twain. Twain took full advantage of the opportunity to promote himself.

Jewett's homestead, known as Willow Lawn, sprawled across the northern edge of the city limits on Main Street, in an area formerly called the Buffalo Plains. His mansion was surrounded by 450 acres of lawns and extensive gardens. A major portion of the flatlands at the base of a slope behind his home was being transformed by landscape architect Frederick Law Olmsted into a public greenspace soon to be named Delaware Park. Buffalo's first tomatoes are said to have been raised on Jewett's model farm. The centerpiece of the grounds was a great willow tree whose massive trunk measured six feet in diameter.[3]

Image 1.1. Elam Jewett's estate, Willow Lawn, where the Western New York Press Club feted Twain in August of 1869. (Image courtesy of the Buffalo State College Archives, *Courier-Express* Collection.)

During Jewett's residency there, Willow Lawn served as a station on the Underground Railroad. Jewett was a good friend of Millard Fillmore; they had traveled to Europe together in 1856. By 1869, Jewett's home was a rendezvous for the elite and fashionable of Buffalo society. Twain was excited about the occasion and wrote about it to his publisher, Elisha Bliss, twice in two days.[4]

At dinner, Twain rubbed elbows with his fellow reporters and editors and charmed them into promising him favorable reviews of *The Innocents Abroad*. He may have entertained his new colleagues by reading selections from the book—his first public reading in Buffalo.[5] At some point, Twain strolled the grounds at Willow Lawn, picking flowers and making impromptu boutonnieres for himself and other guests.

During a recent visit to Elmira, Twain had refused to adorn his lapel buttonhole with flowers. So, shortly after the Press Club fete, he joked with Olivia about his newfound enthusiasm for boutonnieres. His letter is a masterpiece of comic exaggeration.

Twain begins by telling Olivia that at Jewett's reception (he misspells the name as "Jewell"), he decorated himself in pansies and persuaded the other journalists to join him ("We all wore them.").[6] Then Twain claims to have ordered Jewett's gardener to pick a bouquet for every journalist as they were leaving. He closes the letter by telling Olivia that normally he wouldn't wear flowers in public because it seems "snobbish." However, he would gladly "wear a sunflower down the street if you say so," as penance for hurting Olivia's feelings in Elmira.

The press dinner capped a momentous Saturday for Twain. Earlier in the day he had closed the deal in which he purchased one-third ownership of the *Buffalo Express*. Jervis Langdon had forwarded $12,500 toward half the asking price of $25,000, Twain contributed $2,500 of his own toward the down payment, and Langdon guaranteed the balance. Langdon secured the services of Bowen and Rogers, a prestigious law firm, whose impressive staff had so far included a mayor, a three-term congressman, a postmaster general, a past US president, and a US president-to-be.[7] In their offices at 28 Erie Street, the articles of agreement on the sale were drawn up and signed.

The *Buffalo Express* enjoyed a solid reputation and healthy circulation. Founded in 1846, it was strongly Republican and described itself on the local news page as "The Official Paper of the City." The *Express* appeared every morning and evening except Sundays. The evening version was published in two editions at two o'clock and four o'clock in the afternoon. The subscription rate with local delivery was sixteen cents per week. The *Express* was also available in a weekly format on Wednesdays for $1.50 annually. The paper came off the presses in large sheets (weekdays, four pages long; Saturdays, six pages), which newsboys then folded for sale on street corners and delivery to subscribers.

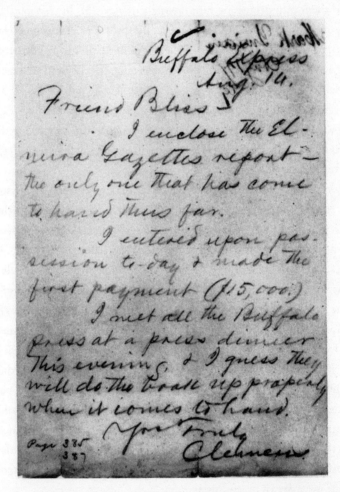

Image 1.2. Twain's August 14, 1869, letter to Elisha Bliss, written from his *Buffalo Express* office, citing his purchase of a one-third share of the *Buffalo Express* and the press dinner in his honor. (Image used by permission of the Collection of the Buffalo and Erie County Historical Society.)

Page 1 summarized national and world events under headings such as "Washington" and "Europe." The second page consisted of legal notices, obituaries of prominent local residents, and farm and garden stories. Page 3 focused on finance and trade, featuring a list of ships and cargo arriving at Buffalo's bustling port.[8] The fourth page contained editorials, local feature stories, and works by well-known authors.

In the mid-1860s, the *Express* had moved from 158 Main Street, between Seneca and Exchange Streets, to 14 East Swan Street. The block on which Twain's *Express* building stood was historic—it occupied the southern border of what in the earliest days of the city had been Joseph Ellicott's one-hundred-acre reservation. The building sat on city land that was part of what the British had burned down during the War of 1812. In the ensuing decades, the city had rapidly rebuilt itself, becoming a major shipping and railroad center, home of iron works, brass foundries, leather and clothing manufacturing plants, and some of the largest breweries in the country.

The Swan Street building was ideally located. The waterfront, Buffalo's commercial heart, was within easy walking distance. The *Express* helped form a tight geographical triangle of Buffalo's three big newspapers. Less than two blocks to the southeast, at 253 Washington Street, was the *Commercial Advertiser*. At 197 Main Street, the *Daily Courier* was less than two blocks southwest of the *Express*. As is so often the case with symbiotic newspaper and tavern cultures in America, there was no lack of watering holes nearby. Within the journalistic triangle, there were five saloons. William Storey's was on Swan Street, Henry Gillig's was on Washington, J. Noe's and Samuel Boas's were across from each other on Main Street, and the legendary Tiphaine's was at 245 Main Street, which was conveniently equidistant between the *Express* and the *Courier*.

The downside of 14 East Swan Street was that to call the building plain was a compliment. William Kennett, whose brother sold his *Express* share to Twain, remembered it as "a very tough looking affair."[9] It was a four-story brick building just twenty-five feet wide. Along its west side, an alley bisected the block northward from Swan to South Division Street. Except for the twelve-foot-tall display windows on the ground floor and cornice trim decorating the top front, the structure was nondescript. The second-, third-, and fourth-floor fronts each had three plain rectangular windows providing bird's-eye views of Swan Street.

Image 1.3. Block of East Swan Street, north side, between Washington and Main Streets. The *Buffalo Express* building at no. 14 occupied all four floors of the left half of the tallest building. (Image used by permission of the Collection of the Buffalo and Erie County Historical Society.)

Image 1.4. The 14 East Swan Street front street entrance of the *Buffalo Express*. (Image used by permission of the Collection of the Buffalo and Erie County Historical Society.)

The interior of the *Express* building was unremarkable as well. The printing press was in the basement, and the business office was on the ground floor. The job-printing office ("Satisfaction Guaranteed in Every Respect," according to its ad in the Buffalo City Directory), which filled orders for posters, programs, checks, streamers, bills of lading, invitations, placards, and street bills, was on the second floor. Editorial rooms were in the front of the third floor. The top floor housed reporters and the city editor/reporter in the front and layout personnel in the back area. Rooms were unpainted, unadorned, and cheaply furnished.

The drabness of his new work environment did not dampen Twain's initial enthusiasm for his *Express* duties. He made himself at home, climbing the "rickety, grimy stairs"[10] to his third-floor cubicle at the center front of the *Express* building, at the head of the staircase. At first he had only an old wooden chair, a plain table, a makeshift bookcase along the wall, and a wastebasket. Soon he added a comfortable, bright-yellow, wooden lounging chair with a writing board hinged on one arm and a stout, basket-woven seat.[11] Outside Twain's small office was an open editorial work area with a crude row of bookshelves lining the wall. A long, antique, black-walnut table featured a two-quart tobacco jar of yellow earthenware in the center and had edges worn from boot heels of staffers and visitors who sat tilted back in editorial chairs, their feet "forming practically a barricade around the editor."[12] Clay and briarwood pipes were scattered about. Twain and his coeditor often spread out proof sheets to read on this table.

Twain attacked his writing and editing chores zealously for the first six weeks. The routine shift for editorial staff was from 3:00 p.m. to 2:00 a.m. (The *Morning Express* was the paper's bread and butter). But Twain often devoted longer hours to his new job, from 8:00 a.m. until well past midnight. Except for the end of August, he worked weekends, too, through September.

During the dog days of the summer, Twain plotted a series of improvements, conferred with reporters and compositors, and wrote several stories. Sweltering heat struck by the end of Twain's first week at the *Express*, making working conditions uncomfortable. Colleagues recall Twain's informality as the workday progressed. He worked in shirtsleeves, smoking a meerschaum pipe, through those busy six weeks and littered his small office with clothing and papers: "Coatless, sometimes vestless, he lolled in his chair with one shoeless foot on the table and the other in the wastebasket. His collar, cuffs and tie were strewn on the floor with the papers, and his hat lay just where it happened to fall when brushed off the back of his head."[13]

Twain's quirky behavior fit right in with the casual atmosphere at the *Express*. Republican pundits wandered in and out of the editorial room, kibitzing and leaving a trail of cigar smoke. In addition to *Express* staffers, the politicos lounging around might include the collector of the port, the postmaster, the superintendent of canals, and an assemblyman or two. Visiting celebrities added an unpredictable, festive touch to the place. At one time or another (not just during Twain's tenure), public figures such as Grover Cleveland, Millard Fillmore, Henry Ward Beecher, "Petroleum Nasby" (David Ross Locke), Oliver Wendell Holmes, and actor John Raymond stopped by. Raymond even sat in Twain's yellow chair.[14]

On one memorable occasion in 1869, a "healer" called on the *Express*. Twain dropped what he was doing and consulted with the visitor. While his newspaper colleagues and other hangers-on watched, Twain held his hands above the healer's bald head. He claimed to feel a cool, curative power radiating from the polished pate. Others apparently felt it, too.[15]

Twain even enlivened the *Express* in his absence. While he was out of town lecturing in December of 1869, an anonymous prankster from Chicago sent Twain a live fox care of his office at the *Express*.[16]

While open to playfulness, Twain was serious about making over the newspaper in order to improve circulation and its reputation. He wanted to do for the *Express* what humorist and friend Petroleum Nasby was doing for the *Toledo Blade*. Twain had a multifaceted plan. One of his first priorities was to insist on clear writing. He intended to teach reporters to "modify the adjectives, curtail their philosophical reflections & leave out slang." He also vowed to alter the appearance of the *Express* by toning down dramatic headline typefaces: "I have annihilated all the glaring thunder-&-lightning headings over the telegraphic news & made that department look quiet & respectable."[17]

Years later, reporter Earl Berry remembered that Twain instilled in his reporters a strict, rule-governed sense of correctness and simplicity when using the English language. However, Berry noticed a double standard in Twain's own *Express* stories. As much as Twain was a stickler with reporters about employing "plain Saxon," he himself was guilty of producing flowery prose.

As for changing the cosmetics of the *Express*, Twain did create a more dignified-looking front page. But it was less appealing, more "gray," to the eye. Formerly, the *Express* mixed type fonts (serif and sans serif) and sometimes varied all uppercase with all lowercase in the stacked headlines. Under Twain's direction, *Express* headlines were much smaller in type size, seldom boldface, all uppercase, and in the same font (serif) as the text of the story. In fact, the headlines and story ran together. Twain also introduced occasional italicized headlines. Overall, Twain's typographical modifications, which he said resulted from two days of consulting with layout foreman John J. Hall, made little impact, which is surprising given Twain's printing background. He did achieve a greater uniformity of appearance, especially on page 1, but made the *Express* look more staid than inviting for readers.[18]

Twain aimed to revamp the *Express* in other ways, too. He wanted to pump new life into the stale People and Things column, which published bits and pieces of news items gleaned from newspaper exchanges. For as long as he supervised that assignment, for sixteen People and Things installments in August and September of 1869, Twain accomplished his mission. The column took on a gossipy, sarcastic, and humorous flavor. He sprinkled in editorial comments, zingers, and hyperbolic statements among the factual tidbits.

Another area that Twain successfully transformed was the coverage of police matters. Previously, news from the police blotter had been delivered straightforwardly. Under Twain's leadership, the police reporter jazzed up the stories via humor and satire. Activities of City Police Justice Isaac V. Vanderpoel's courtroom, as reported in the November to December 1869 editions of the *Express*, reflected Twain's new policy of spicing up police reporting.

Perhaps the most significant change Twain instituted was to shamelessly exploit the *Express* as his personal self-promotion machine. At times during the fall of 1869, the *Express* was so saturated with his name, it could have been renamed the *Buffalo Morning Twainian*. The August 21 issue contained Twain's "Salutatory" introduction to *Express* readers, "A Day at Niagara" (a lengthy front-page feature story), his People and Things compilation, and "Napoleon and Abdul" (excerpted from *The Innocents Abroad*). Then there was the October 9 *Express*, with a two-page insert reprinting thirty-nine notices of Twain's new job at the *Express* and favorable reviews of *The Innocents Abroad*. Twain was not bashful about advertising himself in his newspaper. He also launched a series of his own original feature stories in Saturday editions. On weekdays, full-column ads several inches long alerted readers to each new Saturday feature.

Along with writing and editing like a whirlwind during his first weeks at the *Express*, Twain also cultivated a sense of camaraderie among his new newspaper colleagues.

Twain's *Express* comprised an eclectic and talented crew. Among the staffers with whom he worked were academic scholars, Union Civil War heroes, painters and sculptors, poets, and career journalists. Twain referred to his *Express* associates as "the boys."

SCHOLAR

Twain took an instant liking to Josephus Nelson Larned, his coeditor and co-owner. Aptly named, the "learned" Larned reported on local and state political matters. Twain called Larned, a voracious reader who later wrote a five-volume history of the world, "the human encyclopedia."[19] His twelve-volume *The New Larned History for Ready Reference* consisted of more than ten thousand pages and twelve million words.[20] Larned had moved to Buffalo from his native Canada at the age of twelve. He had been at the *Express* for ten years and had established his solid reputation for stirring editorials during the Civil War.

Image 1.5. Josephus Nelson Larned, Twain's friend and co-owner at the *Express*, who served as political editor. (Image from the *Buffalo Times*, November 4, 1928.)

Larned is usually depicted as a bespectacled senior, a serious intellectual, and a journalist of unimpeachable character. In reality, Larned was six months younger than Twain, had a sense of humor, and was a rowing and card-playing crony of Twain's. At one meeting of Buffalo's private Young Men's Association, Larned responded to jokes about his aversion to tuxedos with the quip, "Well, I might allow the dinner-coat, but it is the tails that make a monkey of the man."[21] Despite Larned's ability to make witty remarks, Twain urged him to stick to serious political commentary. Once when Larned attempted a light story at the

Express, Twain reportedly told him, "Better leave the humorous writing on this sheet to me, Larned."[22]

Twain and Larned worked in close quarters together on the third floor of the *Express*, which created some light moments. Twain wrote Olivia that they would sit across from each other at the big editorial table and exchange manuscripts when they got frustrated. "Then we scribble away without the least trouble, he finishing my article & I his," which produced "patch-work editorials" that were much better due to "crossing the breed."[23] One time, Larned slipped, knocking down rows of books from the rickety shelves lining the editorial-room wall. Twain wisecracked, "Any blessed fool can drop one or two books, but it takes a genius to drop a whole library."[24] Twain also wrote Olivia that he jokingly told Larned, "I wish I had his industry & he had my sense."[25]

The two editors liked each other. On consecutive September weekends, Twain told "Joe" to leave work early so that he could dine at home with his wife, Frances. Twain then handled double the editorial duties for the remaining hours of each shift. He was merely returning a favor. A week earlier, so that Twain could travel to Elmira for a long weekend with Olivia, Larned had covered for him at the *Express*. Twain wrote that Larned was doing "the work of both of us from 3 P.M. Friday till Monday noon . . . the equivalent of getting out two editions of the paper alone."[26] Twain admired Larned's work ethic, his ability to work "straight along all day, day in & day out." He compared Larned's dedication to that of "an honest old treadmill horse."

Larned helped ease Twain's lonely bachelor existence in Buffalo. He sponsored Twain's membership in two local literary organizations, the Nameless Club and the Young Men's Association, to which Twain belonged through 1871. Sometimes, while waiting for page proofs of the *Express* to be printed for final penciled corrections, Larned accompanied Twain to 98 East Swan Street, the home and office of Dr. Alexander T. Bull, where they would play cards and share stories. Another joint outing on a balmy evening in late August turned out to be a harrowing experience.

Larned, Twain, and *Express* bookkeeper William H. Johnston, whom Twain had first gotten to know when examining the paper's ledgers, took a small boat out for a pleasurable row on Lake Erie. In order to reach a patch of sandy beach on which to bathe, they rowed beyond the protective stone break wall of Buffalo's inner harbor. When the wind suddenly whipped up off the lake, choppy waves nearly capsized their frail boat. With Larned, a nonswimmer, and Johnston at the oars, Twain managed to navigate them through the rough waters to a tranquil area within the break wall and then safely back to shore. Larned and Johnston had wanted to row directly to land, but Twain persuaded them to row with the waves farther out into the lake and then steered them tack-like gradually toward shore. Twain later boasted to Olivia that he had been worried about saving Larned if he had gone overboard, but a rescue was unnecessary because of Twain's expert nautical skills.

In Twain's early weeks at the *Express*, he and Larned cemented a life-long friendship. More than thirty years later, Twain looked back at their time together at the newspaper with affection and pleasure.[27] For his part, Larned later reminisced about his good fortune at being associated with Twain at the *Express* and remembered Twain's great charm.[28] In the fourth volume of his five-volume 1915 history of the world, Larned names Twain as one of a handful of masterful fiction writers during history's "sixth epoch."[29]

SCULPTOR AND WAR HERO

Colonel George H. Selkirk was the other co-owner of Twain's *Express*. Selkirk supervised business affairs—circulation, advertising, and the job-printing office. Like Larned, Selkirk was Twain's age, a mere nine months older. And like Twain, Selkirk had already had an eventful life.

George Selkirk was the son of John H. Selkirk, a prominent Buffalo architect. At age nineteen, he traveled to Florence, Italy, to study sculpture. Upon returning to Buffalo, Selkirk continued to study art and sculpted busts of well-known Buffalonians such as former president Millard Fillmore and Rev. John C. Lord of Central Presbyterian Church. But the Civil War altered the course of Selkirk's life.

In August of 1861, Selkirk enlisted as a second lieutenant in the Forty-Ninth Regiment of New York Volunteers, the second regiment to leave Buffalo. He participated in the battles of Gettysburg, Antietam, and Fredericksburg, and in May of 1864 he was seriously wounded in the Battle of the Wilderness. He knew Generals Ulysses S. Grant and Philip Sheridan, under whom he had served at Cedar Creek. By the end of the war, Selkirk had been twice decorated, had been promoted to lieutenant colonel, and had abandoned his sculpting aspirations. Instead, he entered the business world.[30]

Image 1.6. Col. George Selkirk, sculptor and Civil War hero, Twain's other *Express* co-owner who handled business operations. (Image from the *Buffalo Times*, November 4, 1928.)

When Twain arrived at the *Express* in August of 1869, Selkirk owned one-third of the paper and was its business manager. That summer, Selkirk had married Emily Peabody of Buffalo. Tall and mustachioed, he puffed cigars most of the day. Twain and Selkirk appear to have gotten along fairly well. Selkirk was a member of the Nameless Club, whose members met for dinner, drinks, and readings at St. James Hall, and whose ranks Twain joined in 1869.

There is no record of rancor between Twain and Selkirk. However, their mutual cordiality may have been strained at times. Perhaps it was because Twain, while professing to hate business, meddled in how the *Express* was run. Selkirk may have caught wind of Twain's plan to hire his book publisher, Elisha Bliss, and his own brother Orion Clemens to operate the paper more imaginatively and profitably. Perhaps there was lingering North–South tension between the two. Maybe it related to Twain's directives to Selkirk, sent while on a lecture tour, insisting that free exchange copies of the *Express* be given to several newsmen he met on the road. Selkirk, after all, was accustomed to giving orders, not taking them. Selkirk may well have resented how Twain appropriated potential ad space in the *Express* to promote his upcoming stories and *The Innocents Abroad*. It is likely that Twain was bitter at selling his one-third share of the newspaper to Selkirk in 1871 at a $10,000 loss.

Whatever the reasons, there was distance between Selkirk and Twain that did not exist between Larned and Twain. Twain addressed Selkirk formally as "Colonel." A sense of courteous reserve might even be gathered in Twain's wording of an inscription for Selkirk's first edition copy of *The Innocents Abroad*: "With assurances of distinguished consideration &c, &c, your friend."[31] Fifty-five years after they worked together under the same roof, Selkirk recalled that Twain was not a personable *Express* colleague: "Twain, by the way, confined his humor to his writings. He was a very ordinary chap otherwise and was not given to wise cracking or the amusement of his associates."[32]

Another of Twain's fellow workers at the newspaper had fonder recollections of their association. He, too, was a soldier and artist.

ARTIST, POET, AND WAR HERO

John Harrison Mills was in his late twenties when Twain first came to the *Express*. He was the composing-room artist, responsible for converting drawings into woodcuts capable of being reproduced in print. Mills was also a poet, a painter, and a member of the Nameless Club.

In May of 1861, the nineteen-year-old Mills left Buffalo as a private with Company D of the Twenty-First New York Volunteer regiment to join Union forces at the warfront. Three months later he was badly wounded at the Second Battle of Bull Run by a bullet that passed through his knee and hip and lodged in his back. After months of treatment in an Alexandria, Virginia, hospital, the short, slightly built Mills returned to Buffalo on crutches.

Mills grew his hair long, in the style of artists of his time, and established a reputation in sculpture (fashioning busts of Abraham Lincoln and one admired by St. Gaudens called *The Young Athlete*), landscape painting (particularly Colorado scenes), and as a portraitist. Mills painted a portrait of Twain from studies that he made in 1870. The portrait captured Twain's "reddish yellow bush of hair towering above his broad white forehead and dark, eager eyes."[33]

Image 1.7. John Harrison Mills, painter and wounded Civil War veteran, was the staff artist at the *Express* and painted Twain's portrait. (Image from the *Buffalo Times*, October 23, 1904.)

During Twain's first weeks at the *Express*, he and Mills worked closely together on the third floor. Twain either sketched or suggested ideas for illustrations to accompany four of his stories, and Mills engraved them in woodcut. Mills remembered Twain as a diligent worker: "He came here to work, and to make good, and he got right about it."[34] Years later, Mills supplied a grandiloquent description of Twain's presence at the newspaper:

> I thought that, pictorially, the noble costume of the Albanian would have well become him. Or he might have been a Goth, and worn the horned bull-pate helmet of Alaric's warriors; or stood at the prow of one of the swift craft of the Vikings. His eyes, which have been variously described, were, it seemed to me, of an indescribable depth of the bluish moss-agate, with a capacity of pupil dilation that in certain lights had the effect of a deep black.[35]

JOURNALIST

Earl D. Berry was born with printer's ink in his veins. His father, Clinton, had been marine editor at the *Express*. Earl Berry started as an office boy at the *Express* in the late 1860s shortly after graduating from Buffalo High School. He was soon promoted to hotel reporter, making the rounds to hotels late at night to copy the list of that day's arrivals and soak up any newsworthy gossip. He next moved up to theater reporter. Berry was not yet twenty years old when Twain joined the *Express*, but Twain quickly recognized young Berry's talent and promoted him to city editor. Twain handpicked Berry to oversee changes in police coverage and trusted him with other special assignments. Berry reported directly to Twain.

Berry, who went on to have a long career at the *New York Times*, was popular at the *Express* and widely admired for his ability to "cover ground."[36] Berry was impressed with Twain's efficient writing under deadline pressure: "The humorist writes with great ease and accuracy and sends a clean first manuscript to the compositor's case."[37] The young reporter also praised Twain's journalistic integrity, saying that Twain was "scrupulous" of the "purity and dignity" of the press.

However, Berry did note Twain's irascible personality. He remembered Twain as "a quiet, reserved and irritable man." When Berry published his memories of working with Twain at the *Express* in an 1873 issue of *Globe* magazine, it provoked a response by Twain. In the next issue, Twain humorously acknowledged Berry's appraisal of his volatile, egocentric nature: "I perceive that the writer has discovered my besetting weakness, which is unreflecting and rather ungraceful irritability. It isn't a pleasant trait. I *have* some pleasant ones, but modesty compels me to hide them from the world, so no one gets the benefit of them but myself."[38]

POET

Although David Gray edited the *Buffalo Daily Courier*, he counts as an unofficial "boy" of the *Express*. Once when a family crisis called Larned away from the *Express* and left the paper shorthanded, Gray stepped in as guest editor of that day's edition. Gray also met Larned and Twain at Dr. Bull's for cards and small talk while proofs of their respective newspapers were being printed. Gray and Larned once challenged Twain to a swimming match off downtown Buffalo's Lake Erie shore. Twain declined, perhaps in deference to Larned's inability to swim![39]

Image 1.8. David Gray, poet and editor of the rival *Buffalo Daily Courier*, became one of Twain's closest friends. (Image from the *Buffalo Times*, November 4, 1928.)

Gray expressed his preference for poetry over journalism: "I am a poet by nature, and a journalist by compulsion. I am more proud of my iambics and hexameters than any laurels I ever won, or expect to win, in the editorial chair."[40] Although he had been city editor of the *Courier*, a Democrat-loyal rival of Twain's *Express*, since 1859, Gray had a poet's soul.

The native-born Scot was thirty-three years old and had recently married Martha "Mattie" Guthrie of New Orleans when he and Twain first met in August of 1869. Gray and Twain struck up a friendship that would last a lifetime. Soon their wives became close, too. When Twain was still a bachelor in Buffalo, Gray helped guide him around town. Gray not only belonged to the Nameless Club, but he had also founded it. He, Larned, Mills, and Selkirk helped fill some of Twain's lonely evenings in the fall of 1869 with the club's literary events. At Nameless Club meetings, Twain met Buffalo's literati—Captain

John Wayland, Jerome Stillson, Otto Besser, William P. Letchworth, Tom Kean, James N. Johnston, Mrs. C. H. Gildersleeve, and Amanda Jones. The agenda included dinner, debates, and poetry and essay readings. Evenings were capped off by late-night toasts (as many as nine), a favorite being, "Lager beer, a great civilizer!"[41] If Nameless Club outings weren't enough, Gray and his new wife likely invited Twain to their occasional "Saturday night at the Grays" at their cottage home at 192 Niagara Street, where friends read works in progress to each other. Gray was a prolific and accomplished poet who took an interest in Twain's work. In 1870, Twain mentioned his idea for *Roughing It* to Gray, who encouraged him to follow through on writing the project.

OTHER *EXPRESS* "BOYS"

In addition to John Hall, a printer and foreman of the composing room, with whom Twain consulted to redesign typefaces and headlines, there were other key staff members of Twain's *Buffalo Express*. Two other printers, who operated the presses in the basement, were William Gatchell and Horace Wilcox. Francis Wardell worked under Selkirk as head of circulation. In the editorial department there were George A. Martin, the commerce editor, and Chester A. Wilcox, a general editor. George Leader, a clerk who became a reporter after Twain left, was a star player on the *Express* baseball team. One day after Twain joined the paper, second baseman Leader scored four runs in a thirty-three to sixteen victory over their rivals from the *Buffalo Commercial Advertiser*.

There is evidence that corroborates Berry's memory of Twain as sometimes rude and impatient with fellow workers. Jimmie Brennan, a fourteen-year-old office boy (and Francis Wardell's nephew) recalled how he and other young employees of the *Express* teased Twain by walking slowly past his office with squeaky shoes until he would shoo them away.[42] W. Landsittel was a printer's devil (an apprentice) during Twain's *Express* tenure and remembered Twain's sloppy, indolent habits and condescending attitude toward young helpers. He claimed that Twain once gave him a nickel to dot an *i* in his copy for him and that Twain would refuse to move his feet that were propped up on his desk and would bribe Landsittel not to sweep his messy office floor.[43]

Then there was the apparent friction between Twain and Philip Lee. "General" Lee was an African American who served as janitor and coal shoveler at the *Express*. According to Brennan, Twain wanted to fire Lee for insolence. Perhaps as a measure of revenge, Lee purportedly watched once from the Swan Street sidewalk as Twain laboriously scaled the steep alley-side outer stairs of the *Express*. Lee waited until Twain reached for the door knob of the outside entrance on the second-story landing before calling out to Twain that the door was locked and never used. This incident might fall under the "what goes around comes around" category. Reminiscing in February of 1906, Twain recalled pulling a trick on his brother Henry in which Twain had locked the upstairs outer door to their Hannibal, Missouri, home and waited until Henry ascended the outside stairway. When Henry was stranded at the top of the stairs at the locked door, Twain pelted him with dirt clods.[44] Shortly after Twain moved into his wedding house in Buffalo in February of 1870, the *Buffalo Morning Express* reported that Lee had his pocket picked at a restaurant on Elm Street.[45]

Overall, the convivial climate at the *Express* seemed to ignite Twain's passion for writing in his first six weeks there. The staff must have suspected that the *Express* was simply a stepping stone for Twain's career. Berry recalls Twain giving up on journalism because "he did not like routine work and he could not write fun to order."[46] To their credit, "the boys of the *Express*," so unlike Twain in so many ways (they were mostly Northerners, and most of them were firmly rooted in the city and at the paper), welcomed this celebrated outlier into their fold, for theirs was a tightly knit professional and social circle. When Larned married in 1861, Gray was his best man. At Gray's funeral, Larned was a pallbearer. In 1888, Larned edited the two-volume *Letters, Poems and Selected Prose Writings of David Gray*.[47] When Larned died, Selkirk was an honorary pallbearer, as was Olivia's cousin, Andrew Langdon.

Soon after Twain's departure from Buffalo in 1871, the complexion of the *Express* changed, too. Larned accepted the post of Buffalo school superintendent and left the paper. Two years later, Selkirk moved on and eventually became secretary and treasurer of Buffalo's Park Department, a position he held for thirty-seven years until his death at the age of ninety. Mills and his ill wife, Henrietta, moved to Colorado, although they later returned to Buffalo.

Twain had worked at daily, weekly, and monthly newspapers in Hannibal,

Missouri; Keokuk, Iowa; Virginia City, Nevada; New Orleans; and San Francisco before coming to Buffalo. But the *Express* would be his last full-time newspaper job. The writing he generated and the friends he cultivated at the *Express* must have struck him at the time as a solid foundation onto which he could build a career and domestic pyramid, one that would not tumble down. The *Express* "boys,"[48] several of them Twain's age and, like him, newly married and just starting families, embraced Twain, warts and all, into their family. Their support helped fuel Twain's writing engine, for he wrote like fury during his first six weeks at the newspaper.

2

I WOULD RATHER SCRIBBLE

F or Mark Twain, the week beginning Sunday, September 26, 1869, his sixth
   at the *Express*, was hectic. At week's end, he started an extended hiatus from
Buffalo. Before leaving town, however, he hustled to fulfill his many *Express*
responsibilities. Monday's edition saw the last of his People and Things com-
pilations. That same day he followed Prince Arthur, Queen Victoria's seventh
child, around Buffalo during a last-minute visit and wrote a report on it. By the
middle of the week, he found himself alone in charge of editorial matters. Joe
Larned had departed for Wednesday's state Republican convention in Syracuse.

Twain put in extra-long hours in Larned's absence. He fine-tuned an editorial about murder in Mississippi and composed a feature story for Saturday. He
dealt with frequent interruptions by reporters and compositors asking routine
questions that Larned normally helped answer. Making matters worse, the office
was chilly. The previous weekend of sunny, eighty-seven-degree warmth suddenly gave way to a week of overcast days with temperatures in the fifties and
threats of an early frost. The old coal furnace in the corner of the third-floor
editorial room was proving inadequate.

Amid these less-than-desirable conditions, Twain received a telegram from
Larned with the Republican convention results. Larned sent the slate of nominees for nine Republican posts for November's nongubernatorial election. Twain
had only to write it up. Knowing nothing about state politics, and swamped
with supervisory chores, Twain crafted a humorous "noncommentary" on the
Republican choices that Buffalonians remembered for years afterward.

Twain's "The Ticket—Explanation" appeared on Thursday, September 30. He used a favorite narrative pose, the "inspired idiot," to derive humor from his predicament. He warned readers to await the return of "the political editor of this paper, Mr. Larned" if they sought an expert opinion on the Republican slate. Twain confessed, "I do not know much about politics, and am not sitting up nights to learn." Nevertheless, he dove in. Despite his admitted naïveté, he was ready to back George William Curtis for secretary of New York State and "take the chances." As for the other seven nominees, Twain continued, "They may be a split ticket, or a scratched ticket, or whatever you call it."

Twain poked fun at Larned (and perhaps political pundits in general) as an analyst who "whether he knows anything about a subject or not . . . is perfectly willing to discuss it." Twain promised *Express* readers that upon his return from the convention, Larned will "tell you about these candidates as serenely as if he had been acquainted with them a hundred years although, speaking confidentially, I doubt if he ever heard of any of them till to-day."

To milk humor out of his political editorial, Twain used the vantage point of an innocent thrown into an unaccustomed role. His unorthodox, entertaining endorsement may have embarrassed Larned. Twain was ridiculing the party supported by the *Express*. When Larned returned from Syracuse, he tried some damage control. In the *Express* of Friday, October 1, Larned published a serious commentary praising Curtis and the distinguished Republican ticket. Larned did not allude to Twain's mock story. In an amusing historical footnote, George Curtis declined the nomination a day later.

"The Ticket—Explanation" was among Twain's last Express stories at the end of the remarkable six-week writing streak. "Ticket" is also a bookend to "Salutatory," his inaugural address to the Express at the beginning of that intense work period. Twain took Buffalo readers by storm on August 21 with this offbeat explanation of his journalistic goals. In "Salutatory," he promised to "not often meddle with politics, because we have a political editor who is already excellent, and only needs to serve a term in the penitentiary in order to be perfect." It took Twain just six weeks to violate his vow by writing the politically oriented "Ticket."

Twain was so pleased with "Salutatory" that he sent a clipping to Olivia in Elmira. In his inaugural article, Twain satirized pompous platform statements and promised to stick "to the truth, except when it is attended with inconvenience." Once again, he derived humor from his willingness to blithely write from a position of ignorance: "Your new editor is such an important personage that he feels called upon to write a salutatory at once, and he puts into it all that he knows, and all that he doesn't know, and some things he knows but isn't certain of." Twain closed his "Salutatory" by comparing the format to its genre counterpart, the longwinded, maudlin, valedictory customarily used by journalists to sign off their careers. He likened the valedictory to a corpse that comments on a funeral. Twain's "Salutatory" forecasted a playful, irreverent stay at the *Express*.

From mid-August of 1869 until March of 1871, Twain was associate editor of the *Express*. Though away from his desk for long stretches, his output at the newspaper included nearly thirty editorials and over seventy stories, reviews, letters, and shorter pieces. He also compiled sixteen People and Things columns. During his initial six-week writing spurt, Twain generated over half his editorials, all the People and Things columns, and twelve stories and letters. In other words, in just his first six weeks, he published over one-third of the work he produced in the entire seventy-six weeks he was affiliated with the *Buffalo Express*.

After the previous several months of lecturing, preparing *The Innocents Abroad* for publication, job hunting, and courting Olivia Langdon, Twain was finally focused solely on newspaper writing. During August and September of 1869, in his cubbyhole office at the *Express*, he found a productive comfort zone. His pencil moved with dizzying speed as he composed stories, read and took notes on newspaper exchanges, and edited page proofs. At nine o'clock on the evening that "Salutatory" was published, he sat at his *Express* desk and wrote Olivia that he wanted to cancel his autumn lectures because he "would rather scribble, now, while I take a genuine interest in it."[1]

Among Twain's early scribbles, his two-week package of articles on Niagara Falls deftly merges both mirth and marketing and yet deserves scrutiny.

On Wednesday, August 4, 1869, Twain paid his first visit to Niagara Falls as part of a Langdon entourage from Elmira. He signed the hotel registry at the Cataract House with the distinctive stroke of his "Mark Twain" pen name and was assigned room number thirty-two. His fiancée, Olivia Louise Langdon, roomed next door, and her parents, Jervis and Olivia, were on Twain's other side. Young Charley Langdon occupied a room next to his sister. An A. Langdon from New York City stayed in room twenty-six.[2] Another couple from the party, Dr. Henry Sayles and his wife, Emma, Elmira neighbors of the Langdons, checked in to room twenty-four. The following day, the group swelled to a dozen with the arrival of Henry and Fidele Brooks of New York City along with their son, Remsen, and Fidele's sister Mrs. Josephine Polhemus. They were lodged in rooms eighty-three and eighty-eight, respectively.[3]

Image 2.1.The Cataract Hotel in Niagara Falls, NY, where Twain stayed with the Langdon entourage in July of 1869 and with his family in June of 1886. (Image courtesy of the Local History Department, Niagara Falls (NY) Public Library.)

For Jervis Langdon and Twain, the excursion was part pleasure, part business. At some point during their three-day stay in the Falls, they made a brief side trip twenty miles south, to Buffalo. There, Langdon likely called on his coal company branch office at 221 Main Street and checked his waterfront coal-yard operation. Langdon and Twain also spent time at the *Express* office, scouring the newspaper's financial records to confirm the soundness of their upcoming investment. A few days later, Twain complained about "the bore of wading through the books & getting up balance sheets."[4]

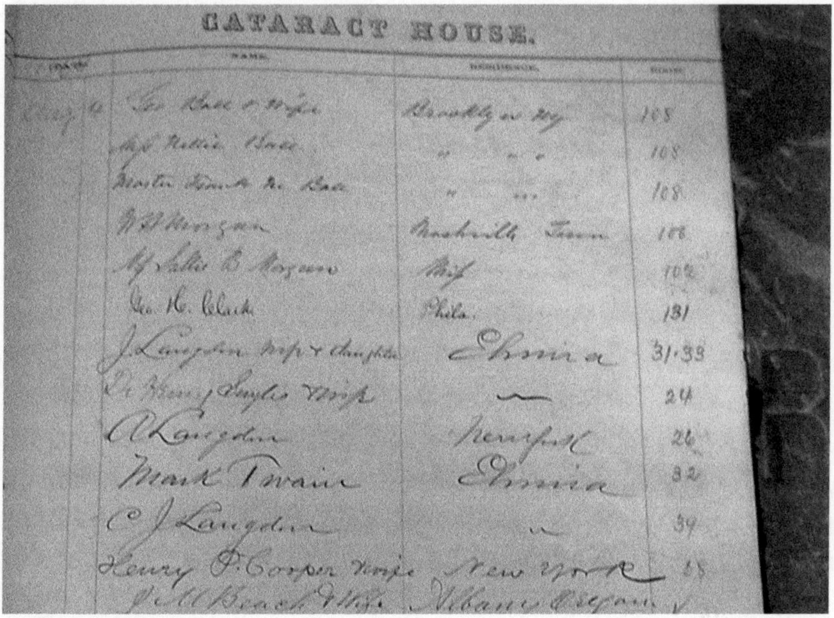
CATARACT HOUSE.

Geo. H. Clark — Phila. — 131
J. Langdon Wife & daughter — Elmira — 31.33
— 24
C. Langdon — Newport — 26
Mark Twain — Elmira — 32
C J Langdon — — 34
Henry P. Cooper Wife — New York

Image 2.2. The register for the Cataract House Hotel, August 4, 1869. Twain and the Langdon family signed in on the middle of the page. (Image courtesy of the Local History Department, Niagara Falls (NY) Public Library.)

For Twain, the pleasure side of the Falls junket ledger meant enjoying a luxurious vacation and reaping a mother lode of comic writing material. In order for him to sample the good life that Langdon wealth afforded, the Cataract House was the place to be.

The oldest, largest, and most grand hotel in Niagara Falls, the five-story Cataract was located on Main Street and Buffalo Avenue, built almost to the edge of the picturesque, wild rapids segment of the upper Niagara River. It boasted an expansive wraparound porch with breathtaking scenic views of the Niagara Falls landscape, a ballroom, entertainment, billiards, and gardens. And fine dining. The French Breakfast Room featured tall window vistas, enough tables covered in white linen cloths to seat seventy-five patrons, and three ornate chandeliers. The Cataract attracted the classiest of guests—royalty and other foreign dignitaries, military heroes, world-renowned artists and authors, politicians, and tycoons. Six weeks earlier, Commodore Cornelius Vanderbilt had stayed there.[5] Within a year or so of Twain's visit, the Cataract clientele also included luminaries such as Charles Dickens, Jay Gould, Generals George McClellan and William Tecumseh Sherman, the Grand Duke Alexis of Russia, members of the Japanese Embassy, and former president Andrew Johnson.

Although Twain took full advantage of the lavish Langdon hospitality at the Cataract, he also spent his three days at the Falls busily collecting story ideas for the *Express*.[6] As he strolled or took carriage rides to the famous Falls tourist destinations, he was bombarded by requests to pose for an inexpensive photograph, buy cheap souvenirs, obey commands posted on the multitude of signs, hire a carriage driver for a ride, and pay for entrance to every key observation point. In addition to the inescapable hawkers, Twain noticed flour and saw mills and shops disturbing the landscape. The sublime natural wonder of the Falls was marred by constant evidence of industry and commerce. He may have overheard talk about the 1869 tourist season's biggest scandal—seedy, swindling hackmen who charged fourteen dollars for carriage rides around the grounds but settled for five dollars, and guides who dogged tourists until they finally gave in to an overpriced tour. It was reported that when visitors left their hotels, twenty drivers would converge on them trying to sell an expensive ride. The *Niagara Falls Gazette* described an unusually large number of hackmen who were "sharpers and blackguards." Then, once visitors arrived at the Cave of the Winds, the Rapids View, Goat Island, Devil's Hole, or the Whirlpool, they had to pay a fee for admission. Twain also got wind of an upcoming circuslike intrusion on the Falls' revered territory, a velocipede daredevil stunt by Professor Jenkins, just three weeks away.

Twain accompanied the Langdon party on their return trip to Elmira, arriving there on Saturday, August 7. But by Sunday morning he was back in Buffalo, settling into his boardinghouse routine, writing Olivia about a Presbyterian-type church service he had just attended, and plotting two weeks' worth of stories that mixed fact, fiction, hoaxes, and self-promotion derived from his Falls adventures and observations.

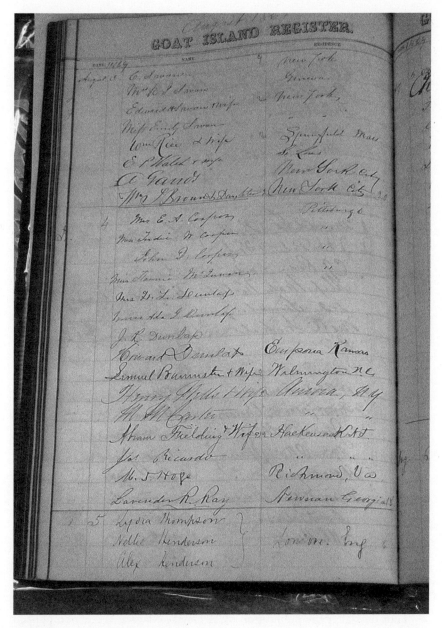

Image 2.3. Goat Island register, August 5, 1869. At the bottom of the page, members of the British Blondes Burlesque Troupe, Lydia Thompson, Nellie Henderson, and Alex Henderson, signed in from London, England. (Image courtesy of the Local History Department, Niagara Falls (NY) Public Library.)

Twain's comic set of Falls writings consisted of two feature stories and two squibs for the *Buffalo Express* and an entry in the *Niagara Falls Gazette*, along with illustrations, short commentaries, and self-advertisements guaranteed to entertain readers and keep Twain's name in the news. Three of the pieces have never before been reprinted in book form.

In the same August 21 issue of the *Express* that carried his "Salutatory," Twain also published "A Day at Niagara. Concerning the Falls." This satirical feature story is vintage Twain. The narrator, Twain himself, is a bewildered, easily deceived, and infuriatingly long-winded bumpkin. He pokes fun at Irish vendors who pretend to be the Tuscarora Indian women known for selling authentic beadwork and carvings, at greedy coroners,[7] and at sentimentalism, particularly ridiculing James Fenimore Cooper's idealized American Indian. Twain jokes about excessive signage that corrupts the pastoral beauty of the Falls ("Keep Off the Grass," "Visit the Cave of the Winds," "Don't Throw Stones Down—They May Hit People Below"), reminiscent of his frustration at "No Smoking" signs aboard ship in *The Innocents Abroad*.[8] Twain's catchy criticism of high fares charged by Falls carriage drivers coined a phrase that soon became popular around Western New York: "They could not dam the Falls, so they damned the hackmen." Throughout the piece, Twain employs stock elements of two traditions of American humor in which he was well schooled, humor of the Old Southwest and literary comedians.[9] In the story, Twain borrows time-honored strategies of fellow comic writers to produce verbal tricks like puns, mangled vocabulary, humorous physical discomfort, incongruous catalogue (when Twain lists Uncas, Red Jacket, Hole-in-the-Day, and . . . Andrew Greeley), climactic arrangement (the increasingly snowballing nonsense of miscommunication when Twain tries talking down to the fake "Irish" Indians), and the anticlimactic sentence, which Twain calls a "nub" or "snapper" (after being beaten, stripped, and tossed over Niagara Falls, Twain dryly concludes, "I got wet."). In fact, the comic storytelling framework in "A Day at Niagara" is the same formula still fresh in Twain's mind from composing *The Innocents Abroad*.

Four days after the publication of "A Day at Niagara," a reaction popped up in the *Niagara Falls Gazette* (see appendix 1) that bears several hallmarks of a Twain creation.[10] In the *Gazette*'s "Mark Twain and Niagara," Twain and/ or his *Express* associate Earl Berry skewers his own inaugural *Express* effort on

the Falls and pokes fun at a long tradition of arrogant authors who try unsuc-
cessfully to put their unique spin on a visit to Niagara Falls. The anonymous
author is identified only with the initial *B*, which could refer to Twain's stand-in,
Berry. The *Gazette* contributor dismisses Twain's *Express* story as just another
cliché-filled travel article by an incompetent, self-important writer. Twain
had just taken a similar stance against hackneyed travel writers when he lam-
basted William Prime's *Tent Life in the Holy Land* (1857) in chapter 50 of *The
Innocents Abroad* for representing a class of books that have been serving up the
same "gruel" about Palestine for ages. Twain's penchant for inventing derogatory
terms for writers, especially hyphenated compounds, is sprinkled throughout
the *Gazette* reaction. The term *penny-a-liner* echoes other Twain creations like
phrase-juggler and *quill-driving scum*. Throughout his work, Twain often substi-
tuted the word *scribbler* for writer. Another Twain trait is to concoct a synonym
for *ignorance*. The *Gazette* contributor attacks Twain's *Express* piece for its "dishwater wit," "namby-pamby wit," "addled brain," and "poor weak brain," which
compare favorably to Twain's use of "sheep-witted" and "wild-brained" in other
writings. And the "mouse" reference and exalted rhetoric mirror language used
by Twain a little over a year later in a *Galaxy* magazine spoof. Therein, he once
again writes his own satirical review of *The Innocents Abroad*, attacking "Twain's"
lack of qualifications for original, informed travel writing: "The poor blunderer
mouses among the sublime creations of the Old Masters, trying to acquire the
elegant proficiency in art-knowledge, which he has a groping sort of compre-
hension is a proper thing for the travelled man to be able to display."[11]

The satirical "Mark Twain and Niagara" was definitely not written by a
Gazette staffer. It appeared on page three of the weekly four-page *Gazette*, a
page devoted to "Local and Vicinity News" and usually filled with accounts of
baseball tournaments, accidents, obituaries, exchange items from Buffalo and
Rochester papers, and signed letters to the editor. "Mark Twain and Niagara,"
with its unprecedented ribbon "FOR THE GAZETTE," departure from the
normal editorial "we," single initial for author identification, and uncharacteristic vituperative tone stands out as a product alien to the *Gazette*'s style.
One week earlier, the *Gazette* had politely welcomed Twain as "one of the best
humorists of the age . . . a valuable acquisition to the editorial fraternity of
Buffalo." The paper would have had no reason to reverse its attitude abruptly

and attack Twain's *Express* story on the Falls. And on September 1, one week after "Mark Twain and Niagara" was printed, the *Gazette* further distanced itself from authorship by quoting a brief purportedly from the *Rochester Chronicle* and then commenting on it. The minor dispute about a Rochester plant show in which Twain is mentioned in the same breath suggests that the *Gazette* did not want credit for "Mark Twain and Niagara." "The Niagara Falls *Gazette* is the only paper among our hundreds of exchanges that says aught about the Century plant. Talk of squeezing is in keeping with a paper that dubs Mark Twain, in the same issue, a namby, pamby, addled-brained wit." The *Gazette*'s September 1 reply read, "We only repeated in substance what we found in our Rochester exchanges. We insist, also, that we haven't said nary a word derogatory of Twain."

The whole issue smells like a hilarious, exaggerated controversy fabricated by Twain himself. Given that he used another Rochester newspaper the next week as part of his continuing Falls hoax, Twain may well have invented the plaintive squib from the *Rochester Chronicle* to get a rise out of the *Gazette* and to keep readers engaged in his silly manufactured saga. In a special touch of showmanship and marketing, Twain placed large ads for *The Innocents Abroad* in the same August 25 issue of the *Gazette* that featured "Mark Twain and Niagara." The ad ran for three weeks and never was seen again.

When readers enjoyed morning coffee with their *Express* on August 23, they saw a front-page splashed with an advertisement taking up several valuable column inches of space. In uppercase print, the ad announced Twain's follow-up to "A Day at Niagara," which would appear again on Saturday.

Twain delivered on the ad's promise on August 28th with another humorous Saturday feature connected to his Falls visit. "English Festivities. And Minor Matters" opens with the absurd logic that because fishing is nonexistent at the rapids, at least fishermen don't come in with false hopes. Twain then lambastes gullible tourists who pay for their photographs being taken at the Falls and think they are the focus, when in reality the powerful Falls in the background humbles any mere mortal. "English Festivities" targets guides and the perilous Cave of the Winds attraction. In his story, Twain crosses the border to the Canadian side of Niagara Falls and gets caught up in a series of parties honoring British royalty and becomes bloated and gassy from drinking kegs and barrels of liquid refreshment.

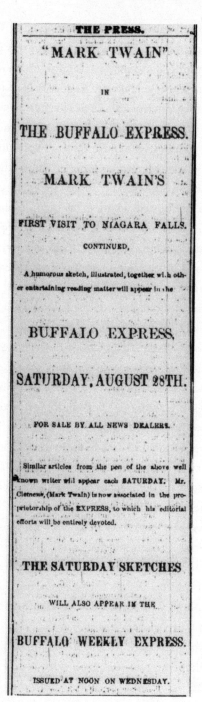

Image 2.4. August 23, 1869, front-page *Express* advertisement for the second in Twain's Saturday features on Niagara Falls.

Cannily, Twain set up Saturday's "English Festivities" with a teaser the day before in the *Express*. In case readers had missed the page-one advertisement, Twain kept Falls zaniness in the forefront with this clever hoax tied to Professor Jenkins's impending "make-up" high-wire performance at the Falls. "In Trouble" (see appendix 2) purports to be a telegram to the editor from a *Buffalo Express* reporter.[12] Reporter "Michael J. Murphy" is in a bind. He has commandeered Professor Jenkins's velocipede in order to write a thrilling first-hand account about defying death, but his bicycle-type machine has stalled on the tightrope midway across the Niagara Gorge. The story plays with a pun on *roost* and a triple pun on *suspend*. Hunters on the Canadian shore are taking potshots at Murphy, and he is missing his own wedding. He asks his boss if he'll still get paid even if he fails to file a story. "Murphy," as *Express* readers probably guessed, and which would be revealed soon, was Twain. And, of course, Twain never really tried to duplicate Jenkins's feat.

When Twain first visited the Falls and read fliers and ads announcing that Professor J. F. Jenkins, known as "the Canadian Blondin," planned a daring tightrope exhibition on a velocipede across the Niagara River on Wednesday, August 25, his humbug detector swung into gear. And when Jenkins's performance was panned, Twain jumped on it. He had already sneered at the Frenchman Jean François Gravelet (a.k.a. Blondin), the world-famous daredevil known for putting on quite a show while tightrope walking across Niagara Gorge. In the summers of 1859 and 1860, Blondin drew thousands of paying spectators, who watched awestruck as he crossed the gorge on a rope while wearing a wig and exotic costumes, drank champagne and Niagara River water yanked up by string in a bottle, pretended to have a sharpshooter on shore fire a bullet through his hat, carried his manager and a stove on his back, cooked and ate a meal, danced and pranced forward and backward, all while balancing with a heavy pole.[13] Twain was not impressed. In *The Innocents Abroad*, Twain found the lovely "Cancan" dancers in the Parisian garden in Asnières more memorable than Blondin's high-wire stunt there. And in his "English Festivities" piece, Twain called Blondin "that adventurous ass."

So when Professor Jenkins, a second-rate Blondin, not only failed to live up to his billing, but also took money from easily duped onlookers, Twain seized yet another opportunity to squeeze fun out of Niagara. The *Buffalo Express* gave

Jenkins a tepid review, commenting on his stunt's low degree of difficulty. The *Niagara Falls Gazette* was harsh: "Jenkins's performance bears about as much resemblance to Blondin's as a poor counterfeit does to the genuine."[14] Jenkins was so humiliated by his initial fiasco that he vowed a "still greater" feat for Friday, September 3, by promising to ride his velocipede forward and backward and to perform on flying rings suspended over the rapids.

His disdain (and, perhaps, begrudging admiration) for frauds and showmen and his desire to expose them likely inspired Twain's sequel to the "Michael J. Murphy" tall tale. In the September 9 issue of the *Buffalo Express*, Twain issued his coup de grâce for the sequence of Falls writings. His "Mark Twain in a Fix" (see appendix 3) added another layer to the absurdity by writing a hoax of a hoax.[15] Twain published a fake anonymous dispatch from the *Rochester Express* (which did not exist), claiming that it wasn't Murphy but Twain who made a fool of himself on Professor Jenkins's tightrope over the Falls. The rest of the report chronicled a hilarious scene of misjudgment and misadventure suffered by the hapless Twain character, written tongue-in-cheek by the real Twain. Murphy's rehearsal on the restaurant dining chair for the high-wire stunt is particularly comical. Twain's vision of himself wearing a white suit, decades before it became his trademark, is also noteworthy. With the pair of Murphy spoofs, Twain seems again to be taking double-barreled aim both at how his fellow editors and reporters flock to sensational stories and at the thrill-seeking public.

Another touch that made Twain's Niagara feature stories so special was their accompanying illustrations.[16] Twain collaborated with *Express* staff artist John Harrison Mills, who produced four drawings to enhance comic elements of each text. For the August 21 story "A Day at Niagara," Mills drew a scene of the coroner trying to light a pipe while Twain flails away in the whirlpool (with the caption, "Got a Match?") and a sketch of a faux Noble Red Man peddling phony souvenirs ("The Child of the Forest"). For "English Festivities" of August 28, Mills's illustrations depicted a Falls landscape dominated by photographers and hackmen ("Niagara as a Background") and a frustrated Twain at the Cave of the Winds thrashing a tour guide ("I Then Destroyed Him"). Before Twain joined the paper, *Buffalo Express* stories were rarely illustrated, and they were never illustrated in-house (see appendix 4).

Mark Twain's comic muse was tickled by his first visit to Niagara Falls. His extended literary daredevil stunt concerning the Falls easily eclipsed Professor Jenkins's physical high-wire antics. And it was accomplished at the same time as the bachelor journalist busily scribbled away on other writing and editing projects during his first six weeks at the *Express*.

As letters to Olivia attest, a typical day at the *Express* for Twain during August and September of 1869 might consist of effortlessly writing "twenty or thirty pages of MS.,[manuscript, or hand-written pages]" the more laborious task of skimming through a large stack of newspaper exchanges (which "takes a deal of time . . . because one gets interested every now & then & stops to read a while"), reading "columns after columns of proof," and dealing with constant interruptions.[17]

Some interruptions were self-inflicted. Within his first six weeks on the job, Twain spent three weekends with Olivia and the Langdons in Elmira. He would leave Buffalo at three in the afternoon or eleven at night on a Friday for the five-and-a-half-hour train ride to Elmira and depart for Buffalo at around the same times on Monday. Twain confessed to another journalist that these weekend shuttles exposed two selves: Mark Twain, the public celebrity journalist of the *Buffalo Express*, and Sam Clemens, the private family man in Elmira adoring his fiancée. "When you happen to be at Buffalo or Elmira, you must come & see me—half of me is at Mr. Langdon's in Elmira, you know, & so I am really writing over a fraudulent & assumed name when I sign myself Twain."[18]

In addition to conceiving the Niagara story cluster, scribbling several other features and editorials, and altering the cosmetics of the *Express* during his first six weeks, the Twain half of his split personality supervised the radical overhaul of two long-standing *Express* columns.

One September day, Twain took his ace reporter Earl Berry with him to Buffalo's Police Court, determined to find a way to improve the boring *Express* coverage of police court news. After an hour of hearing police judge Isaac V. Vanderpoel accompany his rulings with the phrase "I am here to mete out justice," Twain and Berry hurried back to the editorial floor. Twain had a brainstorm. He instructed Berry to use this standing headline over the police court column "Justice Vanderpoel's Mete Shop." With a pun on *meat* and the motif of a judge carving out decisions in a "butcher shop," police court news at the *Express* was turned upside down (see appendix 5).[19]

Although the changeover was short lived, Twain, Berry, and readers had great fun for a while.[20] On Monday, November 8, 1869, under the new heading "JUSTICE SHOP," Berry carried out Twain's wishes with lively, opinionated accounts of the Police Court docket: "Business opened briskly on Saturday, and by ten o'clock the Court room was filled with eager applicants for that ever-desirable commodity—justice." Cases of public intoxication, prostitution, assault, and robbery (frequently occurring in Buffalo's infamous Erie Canal district) were given a light, whimsical touch by Berry—with Twain's blessing. Some headings played with the original, "WEIGHING IT OUT," "JUSTICE FOR ALL," or "METE SHOP." On November 26th, Berry commented creatively on the tedium of court business: "The principal trial yesterday was of the patience of the Police Justice and the officers of the court, who were forced to endure a stupidly tedious examination of witnesses in a small case of assault and battery." In a column published on November 13th, Berry reacted with comically dramatic flair to Judge Vanderpoel's admonition that a man must never strike a woman: "Oh! If women could only vote what an immense majority Mr. Vanderpoel would have at the next election." After the police court column of December 1, only the eighth of Berry's entertaining efforts, "JUSTICE SHOP" was discontinued. Police court reporting reverted to its traditional, straightforward reportage. Twain was out of town on a lecture tour, Justice Vanderpoel may have objected to the disrespectful treatment of his court, or politically savvy Josephus Larned may have halted the experiment in deference to the fact that Vanderpoel was a former law partner to Grover Cleveland, who was about to be elected as the sheriff of Erie County.

Another possibility for the abrupt end to Twain's police court makeover is that Twain was simply becoming disenchanted with his own playful journalistic maneuverings. Another column revamped by Twain, People and Things, met a similar fate.

This semiregular feature in the *Express* had been a grab bag of factual international, national, and state news snippets of general interest lifted from newspaper exchanges, with items presented objectively and arranged in no particular order. Twain seemed to view People and Things as a way to get paid for reading scads of newspapers on the job, to spot briefs that he thought were entertaining, and to troll exchanges for potential story ideas of his own. Earl Berry vividly recalled the zeal and joy Twain exhibited when searching newspaper exchanges for useful or bizarre news tidbits: "He read newspapers like a whirlwind, scattering them, opened, around about him. When not himself writing, he would comment with much versatility and vigor on the contents of the newspapers, regardless of the occupation of any other persons in the room."[21] Twain seemed to have a high opinion of his People and Things duties. He enclosed several clippings of the column in letters to Olivia with instructions to include them in an edited scrapbook of "my 'Works' when I am gone."[22]

Because People and Things columns consisted of unsigned briefs, it is not possible to definitively attribute Twain as the author per se (see appendix 6). But by selecting the contents of the sixteen editions of People and Things, from August 17 to September 27, Twain tilted the column toward the outrageous and comic, yet another step toward his goal of boosting the entertainment value of the *Express*. The *Union*, out of Lockport, New York, noticed Twain's comic transformation, writing that "People and Things sparkles with his refulgent wit."[23] Even though it had been a longstanding department, under Twain People and Things appeared sporadically. Sometimes it was printed three days in a row. Sometimes it skipped several days. During the longest gaps, a week between August 25 and September 2 and twelve days between September 10 and September 22, Twain spent three-day weekends in Elmira with the Langdons. No one else at the *Express* bothered browsing through exchanges and composing People and Things in his absences. The bulleted briefs in Twain's version of People and Things still included straightforward news items, but they also contained lots of sensational, freakish factoids and an occasional local fragment.

Twain settled into a rhythm of plucking a newsworthy bit from the exchanges and concluding it with his own nub-like, wry, editorial comment. Likely the first People and Things that he handpicked and redesigned, in the August 17, 1869, *Express*, carried this one-two punch: "The river Nile is lower than it has been for 150 years. This news will be chiefly interesting to parties who remember the former occasion." So did his penultimate column of September 25 include an entry on a factual incident followed by a line poking mild fun at a crew member related to his former profession: "A Mississippi steamboat recently ran half an hour without an engineer. The passengers had a chance to be safe for a little while, at any rate."

I WOULD RATHER SCRIBBLE   73

The former style of People and Things had focused the news roundup on other regions of the country and world. Under his editorship, Twain sometimes inserted local references. He ended a brief about an alleged seer in Illinois who could tell what was in coat pockets with her eyes closed by hoping the clairvoyant would stay away from "our Buffalo families" because she might be tempted to pick their pockets.[24] In the heat of August, with his *Express* office window facing East Swan Street wide open, Twain must have been distracted enough by the single song played over and over by an organ grinder across the street that he issued a witty personal appeal to him via a People and Things item. It incorporates classic Twain understatement and punning: "The foreign gentleman who has recently located himself on the opposite sidewalk with a hand organ of two-tune capacity will oblige us if he will play the other tune sometimes. 'Buffalo Gals' is fresh and exciting, but one notices after several days that it lacks variety. This person's organ is a greater bore than the Hoosac tunnel."[25]

Then there was the lengthy piece in the People and Things of August 25 about John Wagner, "the oldest man in Buffalo." This sketch was part of a weeks-long running gag about a trend by journalists to sensationalize feats of the elderly. At the age of 104, Wagner absurdly takes two weeks to walk over one mile and has been engaged for 89 years, still awaiting permission to wed from his fiancée's parents.[26] Three other People and Things briefs in August and September lampoon the print media's continued fascination with special accomplishments of the aged. A September 25 item insists that centenarians are not news anymore. Instead they are "pestilential old prodigies, who have broken out like a rash all over the whole country lately." In another tidbit, Twain cites a 107-year-old Ohio man who is such an abnormally normal "driveling old idiot" that Twain believes he should be put on display.[27] Another locally oriented brief wonders why men, unlike women, swing their arms when they walk and invites readers to drop off written answers at the *Express* office.[28]

A brief headlined "Personal" above the September 25 People and Things column is a humorous follow-up to a comic *Express* story that Twain contributed seventeen days earlier called "The Last Words of Great Men." The brief is a humorous poem addressed to Twain (perhaps written by him or another *Express* staff member) in reaction to "The Last Words." The ditty, signed "Yours truly, Some of the Little Women," closes with "A man with a wife *never has a last word*."

Twain adds "S'cat!" and his initials "M.T." Three days before Twain published "The Last Words of Great Men," he showed an interest in last words by selecting an exchange tidbit for People and Things: "There has been some dispute as to the last words which Lamartine uttered on his death-bed. The last version is, that the poet, a few moments previous to his death, said: 'Do not disturb me!' Marshal Neil's were '*l'Armée française!*' (the French army)." This brief served as a seed from which a story germinated. In "The Last Words of Great Men," Twain even duplicates the Neil quote as its inscription. In an amusing postscript, Twain adds that staff artist John Harrison Mills did not supply a drawing because he "finds it impossible to make pictures of people's last words."

Still other People and Things items proved "excellent, as texts to string out a sketch from,"[29] spinning off into *Express* stories. In the column of August 24, Twain suggests a disapproving attitude toward the naughty Blondes Burlesque Troupe (which had opened their American tour recently in Buffalo): "The Blondes will expose themselves in Elmira to-night." This item took longer to blossom in Twain's creative imagination. Five months later, his *Express* article titled "The Blondes" weighed in on the group's scandalous episode in Chicago. A succession of three People and Things notes about Prince Arthur's visit to Canada prepared Twain for his story "Arthur" in the September 28 *Express*; an entry about a fossilized man dug up in Alabama from the August 19 column developed into two later *Express* articles also inspired by the recent Cardiff Giant hoax[30]; and a brief that needled Brigham Young ("Brigham Young has lost his family Bible, and is in trouble to find out how many children he has or what their names are.") was filed away for ridiculing Young and the Mormons in chapters 12 through 16 of *Roughing It* a couple of years later. Twain conveys a theme of social justice by attacking Commodore Cornelius Vanderbilt over five items in People and Things.[31] Two days later, Twain built on his first August 21 Vanderbilt scrap to construct an *Express* story, "Uncriminal Victims," an editorial on the social-class divide in the United States. The subsequent People and Things items on Vanderbilt continued to hammer away at Vanderbilt's elitism.

People and Things, then, was not just a casual cobbling together of disparate exchange-news items for Twain. His decisions about what bits and pieces to include offer a window into his thinking and composing processes. He put in briefs that intrigued him and that he felt his reading public would or should find equally absorbing and entertaining. Across the sixteen columns compiled by Twain, other topics pop up time and again. He was interested in baseball (three items cite the Cincinnati Red Stockings), freaks (like the Siamese Twins, a two-headed girl, an amazingly short princess, the marriage of an albino male and an obese female), aberrant family configurations (at least five items comment on strange cases, such as a soldier with sons aged sixty and two), European monarchs (there are countless items about Napoleon's family and the royalty of Prussia, Sweden, and Denmark), and the controversy that had just erupted over Harriet Beecher Stowe's published accusation that Lord Byron had committed incest with his half sister. (Twain devoted seven entries to this subject and addressed it in numerous *Express* stories in the fall of 1869. He was almost always sympathetic to Stowe and critical of Byron.) He was not above using People and Things blurbs for self-promotion (alerting readers to information about his autumn lecture schedule and pasting in an exchange item about how he judges the distance of a coast-to-coast train trip by the number of cigars smoked—117!) and inside jokes (he ribs fellow literary comedian and journalist friends like Josh Billings and Horace Greeley—several times). Twain even resurrects an ancient gag about cops asleep on the job in a People and Things item that echoes an *Innocents Abroad* comic bit at Pompeii.[32]

Abruptly, when Twain left Buffalo at the end of September, the new light, bright People and Things department was extinguished. Without Twain's creative force behind it, by September 30, the *Express* staff renamed the column Gleanings. By June of 1870, it was changed again to Varieties. It slumped back to its former bland tone. There would be no further input from Twain for the entire time he was associated with the *Express*. Similar to Twain's flickering influence on police court reporting, the entertaining version of People and Things flamed out after just six weeks.

Incredibly, Twain's frenzied opening six-week stint at the *Express* involved more than just supplying the humorous sequence of Niagara Falls stories, pumping life into police court coverage and modifying People and Things, handling proofreading chores and layout innovations, and initiating Saturday feature articles. He also regularly contributed editorials, news reports, and other comic articles.

Image 2.5. A front close-up of the *Buffalo Express* building at 14 East Swan Street. (Reproduction by permission of the Buffalo and Erie County Public Library, Buffalo, NY.)

"Only a Nigger"[33] is an antilynching editorial that is important as an early public stand by Twain against racism. It suggests the influence of the Langdons and his own growing social consciousness, which was fully evident by the time of *Adventures of Huckleberry Finn*, published fifteen years later. Twain also scribbled three more humorous Saturday features with a common theme. Twain's illustrated[34] "Journalism in Tennessee" in the Saturday, September 4 edition of the *Express* takes a sarcastic look at the newspaper profession. In the story, an editor spices up a reporter's copy with no regard for factual accuracy. At the same time, the editor is repeatedly assaulted by outraged readers. There is violence done to written drafts and to people. The editorial staff and office are left in ruins. This fable is the first of several *Express* stories that points to Twain's steadily growing uneasiness with journalism. Twain used the next Saturday feature to complain again about sensational journalism. In "The Wild Man Interviewed" of September 18, an immortal, protean creature named Sensation is hounded by the press and obliged to join the Stowe-Byron controversy. It is the last of Twain's stories to be illustrated by *Express* artist Mills.[35] The final Saturday feature continues to ridicule journalism's passion for sensationalizing the news. Twain begins "Rev. H. W. Beecher—His Private Habits"[36] with a satirical, shocking line, "The great preacher never sleeps with his clothes on." Twain invents more mundane minutiae about Beecher's personal habits—going hatless at dinner, never cursing, operating a farm—that mock both the American public's insatiable desire to know everything about renowned personalities and journalists' eagerness to deliver the sensational information. The *Express* paid Twain twenty-five dollars for each of his six Saturday feature stories.

During the final and busiest of Mark Twain's opening six weeks at the *Express*, nineteen-year-old Prince Arthur came to town. Twain had a chance to be a reporter. Prince Arthur, later Duke of Connaught and the seventh of Queen Victoria's nine children, was touring Canada. On Monday September 27, 1869, the prince, his tutor, the governor general of Canada, and other dignitaries decided on an impromptu train ride to Buffalo from Niagara Falls. The prince was given a hastily arranged lunch at the Tifft House and a tour of Buffalo, its waterfront, and elevator alley. The prince likely saw the recently built fireproof Niagara and Plimpton grain elevator on Ohio Street, one of thirty such structures that made Buffalo's harbor the world's largest grain port of the time. Twain covered Arthur's visit and was put off by the prince's haughtily regal bearing. Twain's story, "Arthur," which has never before been reprinted in book form,[37] pokes fun at Arthur's lineage in an opening paragraph that includes a remarkably long sentence with one of Twain's favorite rhetorical devices—that is, the exaggerated build-up that soon yields to disappointment (see appendix 7). Twain also rips the prince's snotty attitude, his voracious appetite, and his seeming lack of interest in Buffalo and the press during his two-and-a-half-hour visit. Twain's ego was probably deflated, since he was just a member of the press corps, kept at arm's length from the prince and his entourage. At the Tifft House, Twain looked on from a distance as distinguished diners, including former president Millard Fillmore, a resident of Buffalo, were served in the main parlors. (This instance was only the first of Twain's two brushes with Fillmore in Buffalo.) Following the hotel luncheon, Twain rode in the last of six carriages with the other local reporters, tailing the prince around the city's principal streets as he paused to ogle mansions such as William G. Fargo's newly built residence on the city's west side. Twain did not realize it at the time, but the prince's tour took them all past the house on Delaware Street where he would be living in just four months. Compared to similar coverage of the same event in the *Buffalo Daily Commercial Advertiser* and in David Gray's *Buffalo Daily Courier*, Twain's report on Arthur's visit to Buffalo was irreverent and tongue-in-cheek.

Two days after "Arthur" was published, Twain was off to Elmira for a month. He then spent the next three months lecturing on the road. He would return to his desk at the *Express* as a married man in February, but with a diminished sense of journalistic purpose and commitment. Twain never duplicated the scribbling feats of his first six weeks at the newspaper.

He had been given carte blanche to make over chunks of the *Buffalo Morning Express* in order to improve the paper's quality and boost circulation. Selkirk on the business side, Larned and Berry in editorial, and the entire production crew pitched in to enact Twain's many innovations. The full resources of the newspaper had enabled him to creatively promote the Mark Twain brand name and dominate its pages. The long-term impact of Twain's changes proved negligible. Years later, Larned recalled Twain's frustration that *Express* sales had not spiked: "I think that Mr. Clemens expected a more rapid increase and wide extension of circulation for the paper to be caused by his writing in it, than occurred, and was disappointed by the result."[38]

Twain had spent those productive days and nights of August and September immersed in his work in the company of his *Express* colleagues and *Courier* editor David Gray. But due in part to Langdon business contacts, Twain had a life in Buffalo outside the *Express*, too. Perhaps Twain's most loyal companion as a bachelor editor was the large, tawny, scarred office cat that followed him back and forth from the *Express* to his boardinghouse.[39]

3

THIS CARAVANSERY

Mrs. J. C. Randall's boardinghouse catered to an upscale clientele. Like Mrs. Andrew Lee's boardinghouse next door, Randall's was a handsome, four-story former mansion of dark brick converted into one- and two-room apartments. Her fashionable boardinghouse attracted lodgers a cut above the usual class of laborers and tug men. Her roomers were clerks, bookkeepers, insurance agents, bank cashiers, telegraphers, oil and lumber dealers, surveyors, small business owners, and office managers. And, for two months, a newspaper owner and editor named Mark Twain.

An account of Twain's introductions upon moving in at 39 East Swan Street in early August of 1869 describes Ms. Randall in "rustling black silk, point lace collar and cameo brooch"[1] taking charge. On his first night there, Mrs. Randall formally presented Twain to some of the other guests, including Major and Mrs. James Dickie, who saluted and curtsied, respectively; William E. Foster, managing editor of the *Buffalo Commercial Advertiser*; Mrs. Kitty Blanchard, a widow; Blanchard's young son, Arthur; and George Brewster Matthews,[2] a twenty-one-year-old bookkeeper with L. Enos and Company. One night, after a stressful shift at the *Express*, Twain leaned across the dining table at the boardinghouse and joked to Matthews that he had "smoked only twelve cigars today, but I feel like a whole tobacco warehouse with the wooden Injun thrown in." Years afterward, Matthews, whose customary spot at the table was opposite Twain, remembered Twain's magnetic personality: "There was something which held and fascinated one about Clemens."[3]

Image 3.1. The dark brick building at 39 East Swan Street, midway between the two steeples, is where Twain boarded in August and September of 1869. (Image courtesy of the Lower Lakes Marine Historical Society.)

Twain habitually awakened at 7:00 a.m. Breakfast was served at 7:30. The *Express* was only a few steps away. Suppers at the boardinghouse were apparently not always appetizing. Earl Berry recalls a conversation late one Sunday night at the *Express* between Twain and Larned as they closed up shop. The coeditors had emerged from behind the editorial-room door, which they often locked in order to work undisturbed, their exhausting work on the next morning's edition completed. When Larned started heading home for dinner, Twain jokingly said, "Say Joe, come down to my shack and have supper with me. We are going to have beaten biscuit tonight. They are the kind your mother used to make. We have them every Sunday."[4] Larned replied that his mother never made biscuit. Twain answered that Larned was fortunate, then, to pass up Mrs. Randall's indigestible fare: "I guess you are right about that. I don't believe that the mother of a decent man like you could make any such biscuit as these beaten biscuits that my landlady sets out."

In the same way that Twain could be irascible at work, he was not always friendly at the boardinghouse, either. John Harrison Mills remembers that Twain was "little inclined to sociability with his fellow boarders."[5] He whiled away the time in his room reading and writing letters in bed, sometimes as late as two in the morning, to his sister in Missouri and to Olivia. Although Olivia preferred letters written in ink, Twain used pencil when writing in his boardinghouse room so that ink would not leak onto the bed linen. Sometimes being isolated in his room drove Twain to overwhelming loneliness. One such night was Tuesday, September 7. Twain had stayed alone at the *Express* listening to the pounding rainstorm outside until ten at night. Larned had long since made his way home to his wife. Before walking the short half a block to his boardinghouse, Twain wrote an eloquent albeit self-pitying letter to Olivia about the desolate life in his room: "I shall have to go to a solemn, silent room, presently, & if the speechless furniture welcomes me, well & good—if the dumb emptiness has a word for me, well & good again—otherwise the day will have passed & the night waned apace without a sentence of conversation, for both us have sat still & busy since breakfast."[6]

Occasionally on Sunday mornings Twain would rouse himself from bed to attend church. His boardinghouse was located behind St. John's Episcopal Church on the east side of Washington Street at East Swan. The Washington Baptist Church stood on the opposite corner across from the boardinghouse. It is likely, however, that Twain attended nearby Lafayette Presbyterian Church or Central Presbyterian Church, for he soon became friends with both pastors.

Twain also probably filled some of his spare time with his favorite exercise, which was walking around the neighborhood. His Swan Street neighborhood represented "boardinghouse" row, a mixed use of residential and commercial buildings. Directly across from Twain's boardinghouse on East Swan Street was the home and office of husband and wife physicians Elihu and Mrs. E. G. Cook. Next door to the Cooks was Pierce and Polley livery stable. One more block away was the home and office of Dr. Alexander T. Bull, where Twain frequently met for cards with Larned and David Gray while waiting for newspaper page proofs to be prepared for editing. If Twain wanted to avoid Mrs. Randall's cooking, he could buy a light lunch at a popular bar/oyster house on East Swan that served oysters for ten cents a plate, a variety of stews for fifteen to twenty cents, and pork and beans or hot coffee and a roll for a dime. Or he could enjoy fresh lager on tap—except on Sundays.

Although Twain may have slighted his landlady's skills at the stove, he was grateful for her recommendation of a local photographer. He thanked Mrs. Randall and her Swan Street neighbor, photographer Edward H. Paige, for "by far the best picture I ever had."[7] By May of 1870, Twain's photo portrait was on exhibit at Paige's gallery above 446 Main Street. Twain sent card versions of the photo by Paige to several friends. Twain also had another photo portrait taken in Buffalo in the fall of 1869. He posed this time at the studio of Jefferson T. Upson and Andrew Simson, 456 Main Street, just around the corner from the *Express*. Simson had worked at the *Express* as a compositor in the early 1860s.

Another recommendation that Twain had followed up on was to board at Mrs. Randall's. The tip came from John James McWilliams, who already lived there with his wife. McWilliams, John D. F. Slee, and later Charles M. Underhill were key employees at the Buffalo branch office of Jervis Langdon's Elmira-headquartered coal company. In the late summer of 1869, as plans for Twain's purchase of a share of the *Buffalo Morning Express* crystallized, Langdon likely charged McWilliams, the coal company's bookkeeper, with finding a suitable dwelling place for his daughter's fiancé. McWilliams probably nudged Twain to room at Mrs. Randall's. And Langdon was probably pleased to have a trusted employee living there who could look after Twain in his remaining months of bachelorhood. Twain's connection to McWilliams and Slee, established during those first days in Buffalo, broadened his social circle beyond the *Express* and developed into life-long friendships. Part of the camaraderie among Twain, McWilliams, and Slee was due to their compatibility in age and station. Each was in the formative stage of a distinguished career. Twain was only thirty-three when he arrived in Buffalo. Slee, too, was in his early thirties, and McWilliams was in his late twenties.

After Twain finished a typical long day at the *Express* during his first six weeks on the job, McWilliams and his wife, both of whom came from Elmira, helped fill his lonely leisure hours with companionship and homey touches. Sometimes after supper, Twain visited the McWilliamses' two-room apartment above his at the boardinghouse. On other occasions in August and September of 1869, he and McWilliams (whom Twain affectionately referred to as "Mac") walked from the boardinghouse to the waterfront for a refreshing swim or a row in Lake Erie.[8] A few days after Twain arrived in Buffalo, he received a letter from Slee on Anthracite Coal Association letterhead.[9] Slee informed him that the $12,500 in two checks from Jervis Langdon would be in hand to close on buying the *Express* share the next day. Twain probably did not have a mail slot set up yet at the boardinghouse, since Slee addressed the letter to "S. L. Clemens" care of "J. J. McWilliams." Several months later, Twain relied on McWilliams's accounting expertise to assess the health of his *Express* stock. Twain wrote Jervis Langdon on March 3, 1870, that an analysis completed by McWilliams and Slee showing the *Express* to be financially sound convinced him to continue paying on his debt to Thomas A. Kennett.[10] Twain had bought his one-third share of the newspaper from Kennett the previous August. He wanted to be sure that Kennett hadn't swindled him before proceeding with several payments over the next few months and years.

Image 3.2. John J. McWilliams, clerk at the Langdon coal company's Buffalo branch, who lived in the same boardinghouse as Twain. This photograph was taken years later, as McWilliams was Twain's age. (Image used by permission of the Collection of the Buffalo and Erie County Historical Society.)

Twain depended on the McWilliamses for business acumen, friendship, and a model of domestic stability. He liked Esther McWilliams "very much." She sorted and made a list of Twain's dirty clothes, took them back and forth to the laundress, and handled the bill. She even offered to do any necessary mending. Throughout August and September of 1869, Twain and Olivia weighed the pros and cons of either boarding in Buffalo or buying a house once they were married in February. One of Twain's arguments to Olivia in favor of boarding was that John and Esther McWilliams seemed "happy & happily situated in their two unpretending rooms."[11]

McWilliams worked for J. Langdon and Company in Buffalo until 1879. Through the years he was active in the community, serving as a trustee and long-time Sunday school superintendent at the First Congregational Church.

While rooming in the same boardinghouse for six weeks in 1869, McWilliams and Twain probably took a pleasant evening stroll or two together to inspect the Langdon and Company coal yard and docks at the Erie Basin. Langdon's waterfront property was at the foot of Genesee Street, at River Street and slip number two, facing the Buffalo Harbor, with the Erie Canal running behind on the lot's north side. They might also have left the boardinghouse to socialize with Slee and his family. "Mac" and Twain would have walked a short distance west on Niagara Street, through one of the city's better residential districts, past David Gray's charming cottage at 192 Niagara and Selkirk's stately, square, gray-stone house (built by his father, John, with a mirror image of it sitting next door, where his brother, Charles, lived) at number 207, until they reached 462, where Slee and his family lived.

Twain had met John De La Fletcher Slee, whom he called "Fletch," months before coming to Buffalo. He liked Slee immediately. Soon after he and Olivia were engaged in February of 1869, Twain sat in on a coal business meeting held by Langdon and his managers at the St. Nicholas Hotel in New York City. Twain wrote Olivia a tongue-in-cheek letter about the invigorating, cutthroat corporate world. Twain observed a "notorious" character by the name of Slee who coldly vetoed a raise for a Buffalo employee who would now have to "eliminate" one of his children in order to subsist. Twain described the hotel gathering of "ruthless" capitalists with the line "Business is business, you know" and wrote favorably of Slee: "Mr. Slee gave me a very cordial invitation to visit his home in Buffalo, & I shall do it, some day. I like him first-rate."[12]

Barely four days into his job at the *Express*, Twain declared his allegiance to his future father-in-law's coal interests by publishing an editorial that reversed the paper's antimonopoly stance and praised Slee as a "gentleman of unimpeachable character." On August 20, 1869, the *Express* carried a letter from Slee justifying the practices of the Anthracite Coal Association. In the same issue, Twain's unsigned story called "The 'Monopoly' Speaks" also defended the Anthracite Coal Association against recent accusations of price gouging. Local newspapers, including the *Express* before Twain came on board, had been printing stories siding with organized citizen complaints of high coal prices. Two days before Twain's editorial, the *Niagara Falls Gazette* had covered a public meeting in Buffalo in which enraged citizens squarely placed blame for exorbitant coal costs on Jervis Langdon's marketplace stranglehold. Soon after Twain's *Express* editorial, the *Buffalo Daily Courier* printed a page-one note questioning the sudden pro-monopoly position of the *Express*, coyly closing with "What is the reason for it?"[13] Savvy readers, especially local businessmen and journalists, were likely aware of Twain's financial and familial ties to Langdon. One week after Twain's editorial, the *Express* continued its new function as Anthracite Coal Association public-relations organ by reporting on Langdon's "liberal donation" of fifty tons of coal to Buffalo General Hospital.[14]

Slee befriended Twain during the latter's bachelor period in Buffalo and played a major role in getting Twain and Olivia properly housed as newlyweds in Buffalo. Slee and his wife socialized often with the new bride and groom until Langdon's coal company reorganized and transferred Slee back to Elmira in May of 1870. Nevertheless, Twain and "Fletch" remained as close as brothers for the duration of Slee's life. Not only that, but Slee also handled additional financial details of Twain's co-ownership of the *Buffalo Express*. He advised Twain on an appropriate payment schedule to Kennett and oversaw a $3,000 loan to Joe Larned for which Twain held half of Larned's one-third share as security. Even after Twain moved from Buffalo, he informed Olivia that Slee was trying to collect Larned's debt: "Slee writes that Larned thinks he has sold his interest in the Express & wants to pay my notes."[15] Furthermore, one of the Clemenses' cats in Elmira was named Socrates Goldenrod Slee.

Slee became a leading citizen of Elmira, becoming a partner in J. Langdon and Company and serving as president of the board of education and as a member of the board of managers of the Willard Asylum. He was active in the Langdon family's Independent Congregational Church of Elmira (later known as Park Church). He taught Sunday school and was a church trustee. When "Fletch" died in June of 1901, Twain served as a pallbearer at the funeral services in Elmira. Three months later Twain gave a portrait photograph to Slee's twenty-year-old son, Jay, with the inscription: "To Jay Slee—It is one's human environment that makes climate—Mark Twain."[16]

"Mac" and "Fletch," along with Twain's newspaper colleagues and sometimes his fellow boardinghouse tenants, helped occupy some of his first weeks in Buffalo. And when he wasn't busy scribbling at the *Express* or writing letters, Twain also participated in the Young Men's Association and the Nameless Club. The Young Men's Association, founded in 1836, became the Buffalo Library and eventually today's Buffalo and Erie County Public Library. Since 1857, it had admitted women. In 1869 Joe Larned secured a two-year membership for Twain in the Young Men's Association, a library and lyceum society in Buffalo. Twain in turn recruited McWilliams to join.

Larned went on to direct the Buffalo Library from 1877 to 1897. On behalf of the YMA, Larned twice—in 1873 and 1900—invited Twain, their famous former member, to speak in Buffalo, but Twain politely declined both times. The group sponsored a popular public-lecture series that brought in speakers such as Ralph Waldo Emerson and Henry Ward Beecher, held literary discussions, and provided books, periodicals, and newspapers for its patrons. For several years Larned wrote an *Express* column called alternately New Books or Popular Books, which reviewed books newly purchased by the Young Men's Association. While Twain was a member, the YMA bought eight copies of *The Innocents Abroad*, which were kept "in constant use."[17]

George Selkirk and David Gray belonged to the YMA at the same time that Larned admitted Twain into the YMA fold. Grover Cleveland and Twain's future next-door neighbor James Lyon were also members. When Twain belonged, the Young Men's Association owned the St. James Building, a former hotel, on the south side of Eagle Street between Main and Washington Streets. In August of 1869, the large main hall had new imitation marble pillars installed for distinctive decoration. YMA activities were held in the second-floor library and reading rooms. Several other cultural institutions also met in upper floors of the St. James Building—the Fine Arts Academy, the Historical Society of Buffalo, the Society of Natural Sciences, and the Nameless Club.

Image 3.3.The St. James Building, which housed the Young Men's Association, at the southeast corner of Main and Eagle Streets. Twain met here as a member of two literary circles. (Reproduction by permission of the Buffalo and Erie County Public Library, Buffalo, NY.)

Twain recognized many familiar faces when he attended Nameless Club sessions in the second-floor YMA library room in August and September of 1869. He also met David Gray's wife, Martha, and Joe Larned's wife, Frances. Members included journalists, authors, businessmen, future congressmen, and high-ranking Union Army officers of the Civil War, including Selkirk, General William Sooy Smith, and Dr. Peter Wilson, a Cayuga chieftain who was hospital surgeon of the Army of the Potomac. Twain may have had a brief brush with Guy H. Salisbury, the "Charles Lamb of Buffalo," before Salisbury's tragic drowning in the first week of September 1869. Although Nameless Club meetings featured a club song and a secretary who kept minutes, they offered Twain the informal, convivial company of Buffalonians who shared a love of literature.[18]

Twain was known to cap off an evening out and about town with friends by stopping in for a beer at Victor L. Tiphaine's saloon on Main Street. An amusing blurb in the *Express* bears Twain's playful, punning touch: "Swallows are an indication of early Spring. Several were seen and taken at Tiphaine's."[19] In a 1906 autobiographical dictation, Twain remembered "pleasant times in the beer mills of Buffalo with David Gray."[20] Twain's Buffalo was a beer capital, boasting twenty-five breweries by 1870. During 1869 and 1870, 116,947 barrels of beer were sold in Buffalo, a figure that swelled by approximately 40,000 barrels the following year.[21]

Although Mark Twain's early social circle in Buffalo did not have much of a circumference, it was jammed with people and activities. He did not have to stray far from Mrs. Randall's boardinghouse and rarely needed to hire a carriage. The YMA and Nameless Club meeting places were a short, northerly four-block walk away. The waterfront was close by. Langdon's coal office at 221 Main Street, where McWilliams and Slee worked, was a two-block hike southward toward the lake, and Tiphaine's was a couple of doors from the coal office. And the *Express* was less than a block from Twain's apartment. His boardinghouse at 39 East Swan was an ideal setup for a single, working man like Twain, but he knew it would be insufficient once he got married in February.

Throughout August and September, Twain worried about supporting Olivia's comfortable lifestyle and living in an adequate home. He urged her to consider boarding for the first months of their marriage. Twain doubted that he and Olivia were prepared to jump into running a household, particularly when Olivia would be home alone in the middle of a Buffalo winter. So, he proposed finding a classier, more private boardinghouse apartment, "not in this caravansery, but in a house where there are no other boarders, & where the girl can have somebody to go to & speak to when she is lonely."[22] At the end of September, Twain asked Mrs. Randall to preserve his room and store his trunk, and he entrusted Slee with the task of locating a better boardinghouse. While Twain was away lecturing during the autumn and early winter, Mrs. Randall held out hope that upon his return with Olivia in February he would reside in her boardinghouse again. But, after Christmas, Slee sent word to Twain, who was lecturing in Williamsport, Pennsylvania, that he had found a two-room "place on one of our most pleasant streets"[23] for Twain and Olivia to board once they arrived in Buffalo after the wedding. Shortly after that, a rueful Mrs. Randall told *Express* staffers that Twain "had given up his room and arranged to send for his trunk."[24]

Mark Twain left Buffalo, his *Express* office, his new friends, and his one-room apartment Thursday night, September 30, 1869, and took a train to Elmira for a long hiatus. His adventure with Buffalo was headed for another phase, one in which he would mail stories to the *Express* while on the lecture trail. While on the road, he would be unaware of a charming, intriguing, behind-the-scenes conspiracy in his absence.

4

MY RASCALLY PILGRIMAGE

Members of the Mercantile Library Association committee must have been thrilled that Mark Twain was kicking off their Pittsburgh lecture season. By the time they arrived at the Academy of Music, all twenty-five hundred seats were filled, five hundred customers were standing inside, and hundreds more had been turned away at the door. Their group of twenty committee members and reporters had to sit in chairs set up at the last minute onstage behind the speaker. Twain's successful talk earned rave reviews and what would be the highest fee of his lecture course, $125. Furthermore, he was treated well during his three-day stay, entertaining lots of callers, attending a church featuring a fantastic choir, and being guest of honor at an oyster dinner.

Twain had started his lecture circuit in Pittsburgh on the evening of November 1, 1869, with a bang. Fifty lectures and seventy-seven days later, after his final performance on January 21, 1870, in Jamestown, New York, the circuit ended with a whimper.

He admitted to being tired for his last lecture stop, and the Jamestown *Journal* reports were unflattering. Three days after the lecture, a correspondent signing off as "Many Citizens" took issue with almost every aspect of Twain's Sandwich Islands talk. One day after the lecture, the *Journal* printed a tepid review and an item stating that if Twain's lecture weighed 225 pounds, then 224 pounds, 13½ ounces of it were "nonsense."[1] Jamestown papers sustained the attack on Twain for another two weeks, although he was apparently partly the victim of a local dispute about whether Jamestown YMCA lectures should be humorous or didactic.

Throughout Twain's three-month lecturing sojourn, he sent over twenty stories to the *Buffalo Express* and managed to frequently promote himself in the paper from a distance. He also kept tabs on plans for his wedding ceremony in Elmira and on Slee's search for a proper boardinghouse residency for the newlyweds in Buffalo. Before embarking on the grueling but lucrative lecture tour, Twain spent a month of comfort in the Langdon's Elmira family mansion.

During his October respite in the splendid Langdon home at the corner of North Main and Church Streets, Twain scrapped plans to complete a new lecture on "Curiosities of California" and instead refined his standby talk on "Our Fellow Savages of the Sandwich Islands." When he first took over at the *Buffalo Express*, he had tried to back out of his lecture commitment with James Redpath's Boston Lyceum Bureau. In the middle of August 1869, he wrote Redpath two letters from the *Express* asking to be released from the 1869–1870 lecture series. By early September, however, Redpath had informed Twain that several of the upcoming lecture assignments were ironclad contracts. Twain was also anxious about having enough "money to commence married life with."[2] So the obligations and potential income led Twain to publish a notice in the September 9 *Express* that "after recently withdrawing from the lecture field for next Winter, I have entered it again." Just before leaving for Elmira at the end of September, a questionnaire mailed by a publishing firm crossed his desk at the *Express*. His whimsical responses appeared as "The Latest Novelty—Mental Photographs" in the October 2 *Express*. The questionnaire was designed to create a profile, a veritable "mental photograph album" of the respondent. Twain answered the items playfully. His favorite tree was "Any that bears forbidden fruit." His favorite perfume was "Cent. Percent." His favorite characters in romance were "The Byron Family." He described his personal motto as "Be virtuous and you will be eccentric." And his favorite season of the year was "The lecture season." While in Elmira, he gathered strength for the lecturing life, and he continued writing for the *Express*. Some of the *Express* stories involved an Elmira professor.

In October of 1869, Twain praised Professor Darius Ford as a man of "unspotted character" and a "warm personal friend" who he expected would collaborate on a series of travel letters "in all good faith and honesty."[3] Five months later, a sour Twain ridiculed Ford's slow writing pace and abandoned the team project.

Darius Reynolds Ford was born in 1824 in the small town of Belfast, located in southwestern New York approximately seventy-five miles west of Elmira.[4] Ford graduated from Brown University and joined Alfred Academy's faculty, where he taught Greek for nine years until 1861. His academic career was interrupted for two years by service in the Civil War as a Union Army chaplain. After the war, he began a forty-year association with Elmira Female College as a professor of physical science, mathematics, and astronomy from 1863 to 1899, and as a professor emeritus until his death in 1904. By January of 1869, one of Ford's Elmira students was Olivia Langdon. Professor Ford tutored her and her friends Alice and Clara Spaulding in chemistry twice each week at the Langdon home. The Langdon household was busy that winter, since Twain was a frequent guest, campaigning for Olivia's hand in marriage. Twain and Ford met in early 1869. Twain was thirty-three years old; Ford was ten years his senior.

Image 4.1. Professor Darius R. Ford of Elmira College, with whom Twain planned to collaborate on an Around the World series in the *Express*. (Image courtesy of the Mark Twain Archive, Elmira College.)

Not long after Twain and Olivia announced their formal engagement in February of 1869, Ford played a role in one of Twain's comically worrisome dreams. Twain wrote Olivia of a dream in which she had rejected him in favor of a tutorial lesson, and that as Twain departed, he "heard yours & professor Ford's voices discussing the properties of light, & heat, & bugs."[5] Incredibly, several months later, Twain agreed—if only to calm Olivia's fears of leaving her family nest—to have Ford and the Spaulding sisters move in with them once they were married and settled in Buffalo. Nothing ever came of that plan.

Amid his initial writing spurt at the *Express*, Twain hatched the idea of collaborating with Ford. The Langdons had persuaded Ford to accompany their son, Charley, as both tutor and companion on an eighteen-month journey around the world. The family's motives weren't entirely academic. Family lore suggests that Ford was also expected to reform young Charley's drinking problem.[6] The itinerary meant that Charley would miss Olivia's wedding. The Langdons must have made Ford a generous offer, since the college had recently awarded him a one-hundred-dollar raise, hiking his annual salary to $1,300. When Twain learned that the trip was on, the joint writing venture with Ford was born. The concept was simple: Ford would send dispatches to Twain based on his travels, Twain would then revise and expand on them for an Around the World series in the *Express*.

Even though he was relaxing in Elmira, Twain dove into the project enthusiastically. He wrote Mary Fairbanks, his surrogate mother on the *Quaker City* tour, that he was itching to join Ford and Charley Langdon. In a publicity ploy, he teased Elmira newspapers into thinking that he would accompany them as far as San Francisco. He also directed his own newspaper to add to the Around the World fanfare. Three consecutive issues of the *Buffalo Express* in mid-October published one-column display ads with the same message repeated in four blocks, consuming six inches of valuable page space. The ads, on the front and back pages of the *Express*, trumpeted the first installment of the Ford-Twain collaboration.

Twain instructed colleagues back at the *Express* to run the first three Around the World stories—October 16 and 30, and November 13—prominently on the front page. In a move that perhaps signaled his already dimming interest in the team project, Twain allowed the fourth Around the World story on December 11 to be buried inside, on page 2. The remaining six entries, published over the next four months, continued to be scattered randomly in secondary pages of the *Express*. Even as late as January of 1870, though, Twain exhibited some of his old entrepreneurial spirit. He had just printed the seventh letter in the *Express* and wrote his book publisher that he preferred not to copyright the Around the World series, in hopes that they would be picked up by newspaper exchanges, thus supplying free advertising.[7] But the original scheme was pretty well dashed by then. The Ford-Twain pairing had started off with such grand plans. Twain had envisioned Around the World as a series of at least fifty letters because the world tour was so ambitious. Twain was practically salivating at the long-term nature of the writing project when describing the itinerary to Mary Fairbanks: "They start next Thursday & go overland to California & Denver & Salt Lake & Nevada mines & Big Trees & Yo Semite,—then a 25-day voyage to Japan—then China—then India,—Egypt & away up the Nile—the Holy Land all over again—Russia & the Emperor all over again—& we are all to meet them in Paris 12 months hence & make the tour of England, Germany, &c, with them."[8]

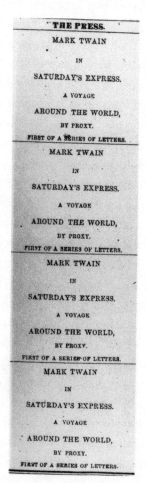

Image 4.2. In mid-October 1869, the *Express* ran these space-consuming, redundant ads for Twain and Ford's Around the World series.

Twain had barely arrived at the Langdons in Elmira when Ford and Charley Langdon departed by train on October 4, 1869. For several months the trip proceeded, with the travelers meeting most of their destinations in a leisurely manner. The global tour came to an abrupt halt, however, in the third week of June, 1870, when the Langdons reached Charley in Bavaria with instructions to return home immediately because Jervis Langdon was dying. The tour ended in June, but the Around the World series had been dropped long before that. In March the newly wed Twain wrote the Langdons with bitterness and sarcasm that he "had given up on Prof. Ford, & shall discontinue the 'Round the World' letters—*have* done it."[9] Twain blamed the failure of the series on Ford's snail's pace as a correspondent: "The Prof. has now been 6 months writing 2 little letters, & I ten—making 12 in all. If they continue their trip 18 months, as they propose, the Prof will succeed in grinding out a grand total of 8 letters, if he keeps up his present vigor." In fact, the collaboration never happened. Twain wrote the first eight—not ten, as he claimed—and Ford the final two Around the World sketches for the *Express*. Ford has been sloughed off by scholars as a stodgy mismatch for Twain, as the stuffy "Socrates of Elmira Female College"[10] whose pedantic pokiness and delinquency as a correspondent were chiefly responsible for Twain's sagging energy toward the joint Around the World scheme.

However, Ford may have been a more faithful contributor than is believed. He certainly wasn't given much of a chance by Twain. And there was more to Darius Ford than the stereotypically bookish professor. He and Twain may have been more alike than different, for Ford had a vigorous, rough-and-ready side to him. In 1867 he was granted a leave of absence from Elmira Female College to help open a silver mine in Idaho, where he battled the elements and hostile Native Americans. At the college, he also coordinated field trips to mines in Pennsylvania, caves in Kentucky, and rapids on the St. Lawrence River. As late as 1879, in his midfifties, Ford was chasing and shooting intruders and vandals on the Elmira campus. He seemed like a person Twain would have considered a kindred spirit rather than a pompous stuffed shirt. However, Twain published only two of Ford's letters. They appeared in the *Express* as the final two installments in the short-lived Around the World series on February 12 and May 5, 1870. Both bear the initials "D. R. F." The only scant evidence of "collaboration" is in Ford's second letter when *Express* editors inserted parenthetical factual updates into his account, written from Yokohama, of the tragic collision of the warship *Oneida* with a merchant steam ship. The other published letter by Ford described his overland trip to San Francisco and the voyage across the Pacific Ocean. Even though Twain decided to pull the plug on the series, Ford provided more than just the two letters Twain griped about. From Cairo in late March of 1870, Ford wrote a travel letter on the wonders of Egypt to his college colleague, Colonel H. M. Smith. In that letter, which Twain ignored as *Express* material, Ford comments that his "time and paper are pretty well used up in my newspaper correspondence."[11] And in the mid-1990s, another of Ford's unused travel letters was discovered. Addressed to Mrs. Azuba Sampson, wife of a former business partner of Jervis Langdon, Ford's letter presents his impressions of China and Japan and places he and Charley Langdon planned to visit on the rest of the trip. A note at the top of the January 10, 1870, letter demonstrates Ford's intention to feed the letter to Twain for the *Express* series ("Do not let this get in print;—preengaged for Mark Twain. D. R. F.").[12]

Early on, Twain allowed another agenda to sidetrack his original commitment to the Around the World series concept. Initially it was to be an entertaining, slightly zany batch of loosely coauthored articles. As Twain put it when introducing the first Around the World letter, "As Mr. F. jogs along, I mean to write paragraph for paragraph with him, and I shall set down all that I know about the countries he visits, together with a good deal that neither I nor anybody else knows about them."[13] The priority that soon distracted Twain stemmed from the rush of recollections about his California days. These reminiscences flooded his writer's consciousness as he tried to relax in the Langdon's home before embarking on the lecture tour. As early as May 1869 he had considered a new lecture on "Curiosities of California," but he had not fleshed it out yet. Twain wound up kidnapping the Around the World series and putting it to his own use. He supplied the first eight letters for the *Express*, seven of them centered on his memories of the West, mining experiences, and California. Chunks of these Around the World letters eventually appeared in his book *Roughing It*. In the first Around the World letter, published in the *Express* on October 16, 1869, Twain forecasts his change of plans and impatience with the coauthor arrangement. Ford and Charley Langdon had barely left Elmira before Twain printed the first Around the World entry in the *Express*. He informed readers that until Ford started sending letters, in the meantime he would "begin the journey unassisted, with a sketch or so of my own about the dead sea of California, and some other curious features of that country. The professor will sail for Japan . . . on the 4th of November . . . so his Japanese letters will not begin to arrive before January. However, I can run this duplicate correspondence myself till then." Another factor helped redirect Twain's attention toward California in October of 1869. He received an invitation in Elmira from a group of original "California Forty-Niner" prospectors to a dinner at Delmonico's in New York. His humorous reply recounted his own misadventures speculating and mining in the Humboldt and Esmeralda districts during the Nevada silver rush of the early 1860s. He sent it to the *Express*, where it was published on October 19 as "Mark Twain. His Greeting to the California Pioneers of 1849."

In the end, the *Buffalo Morning Express*'s Around the World series was not delivered as advertised. The series had little "global" matter and it certainly was not a collaborative effort. The Ford-Twain team fizzled from the outset once Twain decided to manipulate the column for his California musings and not wait for Ford's travel letters. It was yet another grandiose plan by Twain for a continuing *Express* feature that quickly ran out of steam, whether due to Twain's disillusionment with his own idea or his energies being pulled in another direction. It is not known if Twain took the trouble to inform Ford of his declining interest in Around the World. Nor is it known how Ford reacted to Twain's fickleness as a writing partner. However, in the lengthy obituary in the *Elmira Daily Advertiser*[14] chronicling Ford's distinguished career, his association with Twain is not mentioned, even though the same newspaper had proclaimed the Ford-Charley Langdon worldwide trip and Twain's writing connection to it thirty-five years earlier.

Twain's interest in self-promotion definitely had not waned. An idea to commandeer the *Express* for advertising *The Innocents Abroad* bore fruit while Twain was still enjoying Langdon hospitality in Elmira. In early September 1869, Twain had asked his publisher to forward a collection of book-review clippings. On Saturday October 9, the *Buffalo Express* published a special two-page advertising supplement that printed two and a half column's worth of announcements under "Complimentary—Press Greetings" by thirty-nine newspapers praising the fact that Twain had joined the *Express*. These newspaper puffs called Twain "a spicy writer" who was "waking up journalism in Buffalo," resulting in the *Express* becoming "one of the most quoted journals in the country." The ad supplement also reprinted, on space adding up to nearly a full page, extracts of forty-five favorable newspaper and magazine reviews of *The Innocents Abroad* (supposedly gleaned from twelve hundred such reviews), along with information on how to purchase the book from canvassers across New York State, as well as from the counting-room office of the *Express*. Whether the revenue gained from thirty-six advertisers of products—such as the Brilliant (a new-style parlor stove heater), Brandeth's Pills, M. H. Birge Window Shades, Ayee's Sarsaparilla ("For Purifying the Blood"), Venetian Liniment, Hostetter's Stomach Bitters, Hall's Vegetable Sicilian Hair Renewal, and Batchelor's Hair Dye—covered expenses to produce Twain's extravagant, self-aggrandizing newspaper insert, only *Express* business manager George Selkirk could have answered.

One last story that Twain shipped from Elmira to the *Express* in October was inspired by a spectacular newspaper item that month. In mid-October, a huge, fossilized man was reportedly dug up on a farm near Cardiff, a village in central New York about eighty miles southwest of Elmira. After much controversy, the find was exposed as the invention of George Hull, who had commissioned the statue's carving in Iowa and then had it secretly buried outside Cardiff. The fake fossil—and a fake version of the fake—soon went on display, drawing large crowds in Albany and New York City. In Elmira, Twain wrote "The Legend of the Capitoline Venus," published in the *Express* one week after the Cardiff Giant story was released.[15] Written as a drama, it is a romantic farce with a happy ending that depends on duping a wealthy American into paying for an inauthentic classic statue. At the end of the story, Twain alludes to the recent furor over the Cardiff Giant.[16]

By the end of October, Twain was refreshed by his month with the Langdons. His dependable Sandwich Islands lecture was in good shape, he had sustained his imprint on the *Buffalo Express* while staying 150 miles away from its exhaustive daily grind, and he had spent quality time with Olivia Langdon. It was time to hit the road and make some money before getting married.

Twain earned one hundred dollars per lecture, although occasionally he was only paid seventy-five. The Lyceum Bureau took 10 percent commission on the fees, and Twain paid his own expenses. After the rousing Pittsburgh start, he lectured from November to the third week of January throughout Pennsylvania, New England, New York, and Washington, DC. He took Sundays and most Saturdays off, which crammed his weekday speaking schedule. In November, he delivered five lectures in seven days. December was even more brutal. On three occasions, he spoke five days in a row, once giving talks nine times in ten days, and in another stretch performing ten times in twelve days. January was even more jammed, with fourteen lectures in eighteen days. Twain closed out his season with five speaking engagements in a row, finishing up in Jamestown. He lectured on his birthday, on Christmas Eve, and on New Year's Eve. Twain's profits added up to about $2,500,[17] but the grueling pace took its toll. He missed rail connections, rode in open buggies during freezing cold conditions, dozed fitfully in train sleeping cars, ran out of clean shirts, caught a cold in November, experienced blowing snowstorms and sleet in New York City and Albany, and fought off a week-long head and chest cold in December that reduced him to a "spiritless state."[18] Above all, he endured the obligatory demands made on his time by small-town lecture committees. He wrote Olivia that the typical wel-coming committee, or in Twain's terms his "insane persecutors," would call on him at his hotel or at the private home where he was a guest and proudly show off the "wonders of the village."[19] Their carriage ride would point out homes of local politicians, the woman's school, the public school, the town square, the factory, the cemetery, and the site of a proposed park. These gushing provincial tours were well meaning, but they exhausted Twain's patience. Sometimes he dodged them by registering at the hotel under "Samuel Langhorne."

In addition to making money on the lecture trail, Twain may have felt doubly fortunate to be out of Buffalo in early December. Anna Dickinson was speaking at St. James Hall in Buffalo on Friday evening, December 3, as part of the lecture course sponsored by the Erie County Suffrage Association. Twain was lecturing in Poughkeepsie. A week later she lectured in Elmira and stayed with the Langdons, her longtime friends. On the same night, Twain was miles away, speaking in Mount Vernon, New York. Twain had met Dickinson months earlier at the Langdons and had seen her lecture. There was tension between the two celebrities. Twain wrote in a review that Dickinson "will make a right ven-omous old maid some day."[20] By the same token, Dickinson once wrote her sister that she wondered why Olivia Langdon ever married such a "vulgar boor."[21]

A comfortable room in Boston's Young's Hotel served as Twain's home base in November and December. Here he received mail—mostly letters from Olivia—read, caught up on his correspondence, met William Dean Howells and Frederick Douglas, and sent stories to the *Express*. Several *Express* entries were editorials reacting to current events. In "Civilized Brutality,"[22] Twain ponders a recent spill by a trapeze artist and questions the motives of thrill-seeking crowds. He mentions Blondin again. "Hanging to Slow Music"[23] is a biting commentary on a case that sentimentalized the hanging of a vicious murderer. And Twain offers his opinion of the newly appointed US ambassador to Paraguay in "The Paraguay Puzzle."[24] He weighs in twice on the controversial murder of his friend and fellow journalist Albert Richardson by Richardson's lover's ex-husband, Daniel McFarland. Twain criticizes the public for not seeking facts and pleas for a middle ground in cases of divorce.[25] Other *Express* stories also demonstrate that Twain was avidly reading rival Buffalo newspapers and responding to world events. He revisits the Stowe-Byron matter, and in two *Express* stories he attacks the *Albany Argus* for its "blasphemous" obituary of former secretary of war Edwin Stanton and slams the rival *Buffalo Daily Courier* for its silence on the issue.[26]

Twain supplied the *Express* with lighter fare, too. In early November he received a letter from his sister Pamela, which might have reminded Twain of a letter her daughter Annie had written nine years earlier. Annie's charming style inspired Twain to write "A Good Letter. Mark Twain's Idea of It,"[27] a story praising eight-year-olds for writing simple, entertaining, and newsy letters. He also sent the *Express* a review of a Shakespeare production he attended in Boston, his impressions of a fortuneteller with bad breath, and a satirical take on a snooty American family on which he eavesdropped while taking a recent lecture-related train trip.[28] And "An Awful-Terrible Medieval Romance," in the *Express* of January 1, 1870, combines two popular genres of the time, the burlesque condensed novel and the literary hoax, to create a romantic spoof requiring the reader to untangle the plot and invent a satisfactory ending. Twain also sent messages to George Selkirk asking that various newspapers be added to the *Express* exchange list, made sure that the *Express* printed favorable reviews of several of his lectures in Massachusetts and New York, and oversaw the publication in the *Express* of additional *Innocents Abroad* publicity. Two squibs on November 29 and December 1 named the new Buffalo canvassers for the American Publishing Company, George B. Briggs and George M. Hewitt, sellers of *The Innocents Abroad* who would call on potential buyers, leaving their address at the *Express* office.

There is further evidence that Twain was gone but not forgotten in the pages of the *Buffalo Express* during his lecturing hiatus. When he was in the midst of his initial writing flurry at the *Express*, the paper carried two briefs about cattle breaking loose from pens at the nearby Buffalo stockyards in the Swan and Seneca Streets vicinity. "Wild Cattle" in the August 31 paper reported on a herd of ninety steers that had stampeded through city streets the day before. A follow-up item the next day, "More Texans," identified the marauding cattle as Texas steers. Two weeks after Twain left town for Elmira, the *Express* printed a humorous spoof letter, "Those Texas Steers. Letter from an Inquiring Texan Who Has Lost Some." Purportedly from a Texas cowboy with the amusing name of Dick Brand, whose rationale for reading the *Buffalo Express* is that he is a native of the city, the letter claims that some of the lost cattle may belong to him. The letter is addressed to "Mr. Mark Twain & Co., Editors of the *Buffalo Express*," and is written in a primitive vernacular with spellings distorted to mimic the voice of a Texas wrangler: "Der Surs I notis that a big herd of Texas Beeves stomp-pedid in yure City a few days ago." He sends an image of his distinctive brand and asks to be informed if some of the wild Buffalo stampeders turn out to be runaways all the way from his Texas herd. Young Earl Berry might have authored the hoax letter. If he did, chances are he ran the idea past Twain in Elmira first. And then there was the fox incident.

The *Express* of January 3, 1870, reported that a fox had been delivered by express mail to Mark Twain, care of the newspaper office from an unknown admirer in Chicago. Twain had just lectured in Williamsport and was spending a couple of days with the Langdons while in between lectures. The report, "New Year's Presentations," includes the comical letter that came with the fox (the letter alludes to characters in Twain's "The Notorious Jumping Frog of Calaveras County") and responds using the "persona" of Twain's office chair at the *Express*. Again, the response is probably the witty work of Berry, Twain's disciple in humor. The *Express* author promises to care for the fussy fox until Twain returns to the paper: "He is going to cost, but if it swamps the Third National Bank that fox shall be kept in provender till Mark comes home." The fun continued four days later when the *Express* published "Cuteness." Again it is a light, bright story allegedly reacting to a reply by the *Chicago Tribune* about "smelling a rat," doubting that such a fox was ever sent. The *Express* reaction, likely by Berry as well, says that the *Tribune* accusation is "lie-bel" and that the collective nose of the *Chicago Tribune* is incapable of smelling a rat from a fox. Extending the metaphor, "Berry" says that if the *Tribune* stretched its "mental nasal protuberance all the way to Buffalo and down into our pressroom," they would indeed see that the fox is there waiting for Twain. The *Express* wonders if the *Chicago Tribune* staff has been poking its "smeller" into the "editorial hash" of the rival *Buffalo Commercial Advertiser*, since the *Advertiser* is mostly "litter-rat-i."

A curious, witty, and satirical story appeared in the *Buffalo Express* on Monday, December 20, 1869. Headlined "Innocence at Home; Or Hunting a Hero in Washington" (see appendix 8), it is signed "LITTLE RED RIDING HOOD." The piece has never been reprinted and may be a Twain original. The lengthy two-column letter "*To the Editor of the Express*," datelined "Washington, December 15, 1869," adopts the point of view of a young girl infatuated with Twain. The long opening paragraph coyly hints that the author of the *Buffalo Express* letter is also the author of *The Innocents Abroad*, that is, Mark Twain. She claims to have attended Twain's lecture in Washington on December 8, but her interest in Twain comes across as absurdly obsessive. The letter contains insider information on Twain's personal habits and lecture-tour details, and it shows elements of Twain's writing style—particularly the usage of semicolons and parenthetical appositives—that suggest a compelling argument in favor of his being the author. The story may be read as a last-ditch bachelor fantasy or a cautionary tale of celebrity life on the road. More likely, it is one more comment on the public's insatiable fascination with the lives of public figures, a theme that had dominated Twain's body of work for the *Express* thus far. Twain's Red Riding Hood expresses her all-consuming admiration for *The Innocents Abroad* by saying, "I don't know now which is Me at home and which is Me Abroad." Before her idolatry of Twain, the author groupie says, she had flirted with Charles Dickens, but then she cut it off, fearing that she would wind up as a "lazy novel-reading woman in a wrapper on a soiled chintz sofa with broken springs" in his next novel. After reading *The Innocents Abroad*, Twain's Red Riding Hood turned her romantic desires toward Mark Twain, "fully determined on capturing that author and having him for breakfast." She admits roaming the streets of Washington, DC, days before the lecture, hoping to meet her new heartthrob, "eyeing every man I met with nothing but a moustache, in the most interrogative manner." She carefully researches Twain's personal life. She doesn't care if he is dead, as long as he is single—a humorous gag echoing the Columbus "Is he dead?" routine in *The Innocents Abroad*.

The slow comic build-up describing her fanatical steps is stock in Twain's trade. Then she buys a new hat (which she calls "MT") and tries sending a note through a friend of Twain who is a cabinet member, perhaps a thinly-veiled joking reference to Twain's friend Vice President Schuyler Colfax. She discovers that Twain enjoys his sleep and lectured in Philadelphia the day before DC. After attending the Washington lecture in Lincoln Hall, Red Riding Hood waits in line to finally meet her adored one. But the line moves so fast she can't pause to ask him where her favorite *Innocents Abroad* character—the Doctor or Dan or Blucher—lives (presumably she has plans to stalk him, too).[29] A likely inside joke here is that Dan Slote was Twain's favorite traveling companion on the *Quaker City* voyage, and Blucher was a fictional creation. She realizes that she is not alone in her Twain fixation because she is competing for Twain's attention in a long line with "thousands of other charming young ladies." The long-awaited personal encounter with her idol is nothing but "a polite greeting in an exasperatingly cold room." She is crushed. Her hero-worshipping days are over. All that Little Red Riding Hood gets for her Twain quest is "a most tremendous cold and what I have suffered since in mustard plasters and whisky punches my feeble pen cannot portray." During much of December, Twain, too, had a miserable sore throat and chest cold. And one week before "Innocence at Home" appeared, Twain, like Little Red Riding Hood, had experienced a nightmare of "black chaos" in which he had lost the affections of Olivia Langdon. [30] "Innocence at Home" is amusing but may be a meditation by Twain about fans who intrude on his private time during the lecture trip, about Americans who live vicariously through their celebrity heroes, about the difficult challenge of separating Mark Twain and Samuel L. Clemens. At the very least, it was a way to remind readers once again of his new book, *The Innocents Abroad*, which Little Red Riding Hood praises as all-consuming and, seemingly, superior to any of

Dickens's works. It would not be the only time that Twain would write positive notices anonymously or under a pseudonym for *The Innocents Abroad*.

During the lecture tour, Twain started receiving the first batch of "pretty gorgeous"[31] royalty checks for sales of *The Innocents Abroad*. He began feeling financially secure as his marriage approached. In Boston, Twain bought his complete wedding outfit and sent the parcel of clothing to Elmira, joking that Jervis Langdon should not go "wearing them around."[32] Twain was also moved to learn that Mrs. Langdon was making a quilt as a wedding gift out of a blue silk dress that held special meaning to Olivia and Twain. Twain's wedding jitters were further eased in a letter from Slee that he received in late December. Slee reported securing a first-rate boardinghouse in which Twain and Olivia could lodge once they arrived in Buffalo after the wedding. According to Slee, it was on one of the city's best streets, close to the *Express*, furnished, and with a bay window. Slee's only fibs were that it cost twenty dollars per week and was cohabited by a small family. Early on the morning of January 19, 1870, Twain departed Ogdensburg, New York, for Buffalo, where he spent part of the day, before continuing by train to Dunkirk. While in Buffalo he probably visited the *Express* office and then attempted to find Slee so that he could see the new boardinghouse. Slee artfully evaded Twain.

If he had not been so busy lecturing and writing, Twain might have connected some of his suspicions in late November regarding Olivia's sketchy whereabouts. On November 24 he wrote Olivia that he was "perplexed,"[33] wondering why she could not tell him more precisely about her plans for a trip to New York City. For the next three days, Twain appealed to Olivia to tell him where and when she expected to be in New York. He even telegraphed Jervis Langdon and got no answer. Eventually he caught up with Olivia and her father and was placated by discovering that she was shopping for her trousseau. It was true that Olivia had purchased over $500 worth of silk, cloth, and satin suits in a variety of colors from Madame Fogarty,[34] but there was much more going on behind the scenes. And Twain had no clue about the scale of subterfuge afoot.

Unbeknownst to Twain, Olivia and her father had traveled to New York City on November 22 and signed in at the St. Nicholas Hotel. Olivia's sister-in-law, Susan Crane, had been there for a week already. They were soon joined by J. D. F. Slee and his wife, Emma, from Buffalo. The "coconspirators" spent several days preparing for the Elmira wedding and buying furniture and fabrics for a house in Buffalo that Jervis Langdon had bought as a wedding gift. On the same day that Twain was lecturing in Norwich, Connecticut, Langdon purchased the house at 472 Delaware Street for $20,000 from Joanna and Prelate Barker. The house was bought in the name of Olivia Louisa Langdon of Elmira. The deed named Olivia, prematurely, as "wife of Mark Twain, Samuel L. Clemmens [*sic*]." The transaction took place on November 13 and was finalized on December 2.[35] Diagrams of the rooms were sent to Elmira, where the Langdons and a New York City firm developed an interior-design remodeling plan. Olivia's mother later arrived in New York to help pick out furniture. The New York designer was dispatched to do the decorating in the Buffalo house, upholstering new chairs and creating a master bedroom motif in blue satin.[36] Carpenters were hired in Elmira and New York to build customized furniture and handcrafted interior trim work, such as escutcheons in the shape of a *T* for Twain to be placed in the center of the heavy cornices. Some of the solid-walnut tables were made by the Langdons' cabinetmaker in Elmira. A handmade book case, which may have been measured by Olivia or Slee to fit snugly into a nook, was too big by an inch and wound up in a Buffalo physician's office instead.[37] Servants for the Buffalo house were hired, and provisions began being delivered. While still in New York City in the middle of December, Olivia projected a household budget of $2,300 at 472 Delaware, based on an annual income of $4,000.[38]

Meanwhile, Twain was blithely unaware of the Buffalo wedding gift skull-duggery. He chugged along in the homestretch of his lecture course, running on empty. In one thirty-one-hour span in New York State, he traveled 350 miles and gave two lectures. He was infinitely weary and frustrated. The best words he could find for his lecture tour were, "My rascally pilgrimage."[39] More accurately, he now referred to the lecture season as "the long agony" and "an eternity."[40] But suddenly, the January 21 Jamestown fiasco was over, and the next day he was back in Elmira, preparing for his wedding day in the friendly confines of the Langdon mansion.

On Wednesday evening, February 2, 1870, Twain and Olivia were married in the Langdon parlor. Between seventy-five and one hundred guests attended the quiet ceremony officiated by Rev. Thomas Beecher, of Elmira's Independent Congregational Church, and Rev. Joe Twichell, Twain's Hartford friend.

Among the guests were Joe Larned of the *Buffalo Express*, Twain's sister and niece from Missouri, Mary Fairbanks and her family, Dr. Rachel Gleason—cofounder of the Elmira Watercure—and her sister, and Olivia's eighty-eight-year-old grandmother. Olivia's gown was white satin with a long white veil and gloves that covered her arms. Afterward, a light supper included boned turkey and nonalcoholic drinks. Late in the afternoon of the next day, about twenty wedding party members boarded a magnificent director's car chartered for Jervis Langdon by the president of the Pennsylvania Northern Central Railroad and James Tillinghast of Buffalo, the general superintendent of New York Central Railroad. As the festive group headed toward Buffalo, Twain entertained them with a slightly inappropriate song about an unfaithful woman:

Image 4.3. Olivia Langdon, circa 1869. She and Twain were married in Elmira, NY, in February of 1870. (Image courtesy of the Mark Twain Archive, Elmira College.)

> There was an old woman in our town,
> In our town did dwell,
> She loved her husband dearily
> But another man twicet as well,
> Another man twicet as well.[41]

Twain also took up a collection totaling one dollar to give Beecher for conducting the wedding ceremony. At nine in the evening, the small group arrived at the train station, stepped out into the snowy darkness of Buffalo, and was greeted by several sleighs pulled by eagerly awaiting horses. But John D. F. Slee had one last trick up his sleeve.[42]

5

ALADDIN'S PALACE

Charles M. Underhill and John D. F. Slee were practically brothers. They were both graduates of Genesee College (which later merged with Syracuse University) in Lima, New York, class of 1860. Then they taught together for a few years at Falley Seminary in Fulton, New York. Slee taught Greek and German; Underhill taught Latin and Intellectual and Moral Science. In the late 1860s, they both left teaching to join the J. Langdon and Company coal business. By 1869 Underhill was general sales agent at Langdon's Anthracite Coal Association branch in Rochester, New York, and Slee managed the Buffalo office. Their marriages took place on the same day in 1862, Slee to Underhill's younger sister, Emma. The Slees gave the middle name "Underhill" to their firstborn. The Underhills gave the middle name "Slee" to their first son. After John Slee's death in Elmira in 1901, he was buried in the Underhill family lot in Buffalo's Forest Lawn Cemetery.

But in early 1870, the "blood" brothers were reunited. Underhill had been promoted from Rochester to Langdon's Buffalo coal office, where Slee had risen to be its highest officer. Underhill, his wife, Anna, and their three small children, ages two to five, moved in with the Slees at 462 Niagara Street. Slee and his wife had a three-year-old daughter. The in-laws and young cousins formed a tightly knit crew in their crowded but cozy Niagara Street home. And Underhill arrived in Buffalo just in time to be recruited by Slee in February 1870 to participate in the charming wedding-gift trick pulled on Mark Twain by Langdon and friends.

Image 5.1. John De La Fletcher Slee, Langdon coal company employee, Twain's friend, and organizer of what Twain called a "first class swindle." (Image courtesy of Charles S. Underhill.)

Image 5.2. Charles Munson Underhill, circa 1861. Langdon coal company employee at the Buffalo branch and lifetime friend of Twain. (Image courtesy of Charles S. Underhill.)

Slee had arranged for horse-drawn sleighs to meet the select Twain-Langdon wedding party at Buffalo's train depot on the snowy night of Thursday, February 3, 1870. He relied on his two trusted Anthracite Coal Association colleagues to assist in the final step of the elaborate hoodwink. Underhill was at the reins of one of the sleighs, with instructions to drive his passengers to the Tifft House hotel. Slee, suffering from a brutal head cold, planned to drive another sleigh, dropping off Olivia Langdon's parents and Twain's sister and niece at the surprise wedding-present home on Delaware Street. Slee assigned the most challenging role to Twain's boardinghouse buddy, John J. McWilliams. McWilliams was to engage in a stalling tactic by guiding a third sleigh with only the bride and groom aboard on a winding, circuitous route through several streets of the city until eventually delivering them to the 472 Delaware address. McWilliams was sworn to silence and stoicism—particularly if Twain grew impatient with the seemingly random itinerary. The stage was set, the actors in place.

For Twain's part, he was enjoying the home stretch of the train ride from Elmira with a handful of family and friends. He looked forward to moving into the stylish boardinghouse that Slee said he had found for him and Olivia on a splendid Buffalo street, with two newly furnished rooms and a bay window facing southward and eastward. The director's private rail car that Jervis Langdon had chartered for this postwedding trip to Buffalo was a treat. Twain admired the richly appointed interior that likely featured partly paneled and partly painted walls with gilt trim, a washroom, three state rooms, and a center sitting area with velvet-covered sofas on plush carpeting. As the elite train pulled into the station, Mark Twain had once again arrived in Buffalo . . . this time in a state of luxury befitting the social class he had married into. He had been told to expect either his new landlady, named Mrs. Howells, or a former Elmira minister now employed in the coal-and-lumber business in Buffalo, Rev. A. M. Ball, to greet them at the train station and escort the entire party to the Tifft House for a small wedding reception. When the luxury train stopped and passengers and luggage were disembarked and unloaded, respectively, Twain saw only his friends Slee and McWilliams and three empty horse-drawn sleighs waiting in the darkness somewhat illuminated by gaslights and gently falling fluffy, white snowflakes.

Charles M. Underhill heard the train's horn, then saw a rare sight: a single heavyweight, custom-built, well-polished, sixty-five-foot-long palace car with an observation platform pulled by a locomotive chugging smoothly into Buffalo's Exchange Street Station.[1] He checked his pocket watch: nine o'clock. When the small Elmira party alighted, he recognized his boss's daughter, Olivia, and the famous Mark Twain. Underhill's group, including Reverend and Mrs. Thomas Beecher and the Fairbanks family, piled onto his sleigh, and after a five-minute ride they were dropped off at the Tifft House for the night. Slee loaded Jervis and Olivia Langdon and Pamela and Annie Moffett onto his sleigh and drove straight to 472 Delaware, a relatively quick trip at that time of night. Twain and Olivia rode with McWilliams, the last sleigh to leave the quiet train station. By all accounts, McWilliams handled the ruse perfectly. To Twain, the round-about route seemed destined for nowhere in particular. As street after street and minute after minute passed, McWilliams in the driver's seat could hear Twain's muffled complaints and mild curses. In later years, Twain remembered the frustratingly aimless sleigh journey as one in which he was "driven all over America" in an itinerary that "turned all the corners in the town and followed all the streets there were."[2] As Twain recalled in an 1884 return visit to Buffalo, he "was the only person this side of Niagara Falls"[3] not in on the secret.

Almost an hour later, McWilliams pulled up the sleigh in front of a handsome house at 472 Delaware Street, Buffalo's most desirable residential boulevard. A landlady, someone the Langdons had hired to pose in this cameo role, emerged from the house and approached the carriage stepping stone at curbside. Twain later sketchily remembered her as being named Mrs. Howells, Mrs. Johnson, Mrs. Thompson, or Mrs. Jenkins. Before Twain had much of a chance to tell her that Slee made a mistake, that he could not afford such opulent lodgings, the "landlady" virtually evaporated and Olivia and Twain were surrounded by Mr. and Mrs. Langdon and Twain's sister Pamela and her daughter, Annie. Jervis Langdon handed Twain a carved box of teakwood containing the deed to the house.

Once inside the gorgeous house, made to feel homey with floral arrangements everywhere, crystal chandeliers shimmering in gaslight in the parlors and dining room, and smells of a late hot supper being prepared, Twain learned the extent of the Langdons' wedding gift. Along with buying the newly decorated and furnished house and attached stable, the Langdons also had hired a cook, maid, and coachman; had purchased a horse, sleigh, and carriage "with their monogram on the panel";[4] had written a substantial start-up check; and had provided an ample supply of food and coal for their beloved daughter and new son-in-law. Twain was bedazzled by the lovely rooms outfitted in satin curtains and upholstered furnishings in a variety of color themes. He was especially taken by the blue drawing room and red study. As reported by Mary Fairbanks, he declared the entire practical joke and surprise wedding present "a first class swindle."[5] Mark Twain, from the dusty little river town of Hannibal, Missouri, had now really, truly arrived in Buffalo and Victorian America's upper crust. That first night before going to sleep in their bewitchingly beautiful new home, Twain and Olivia were asked by coachman Patrick McAleer what his orders were for the next day.

Image 5.3. The original design of the Second Empire–style wedding-gift house at 472 Delaware. Several design details stress the entrance bay as a vertical feature. (Image used by permission of the Collection of the Buffalo and Erie County Historical Society.)

The next morning, Friday, the Tifft Hotel contingent paid a visit to 472 Delaware. The Beechers and the Fairbankses marveled at the lovely interior decorating. Reverend Beecher christened the house by rolling around on a carpet in order "to take the feather edge off." Then, with the small group of well-wishers together in the drawing room, Beecher led them in singing "Heaven is My Home."[6] As the full impact of the Langdons' largesse began to sink in, Twain announced, "Mr. Langdon, whenever you are in Buffalo, if it's twice a year, come right here. Bring your bag and stay overnight if you want to. It shan't cost you a cent!"[7] The genial gathering erupted in laughter. Twain played with that gag for a few days. A newspaper carrier remembered a temporary sign posted on the front entrance at 472 Delaware that read "Mark Twain lives here and my father-in-law pays the rent."[8]

Delaware Street, known to locals as "the Avenue," was already established as one of the grand American boulevards. Within the next ten to twenty years, most of Buffalo's sixty millionaires lived in mansions on Delaware.[9] In August of 1869, the *Buffalo Express* praised Delaware as a broad and beautiful thorough-fare with abundant shade trees and well-tended gardens, "making it an avenue with one of the city's pleasantest drives imaginable."[10] By 1870, a wide, grassy median divided Delaware Street into two parallel east- and west-side strips. The median was beautified by elm, giant horse chestnut, and maple trees, and it featured hitching posts and carriage stones so that passing buggies could stop and allow visitors to inspect the ornate gardens in front of the homes of Buffalo's elite. Years later, French writer Andre Maurois, while visiting as a university instructor, admired Delaware Street's "seas of verdure" from his hotel window, a view which reminded him of his "house at Neuilly and the green waves of the Bois de Boulogne."[11] Residents of Delaware Street in 1870 lived on a typical nineteenth-century urban street of fashion, members of an elite "socially one-dimensional community" in James Howard Kunstler's terms, where hordes of "immigrants were providing a pool of domestic servants at bargain rates—maids, cooks, squads of gardeners, handymen, laundresses—some of whom lived in the house. The home itself became a kind of factory for the production of comfort."[12] Seeing to Twain and Olivia's comforts were three live-in domestics hired by the Langdons: twenty-four-year-old Irishman Patrick McAleer, the coachman; Ellen White, twenty-nine, a cook and housekeeper also from Ireland who had been a family servant for the Langdons; and a young maid named Harriet. McAleer ended up serving Twain and his family for over two decades.

With the number of expensive mansions being erected each year, Delaware Street was a source of civic pride. It was Buffalo's "street of palaces" at the nexus of old and new money in a booming city. Most of Buffalo's leading merchants in 1870 operated "on the dock," conducting their thriving enterprises from offices at the Lake Erie waterfront Central Wharf. And many of those merchants, dealing in grain storage, leather, lumber, and coal, lived in exquisite houses along Delaware Street. At number 472, Twain and Olivia rubbed shoulders with Buffalo's best and brightest professionals, established moneyed class, and newly rich entrepreneurs. Their parklike street lined with a double row of trees spoke of affluence and influence.

Next door to Twain and his bride, at 468 Delaware in a fine, red-brick home with sandstone trimmings, on the northwest corner of Virginia and Delaware, lived James S. Lyon, a prosperous realtor of Lyon and Baker Erie Land Office. Lyon's front entrance was graced by massive bronze doorknobs, each ornamented with a lion's head to remind visitors of the family name. Twain's other next-door neighbor, in the third house above Virginia at 482 Delaware Street, was Dr. Cornelius Cox Wyckoff, thought to be Buffalo's oldest practicing physician at the time of his death in 1903. Wycoff's office was at 8 South Division Street, over the rear of William Peabody's drug store. Peabody himself lived at Delaware and Allen in a Tuscan villa-style house with a "handsome tower and graceful arcaded porch."[13]

At 409 Delaware was the imposing home of Peter C. Stambach, owner of a merchant tailor business; at 452, in an immense, square house, lived James S. Howells, a wealthy Medina sandstone dealer and paving contractor. At 585 Delaware lived William C. Newman of Newman's Akron Cement Company, with offices at the Central Wharf. There was S. Burrell Sears, a commerce merchant at the Central Wharf, who lived at 489 Delaware Street; Ebenezer Guthrie of the firm Hazard and Guthrie, commission merchants, resided in splendor at 435 Delaware. John C. Hazen, a wholesale seed and produce dealer at the Central Wharf, lived at 431; the impressive homes of Henry Janes and Francis King, Central Wharf wheelers and dealers, occupied 591 and 564 Delaware, respectively. At 434 Delaware, the elegant William Dorsheimer house, designed

by Henry Hobson Richardson with a distinctly French influence for the prominent local lawyer, was under construction. And at 414, an enormous Second
Empire–style dwelling was nearly complete and boasted twelve bay windows
and two curved flights of marble stairs. The house was being built at a cost of
$200,000 for Charles F. Sternberg, millionaire owner of an Ohio Street grain
elevator with an office at the Central Wharf.[14] Plush interior details included
heavy, carved black walnut, oak, and mahogany wainscoting and moldings and
fourteen-foot-high ceilings on the first floor. Still another mansion was being
built in 1870 at 506 Delaware for Chillion M. Farrar, who owned two foundries that manufactured locomotive boilers, metal tanks, and propellers. Farrar's
expensive house featured mahogany and walnut paneling and walls covered not
with paper but with dark red brocades and tapestries.

This was Mr. Twain's neighborhood.[15]

Image 5.4. At the northwest corner of Virginia Street, the home of James S.
Lyon sat at 468 Delaware Street. Lyon was Twain's next-door neighbor on
the south side. (Image used by permission of the Collection of the Buffalo
and Erie County Historical Society.)

Image 5.5. The home of Cornelius Cox Wyckoff, MD, sat at 482 Delaware Street. Wyckoff was Twain's next-door neighbor on the north side. (Image used by permission of the Collection of the Buffalo and Erie County Historical Society.)

Accounts of early life at 472 Delaware by Twain and his wife describe it in storybook terms. It was a "palace," with Olivia a "queen" and "princess." The house was "bewitchingly furnished." Twain told his Hartford friend, Rev. Joe Twichell, that he felt like "little Sammy in Fairy Land."[16] Perhaps most revealing was Twain's reference to their honeymoon house as "our Aladdin's palace" in which they were "roosting in the closing chapter of a popular novel."[17] Since childhood, Twain had known the story of Aladdin's magic lamp in *The Arabian Nights' Entertainments*.[18] In December of 1867, while courting Olivia, he wrote Mary Fairbanks despairingly that he likely lacked the social standing and wherewithal to win Olivia's hand: "I can't turn an inkstand into Aladdin's lamp."[19] Almost one year later, his prospects improved, Twain assured Olivia that their mutual love was as secret "as though it were shut within the fabled copper vessel of Arabian story."[20] And the *Arabian Nights* tales motif was fresh on Twain's newly wed mind from having just published *The Innocents Abroad*, where in one span of ten chapters (from chapters 8 to 18), he makes four allusions to the tales, Aladdin, or Aladdin's palace.

Just one month after describing 472 Delaware as "Aladdin's palace," Twain seemed poised to launch a new phase of his writing career from his newfound lofty, secure social and financial standing. He planned to contribute a column to the New York City–based *Galaxy* magazine, which offered an opportunity to produce "higher-class writing—stuff I hate to shovel into a daily newspaper."[21] It appears as though Twain was looking at his sumptuous 472 Delaware honeymoon dwelling as a symbol of his ability to move beyond the newspaper grind toward artistic, literary writing. He had, indeed, married into a comfort level enabling him to convert his inkstand into Aladdin's lamp.

The 472 Delaware Street mansion was fairly new and possibly built by Henry M. Kinne, who had owned the house with his wife, Elizabeth, from 1864 to 1869, before Twain moved in. Kinne had built nine stores on Main Street, three more on Prime Street, three grain elevators, and four private dwellings. Another possible builder of Twain's home was architect George M. Allison, who designed several costly dwellings on Delaware Street in the 1860s and 1870s, including the Sternberg house.

Four seventy-two was the second house on the west side of Delaware north of Virginia, two-and-a-half stories solidly constructed of bright-red bricks larger than standard size. Starting at the rear, the attached two-story brick barn, or carriage house, was almost as spectacular as the house itself. The carriage house was connected to the house proper because the lot was only about 139 feet deep. With walls two feet thick, a concrete floor eight inches thick, like iron, made not out of typical porous cement but of crushed marble so that horse urine would not soak through, and a loft supported by heavy beams where bales of hay were stored, the carriage house was built to last. The loft also had two or three rooms, and the floor was made of very white, white pine two-and-a-half inches thick. On the ground floor, the carriage was parked on one side. A huge garage door opened to Holloway Alley, a private road behind Twain's house that paralleled Delaware Street and extended behind other homes on the block from Virginia to Allen Streets. Inside the carriage house, on the opposite side of the coach-storage area, was a stable with six horse stalls. Early on, the extensive carriage house might have served as a livery for some neighborhood residents.[22] On the stable side, there was a metal circular stairway to the loft, in the style of late nineteenth-century fire stations, to prevent horses from wandering upstairs. A passageway from the stable to the buggy section was nine feet high so that horses would not hit their heads. The carriage house was equipped with gas and water, and the six horse-stall windows were barred.[23]

The main house had thirteen rooms in addition to the kitchen and laundry. It had a mansard roof and an elegant Italianate design, with some Second Empire influences. Bay windows seven feet high projected from the first and second floors on the north and south sides of the house. Windows throughout were tall and arched. The overhanging eaves were supported by decorative brackets, and arched doorways were framed by an elaborate entranceway trimmed by ten-foot-long pieces of hand-carved dark-walnut rope molding.

Image 5.6. A drawing by Helen Durston of 472 Delaware Avenue. (Reproduction by permission of the Buffalo and Erie County Public Library, Buffalo, NY.)

Image 5.7. The house at 472 Delaware, after its front was modified with a wraparound porch once Twain moved out, with a view of the attached carriage house. (Image used by permission of the Collection of the Buffalo and Erie County Historical Society.)

Inside the doors, striking features included a lovely vestibule and grand staircase with a carved newel post containing inlays of contrasting wood. Beneath the staircase, which ascended to the third floor, was a comfortable window seat. Flanking the long front hall were spacious rooms. The largest set of rooms was to the right of the hall (the north side of the building) and included one of the showpieces of Olivia's design handiwork, the drawing room. As with the upstairs master bedroom, Olivia had chosen a blue satin decorating motif for the drawing room. Twain and his wife often proudly displayed this room to visitors, temporarily removing the furniture covers to achieve full effect. The drawing room boasted a long pier-glass mirror between its two windows and heavy blue satin curtains draped from cornices to the floor. Olivia placed two of her favorite objects in the drawing room: a blue enameled clock that rivaled anything she had seen in New York City and a statuette called *Peace*, a wedding present. Also on the north side of the main floor, pocket doors of heavy black walnut opened from the drawing room to the library; from the rear of the drawing room, more doors led into the dining room. The library served as the true family room for Twain and Olivia. When guests called, servant Harriet or Ellen invariably brought them into the library, referred to as a "little sanctum."[24] Olivia had outfitted it in scarlet upholstery. Among the furnishings was a big rocking chair, a sofa lounge that was "awful short" to recline on, a library table, and an inlaid chess table at which the newlyweds sat and played cribbage and "cutthroat euchre." They also spent evenings there, with Twain reading poetry aloud until bedtime at ten o'clock. Perhaps Olivia's favorite wedding present, the Madonna painting from Alice Hooker Day and her husband, John, hung above the intricately carved cherry fireplace and mantelpiece in the library. The fireplace included an attractive insert of mosaic tile. Olivia wrote the Days that the Madonna artwork watched over them and pleasantly spoke to her and Twain "of you two friends away off in Hartford."[25] A few of the books that formed part of Twain's library collection at that time included copies of *Short Studies on Great Subjects* (1868) by James A. Froude, inscribed by Olivia in Elmira in 1869 and Twain in Buffalo in 1870; *The Autocrat of the Breakfast-Table* (1858) by Oliver Wendell Holmes, which Twain had already read twice and annotated and which Olivia and Twain thought of as their "courting book";[26] *The Poetical Works of Jean Ingelow* (1863), from which Olivia copied the poem "We Two" in her commonplace book in February of 1870; and *What I Know of Farming* (1871) by Horace Greeley with an inscription to Twain by Greeley that read: "To Mark Twain, Esq., Ed. Buffalo Express, who knows even less of MY farming than does Horace Greeley. N. York." Twain's library also likely included *History of the Hawaiian or Sandwich Islands* by James Jackson Jarves and *1001 Nights: Arabian Tales*.[27]

The dining room, the last of the three large rooms on the north side of the downstairs and the only one that led directly from the front hall, was stocked with a custom-built sideboard, long table and chairs, and another wedding gift—a full-length mirror in an elegant rosewood frame. The dining table was covered with a fringed red cloth. Olivia installed trains of ivy around the dining

Image 5.8. The foyer of 472 Delaware as it appeared in 1961. The newel post at the foot of the stairway was carved and had inlays of contrasting wood. (Image used by permission of the Collection of the Buffalo and Erie County Historical Society.)

Image 5.9. The library of the Twain house showing paneled wainscot and tiled fireplace. (Image used by permission of the Buffalo and Erie County Historical Society.)

Image 5.10. An antique inlaid chess table from 472 Delaware. It was purchased at a sale of furniture items that Twain and Olivia did not want to take with them when they moved from Buffalo in 1871. (Reproduction by permission of the Buffalo and Erie County Public Library, Buffalo, NY.)

room window. To the left of the front hall, on the south side of the house, there was a big, bright parlor broadened by bay windows and with an ample fireplace and full pier-type mirror mounted on one wall. Downstairs rooms were enhanced by stylish wainscoting of black walnut and curly maple. According to the last owner of the house, hidden tongue-and-groove compartments were found in the early 1960s in some of the wainscoting where panels slid up waist high, revealing long-dried-out, empty, flat pint bottles of whiskey.[28]

Twelve-foot-high ceilings were accented by handcrafted embellishments. Some had beveled corners and, above the windows, specially designed cornices with faces and heads hand carved of mahogany. Other cornices to which valances were attached over parlor windows were framed to casings; in the center of each casing was a shield with the letter *T* for Twain. The tall windows downstairs were surrounded inside by sets of impressive wooden shutters. Each room at 472 Delaware had a lovely fireplace and ornate mantelpiece, sometimes of carved cherry, as in the library, or of rich, dark walnut with burled veneer inlays, as was the case in another room. Most of the other dozen or so fireplaces and mantelpieces were Italianate marble style. Some of the marble fireplaces had slate mantels. Each marble fireplace boasted a custom-designed keystone in shapes such as date clusters, palm leaves, bison heads, elaborate floral patterns, female human heads, and shields.

A handsome black-walnut balustrade accompanied the main stairway up to the second-floor hall, where a small sitting room was positioned at the front of the building facing a hooded window directly above the entrance to the house. Rooms of varying sizes branched off the second-floor hall. The largest room was Olivia's blue-satin bedroom masterpiece. Its low bed was canopied and curtained in pale-blue satin and featured the quilt made by Mother Langdon out of Olivia's blue dress, Twain's favorite. Master-bedroom chairs were also done up in blue satin. Another of Olivia's second-floor creations also spoke from the heart. She had designed a scarlet-appointed den for Twain to write in. Eventually, he settled into a routine of working in his "perfect gem of a little study," rain or shine, from eleven in the morning to three in the afternoon. A small bedroom served months later as the baby's nursery.

Although the third floor was occupied by servants and had a separate back stairwell down to the kitchen, pantry, and cellar, Twain had an idea for remodeling a section of the top story. In May of 1870, just three months after

Image 5.11. An ornate mantelpiece of rich, dark walnut with burled veneer inlays that once graced 472 Delaware. (Reproduction by permission of the Buffalo and Erie County Public Library, Buffalo, NY.)

Image 5.12. Another Italianate marble mantelpiece salvaged from the Twain house. (Image courtesy of Ted and N. Averie Montagu.)

Image 5.13. A third stately marble mantelpiece from 472 Delaware. (Image courtesy of the Buffalo State College Archives, *Courier-Express* Collection.)

Image 5.14. An interior view of the second-floor stair hall looking toward the sitting room at the front of the house. The window is hooded and sat directly above the entrance. (Image from the *Buffalo Evening News*, May 15, 1910.)

moving in at 472 Delaware, Jervis Langdon sent an additional check for $1,000. Olivia wanted to use the money to pay off debts. Twain, however, hoped to use the windfall to build a dream "sky parlor" for a billiard room on the third floor. Years later, he fulfilled that vision when he built such a specialized playroom upstairs in his Hartford, Connecticut, mansion. Although the billiard-sky-parlor renovation never happened at 472 Delaware Street, Twain may have optimistically gone ahead and ordered a pool table in Buffalo in case the room was built. A substantial billiard table made of bird's-eye maple and some rosewood with walnut, with liners of heavy oak and ivory diamond inserts on the ends and sides, manufactured by Braun Brothers on Genesee Street in Buffalo, somehow found its way to the Langdon home in Elmira sometime after 1869 (Frederick and Adam Braun's company operated from 1869 to 1880). The Langdons were not billiards players, but Twain alludes to the table, which wound up in the third-floor playroom of his in-laws' mansion on the corner of Main and Church Streets and remained there until the house was torn down in the 1930s.[29]

By all accounts, 472 Delaware was a palatial dwelling. Elements of its exquisite interior lasted well into the twentieth century. Those who occupied or toured the building as late as the 1950s and 1960s vividly recall details such as the rich Honduras mahogany and walnut woodwork; the unusually high ceilings; the bright, large rooms with tall bay windows and impressive shutters; the natural hardwood floors; and the grand "stairway and balustrade to the second floor from the front foyer and marble fireplaces."[30]

During the first months of their marriage, Twain and Olivia were busy socializing, adjusting to keeping house, and enjoying a prolonged honeymoon. Five days after moving in at 472 Delaware, Twain wrote a somewhat risqué note to his agent's brother that he was "just married, & don't take an interest in *anything* out of doors."[31] Despite Twain's macho claim, privacy must have been a rare commodity. Olivia and Twain did not waste any time before engaging in the Victorian high-society dance of going on calling expeditions and entertaining at home. In the first few days of life at 472 Delaware, Twain and Olivia exchanged a handful of visits with Emma and John Slee, who by now was over his severe sore throat. When they called on the Slees, Twain and Olivia undoubtedly also socialized with Charles and Anna Underhill, who shared quarters with the Slees. While visiting the Slees, Twain said that if he happened to attend a boring theatrical performance, all he had to do was enter his spectacular drawing room and remove the furniture covers, and he would be suitably entertained by the sight. Then, back at 472 Delaware, the two families spent a pleasant evening. Emma Slee, Olivia, Annie Moffett, and Twain played a card game of High, Low, Jack, while Slee and Pamela Moffett chatted.[32] In the early going, the newlyweds had company quite often. Twain's sister Pamela and his niece Annie had left for Elmira following the surprise wedding-gift affair, but they came back to stay at 472 Delaware for a few days. In mid-February, at Twain's suggestion, they investigated Fredonia, New York, just forty-five miles south along Lake Erie, where they arranged to rent a home. By February 16, they returned to stay with Twain and Olivia for a sustained period. Joe Twichell and his wife from Hartford also were houseguests around this time. Twain reveled in telling his story of "Little Sammy in Fairyland" and in giving the grand tour of his "palace," saving the drawing room for last after dinner. Twichell left duly impressed by the grandeur of the home and the scope of the wedding gift.

On Saturday, February 12, they received Rev. Grosvenor Williams Heacock of Lafayette Presbyterian Church. Heacock spoke highly of *The Innocents Abroad* to Twain, and the new married couple enjoyed his company. Twain had attended Lafayette Presbyterian alone on February 6, while Olivia rested at home in the library. But the next Sunday they went to church together and were warmly welcomed by Heacock. Twain joked that it was an opportunity to show off his Sunday attire to the congregation, and he also commented on Heacock's "exceedingly pleasant and hearty" nature.[33]

Image 5.15. The Rev. Grosvenor W. Heacock, pastor of Lafayette Presbyterian Church, attended by Twain and Olivia. (Image courtesy of the Lafayette Avenue Presbyterian Church, Buffalo, NY.)

The carriage ride to Lafayette Presbyterian, located on Washington Street across from Lafayette Square, did indeed afford Twain a chance to advertise his newfound lofty social standing. Patrick McAleer, the coachman, was decked out in a pale-blue livery coat and cape and wore a tall, shiny hat. Twain described the ride to church as a sideshow, with boys attracted to their carriage as if to a circus. In comparison to his flashy coachman, Twain joked that he himself seemed rather dull looking. This observation was in keeping with his pattern of reviving images and themes fresh in mind from *The Innocents Abroad*. In chapter 14, Twain had also described being starstruck by stylish coachmen uniforms. He wrote of a Parisian boulevard where royalty paraded by in carriages attended by "gorgeous footmen" dressed in colorful, "stunning and startling" liveries that made him want to become a "flunky" himself just "for the sake of the fine clothes."[34] Years later, in *The Adventures of Tom Sawyer*, Twain wrote that Tom Sawyer's sole reason for retaining his membership in the Cadets of Temperance was the showy "regalia" and red sash of their marching uniforms.

Image 5.16. Old Lafayette Presbyterian Church at Lafayette Square in Buffalo. (Image used by permission of the Collection of the Buffalo and Erie County Historical Society.)

Reverend Heacock's kindly manner made Olivia homesick for Rev. Thomas Beecher and her family's church in Elmira. Heacock's "exceedingly fine face" reminded her, too, of Anna Dickinson, an association that must have rankled Twain.[35] For that matter, the comparison would probably not have flattered Heacock, either, if he had known about it. For Olivia, a little bit of home came to Buffalo when Beecher and Heacock exchanged pulpits on Sunday, April 10,

1870. Heacock officiated at Beecher's Congregationalist Church in the morning and delivered a sermon Sunday evening at the Opera House in Elmira. Beecher led morning and evening services at Buffalo's Lafayette Church. In a letter to the Langdons, Twain praised Beecher's evening sermon, referred to equally favorable news of Heacock's Elmira talks, and joked about the advantages of preachers occasionally swapping churches.[36] Indeed, the *Elmira Daily Advertiser* reported that Heacock "is justly entitled to the reputation which he enjoys, of being one of the ablest and most eloquent Divines in the State."[37]

Heacock, forty-seven years old in early 1870, had already been Lafayette Presbyterian's minister for twenty-four years. He was from a distinguished Buffalo family—his grandfather had founded the Grosvenor Library. During Heacock's tenure, the Lafayette church had prospered. His knowledge of literature and evangelical fervor made Heacock one of Western New York's most famous and beloved preachers. Nevertheless, despite attending the church regularly through the early summer of 1870, Twain managed to find fault with the choir. In a letter to the Langdons, Twain criticized their singing as bad enough to invite avenging thunderbolts from above.[38] In doing so, Twain was invoking a favorite bit of comic business. Again, in chapter 4 of *The Innocents Abroad*, he had complained that the passengers aboard the *Quaker City* who performed choir singing at church and prayer services were so horrid that they tempted Providence to bring down a storm and sink the ship. On one occasion at Lafayette Presbyterian, when subscriptions for the missionary cause were asked for in the congregation, Twain's pledge had $49.50 for the "Home" and fifty cents for the "Foreign Work."[39] In mid-June, Twain dreaded the prospect of Heacock's upcoming month-long hiatus and planned to attend Westminster Presbyterian Church during his absence. Westminster was just three walkable blocks on Delaware Street north of the Twain home. If they were able to visit Westminster Presbyterian—known as "The Church on Delaware Hill"—that summer, they made the acquaintance of yet another distinguished Buffalo clergyman, Reverend Erskine White.

Meanwhile, Olivia's induction into the vagaries of Buffalo's social-upper-crust etiquette was a rather hectic one. Sometimes Twain accompanied her on the obligatory visits. Sometimes he went on shopping errands with her, too. Usually, though, Olivia was on her own. Less than two months after moving in at 472 Delaware, she had received approximately seventy social calls. Occasionally when the doorbell rang, Twain would interrupt his work in order to play host because Olivia was upstairs taking one of her frequent naps.

When Olivia did venture out on solo calling expeditions, it could result in comic missteps. For example, the Buffalo Wadsworths bewildered her. In early March, Olivia dropped in at Mrs. Charles F. Wadsworth's home on West Ferry Street, seven blocks away. Mrs. Wadsworth, whose husband owned Buffalo Union Iron Works, was not home, so Olivia left her card. When Olivia paid a return visit a week later, she learned that she had left her calling card at the wrong house the first time. To add to the confusion, another Mrs. Wadsworth (Emily Otis Marshall Wadsworth, the wife of lawyer George Wadsworth of the firm Wadsworth and White), a neighbor just three blocks away at 370 Franklin Street, rang Olivia's doorbell at 472 Delaware. The home of Emily and George Wadsworth reportedly had been one of the Buffalo-area "terminals" for the Underground Railroad movement. Olivia described her calling card tribulations to "Mother" Mary Fairbanks of Cleveland as "stupid blunders" and worried about acquiring a reputation as a ditzy young socialite: "I think I shall get the name of leaving my cards at strange houses in rather a peculiar way, if I am not careful."[40] In the same letter, Olivia says that she and Twain find the gaffes amusing, but that Twain is of no help to her in the ways of proper social protocol: "Mr. Clemens is splendid to laugh it off with, but then when it comes to his giving me any practical advice in these matters I find him a little incompetant [sic]. He can't quite understand this call making." Apparently, Twain naïvely expected to simply send word before embarking on a calling expedition to guarantee that the party would be home. Olivia also confided in her friend from Hartford, Alice Hooker Day, that her formal calling rituals could launch a comedy of errors. At times, Olivia wrote to Day, when a servant opened the door, she would freeze, forget whom she was calling on, and silently fork over her card. Then, while the servant delivered her card to the mistress of the house, Olivia would frantically consult her list so she could address the woman by name. Nevertheless, despite a few false starts, Olivia was finding Buffalonians "very cordial and pleasant."[41]

Twain and Olivia did their fair share of entertaining early on, too, besides hosting the Slees, the Twichells, and Reverend Heacock. On Wednesday, March 2, they invited George H. Selkirk, one of Twain's *Express* partners, and his wife, Emily, over for the evening. Later that month, Olivia remarked that *Daily*

Courier editor David Gray and his wife, Martha Guthrie Gray, were "attractive" people who "seem as if they might be friends."[42] In March, one of Olivia's cousins, Anna Marsh Brown, stayed with them briefly. In late February, another of Olivia's cousins, Hattie Marsh Tyler, who lived in the Buffalo area, dropped in. She filled Olivia's ears with complaints about the female "help" available in Buffalo. Around that time, just three weeks into running her new household, Olivia had needed to mildly scold servants Ellen and Harriet. Perhaps Tyler's groaning bolstered Olivia's executive decision making (by mid-April, Harriet was dismissed as a servant).

Two additional February guests, acquaintances of Twain, brought collegiality and snowy boots to 472 Delaware Street. Twain's fellow humorist, David Ross Locke, known as "Petroleum Nasby" (in town to lecture on "The Struggles of a Conservative with the Woman Question"), and Coleman E. Bishop, editor of the Jamestown, New York, *Journal*, called one afternoon. Before allowing them to settle in the drawing room, Twain insisted that they both go back out into the foyer and knock the snow off their feet. After that, as a matter of policy until the snow stopped falling, Twain ordered Harriet to usher visitors into the library first to avoid tracking snow directly onto the drawing-room carpet. February 1870 was so snowy that sleighs were out and about on twenty-four days that month.[43] And if sleighing was good, every cutter in the city was hired, and harnesses were covered with bells. Mabel Dodge Luhan, who grew up on Delaware Street in the late 1800s, recalled "the sharp sound of silver sleigh bells" muffled by the snow that became "fainter and fainter in the darkening evening."[44] Snow, in fact, was a constant companion to Twain and Olivia during their first two months of life at 472 Delaware.

From Twain's first nighttime sighting of his wedding-gift house through a magical curtain of twinkling, gently falling snowflakes through the end of March 1870, it was as though some unseen hand was constantly shaking a giant snow globe, and nestled inside it was 472 Delaware Street. February and March saw an unusually heavy snowfall. However, Twain was no stranger to severe Western New York winters, and the snow, cold, and wind did not seem to faze him. Almost exactly one year earlier, Twain had postponed a lecture scheduled in Lockport, just twenty miles north of Buffalo, due to a vicious snowstorm. However, he did show up in the lecture hall that night, February 27, 1869, and rewarded the hundred or so attendees who braved the "fearful storm" with several minutes of small talk and jokes about the weather before sending them home with tickets for a return make-up performance on March 3.[45] Furthermore, Twain was determined not to allow a little snow to disrupt his expressions of love for Olivia. While riding out the snowstorm on the road, he wrote her a letter sending a "kiss that I set adrift above the wastes of snow that lie between us"[46] and kidded in another letter from Lockport that he "would walk twenty miles through this snow-storm to kiss you."[47] At the end of March 1870, closing in on two months of living in his new home, Twain stared out his window at 472 Delaware on a Sunday afternoon and described his mixed feelings toward the Buffalo winterscape in a letter to the Langdons: "It is snowing furiously, & has been, the most of the day & part of the night. We are glad that you are safe beyond its jurisdiction—for albeit snow is very beautiful when falling, its loveliness passes away very shortly afterward. The grand unpoetical result is merely chilblains & slush."[48] Rather than representing a diatribe on snow's initial picturesqueness yielding to slush and frostbite, Twain seems to be using the occasion to mildly ridicule John Whittaker Watson's popular 1869 poem, "Beautiful Snow." Twain takes a pragmatic view of snow instead of accepting Watson's metaphor that pure falling snow contaminated by the filth of the street is akin to a sinner falling from grace. The City and Vicinity Department of the *Buffalo Morning Express* published complaints throughout March 1870 about residents not cleaning snow off their sidewalks, about children throwing snowballs, and about teamsters being arrested for cruelty to animals because they forced their horses to pull heavy sleighs loaded with stone across the barren boards of a bridge.

The only time Twain lectured in Buffalo while he lived there was three days after the worst snow storm of the 1870 season. David Gray's wife, Martha, on behalf of the local Grand Army of the Republic organization, had persuaded Twain to speak on Tuesday evening, March 15, as part of its lecture series. This was the second-annual GAR lecture course in Buffalo. Single tickets cost sixty cents. Doors opened at St. James Hall (where the Nameless Club gathered) at 7:15 p.m., and the lecture commenced at eight. People ventured out into the wintry night to attend Twain's talk, so chances are many of them kept to familiar lecture-night rituals. For Buffalonians, that often meant a prelecture snack at a downtown eatery of good tea, with oysters and tea biscuit or sliced cold tongue, coffee, preserves, and cake. After the lecture concluded, usually around nine o'clock, lecture-goers would gravitate to a place like McArthur's on Main Street for more coffee and oysters (a popular menu item, indeed) or ice cream. On that March evening, for the first time onstage, Twain read from "The Celebrated Jumping Frog of Calaveras County" and also from a chapter of *The Innocents Abroad* to a very large crowd that had braved bitter ten-degree cold and heavy snowfall to pack the room. Twain shared the bill with English elocutionist Henry Rogers. Although Twain's performance went smoothly and the audience was entertained, the GAR organizers—not Martha Gray—managed to upset Twain so much that he declined to give an encore, frostily informed the crowd that he had fulfilled the terms of his contract, and walked off the stage. Earlier in the evening backstage, GAR officials had told Twain that former president Millard Fillmore would introduce him. Fillmore was willing, but a testy Twain balked, reportedly telling the lecture committee, "I don't want to be introduced by anybody, not even by a former President of the United States. Just as likely as not Mr. Fillmore would say something that would make me laugh—or cry, and that would upset my poise."[49] This turned out to be Twain's second and last encounter with Fillmore during his stay in Buffalo. In September of 1871, six months after moving from Buffalo, Twain vilified the sponsors of his lecture circuit, telling his agent that he refused to lecture in Buffalo because "I mortally hate that GAR there . . . I once gave them a packed house, free of charge, & they never even had the common politeness to thank me."[50]

Despite Twain's hard feelings toward the GAR, he must have been gratified at the heartiness of Buffalonians for turning out for his lecture on such an awful late-winter night. In fact, in his *Buffalo Express* editorial, "Removal of the Capital," Twain praised Buffalo's "agreeable climate" for being "breezy in summer" and "bracing in winter."[51] Three years before his death, Twain playfully told a *New York Times* interviewer that harsh winters had driven him from Buffalo. He said he "couldn't live in Buffalo because of the frequency of fur overcoats."[52] Yet, when Twain was preparing to move to Hartford, Connecticut, it was Buffalo he turned to for proper winter garb. In September of 1871, he returned to Buffalo and purchased a heavy sealskin coat and cap for $250 at Bergtold Bros. furriers, located at 291 Main Street, only four stores around the corner from his former *Express* office. Bergtold Bros. proudly exhibited Twain's winter fur coat at the Rink—an ice skating arena on Pearl Street, just south of Niagara Street, in winter, and a public gathering space with booths and sporting events such as roller skating and billiards during warm months—for two days. A few weeks afterward, Twain bragged that his Buffalo winter clothing kept him toasty warm during a frigid December visit to Chicago. It was "a crisp, bitter day, but all days are alike to my seal-skin coat—I can only tell it is cold by my nose & by seeing other people's actions."[53] Decades later, William Dean Howells recalled walking down Broadway with Twain drawing crowds to admire him in the same sealskin coat.[54]

Image 5.17. Twain wearing the heavy sealskin coat that he purchased at Buffalo's Bergtold Bros. furriers in 1871. (Reproduction by permission of the Buffalo and Erie County Public Library, Buffalo, NY.)

Before two months had passed in his Delaware Street palace, Twain had an opportunity to meet another neighbor while learning that a snowy spring in Buffalo might have its advantages. On the morning of Sunday, March 26, Twain looked out the window of his upstairs master bedroom and noticed flames coming from the roof of a house across Delaware Street. He and his coachman, Patrick McAleer, raced over to 455 Delaware to assist. On the way, McAleer rang fire-alarm box sixty-two at the corner of Virginia and Delaware by striking six times, pausing five seconds, then striking two more times. Meanwhile, Twain reached his neighbor's front entrance, pulled the doorbell, and is said to have drolly introduced himself: "My name is Clemens. We ought to have called upon you before and I beg pardon for intruding now in this informal way—but your house is on fire."[55] After thus meeting the owner, J. M. Gwinn, a teller at Marine Bank, they scampered up the stairs to address the blaze. McAleer climbed out of a window onto the roof and put half the fire out by throwing snow on it. Then Twain and Gwinn passed him buckets of water to extinguish the rest. By the time the two fire department steam engines arrived, led by Chief Tom French of Columbia Hose II, the fire—caused by a defective chimney—was under control.[56]

Image 5.18. Number 455 Delaware Street, owned by J. M. Gwinn, across the street from Twain's house. In March of 1870 Twain rang Gwinn's doorbell, introduced himself, and told Gwinn that his house was on fire. (Image used by permission of the Collection of the Buffalo and Erie County Historical Society.)

As the weather inevitably warmed and the snow melted, Twain and Olivia grew into domestic routines and continued their fast-paced socializing. Publically, at least, Twain appeared to relish his new role as lord of the manor. In private, he may have had a few misgivings about housekeeping. In an otherwise female-dominated household, though, Twain enjoyed the company of his coachman, McAleer, whom he described as a "brisk and electric" young man.[57] The parade of visiting friends and family continued in those early weeks of marriage. Twain and Olivia seemed desperate for company. Among those they invited to stay whenever they were in town were publisher Elisha Bliss and his family; Twain's poet friend Joel Benton; the Paynes of Armenia, New York; Missouri friends Will and Mollie Bowen; Elmira friends and family Ida Clark, Emma Sayles, and Susan Crane; and Frank Fuller, an insurance salesman and Twain's former lecture agent. Twain tried to sweeten the offer by joking that the leisurely life at 472 Delaware operated on the "European plan," in which the hosts and guests "get up & take breakfast when we *want* to,—not when we *have* to."[58] With tongue in cheek he listed the Fairbanks, Langdon, and Twichell families as references who could vouch for the creature comforts available at Twain's Buffalo home.

Although their entertaining tailed off considerably by summer, Robert Howland (a former mining partner from out west) and his wife, Louise, and journalist Edward H. House stayed at 472 Delaware in June. Before that, Allie and Clara Spaulding, Olivia's friends from Elmira, stayed for ten days in April. They barely vacated the two spare upstairs rooms before Twain's mother, sister, nephew, and their housekeeper, Margaret, arrived from St. Louis. Twain's mother, Jane Clemens, stayed for a month. But his sister Pamela and nephew Sammy did not visit too long. They were eager to move on to Fredonia, New York, forty miles south of Buffalo, where they rented a house on Day Street. Twain had offered Pamela $1,000 toward buying a house, but that plan fell through. Several months later, Pamela moved to another Fredonia home on Temple Street that was more ideal for Jane's quirky preference of watching funeral processions. In May of 1870, when Pamela took the train from Buffalo to Dunkirk (and a brief carriage ride onward to Fredonia), she brought with her one of the kittens that had been sent to Twain and Olivia from Elmira. Twain reported to Jervis Langdon that the cat had slept during the entire two-hour train ride, then "stretched & yawned, issuing much fishy breath in the operation, & said the Erie road was an infernal road to ride over." He continued the gag by insisting that the cat was misinformed about the railroad line: "The joke lies in the fact that the kitten did not go over the Erie at all—it was the Lake-Shore."[59]

A month earlier Twain had appealed to his sister-in-law Susan Crane in Elmira to please send them a couple of kittens. He claimed that the "snooty" mice of the house had been avoiding the mousetrap because it was "cheap & small & uncomfortable, & not in keeping with the other furniture of the house."[60]

Their social calendar remained full. Twain and Olivia exchanged several dinner evenings with the Grays. Evidently, vestiges of Twain's Wild Man of the Pacific Slope behavior persisted. Visitors occasionally were treated to Twain's eccentric, slightly improper mannerisms around the house, perhaps illustrating what Twain scholar Louis Budd called the gap between Twain's "showman's swagger and his parlor gentility."[61] By some accounts, he wore lounging slippers all the time, stretched out on the floor in front of the fireplace when he felt like it, and paced around the dining room between dinner courses, talking and waving his napkin as he gestured.[62] Twain's unconventional domestic behavior merely mirrored his odd habits in the first weeks at the *Buffalo Express* office, where he was known to "toss aside his coat, vest, collar, and tie and at times even his shoes to a resting place among the discarded exchanges upon the floor of the office."[63] On the other hand, Twain did limit his smoking at home, and when his old friend Joe Goodman visited Buffalo, he was shocked to see Twain "saying grace and reading the Bible."[64]

Olivia continued her calling expeditions. Occasionally, Twain—whom she began referring to as "Youth"—accompanied her on the obligatory "dreadful calls," but stayed in the carriage when Olivia approached the door with her card.[65] Olivia found her neighborhood "very delightful,"[66] had met four young married couples in their neighborhood, and knew of another "young married lady" set to move in on their block in the spring. And local lore places Twain in the homes of some of Buffalo's best and brightest. He was a guest at William G. Fargo's French mansard-style mansion, part of a five-and-a-half-acre estate on Buffalo's lower west side. Fargo, with Henry Wells, had cofounded the American Express Company and Wells, Fargo, and Company. And Fargo had served as Buffalo's mayor during the Civil War. He was a close friend of David Gray. Twain is also said to have frequented Charles Gerber's home at 821 Main Street, where he would pop in unannounced in the winter, saying he was a burglar "come to steal some heat." In the summer, Twain would visit Gerber, a brewer, for a glass of fresh, chilled water from a nearby spring.[67]

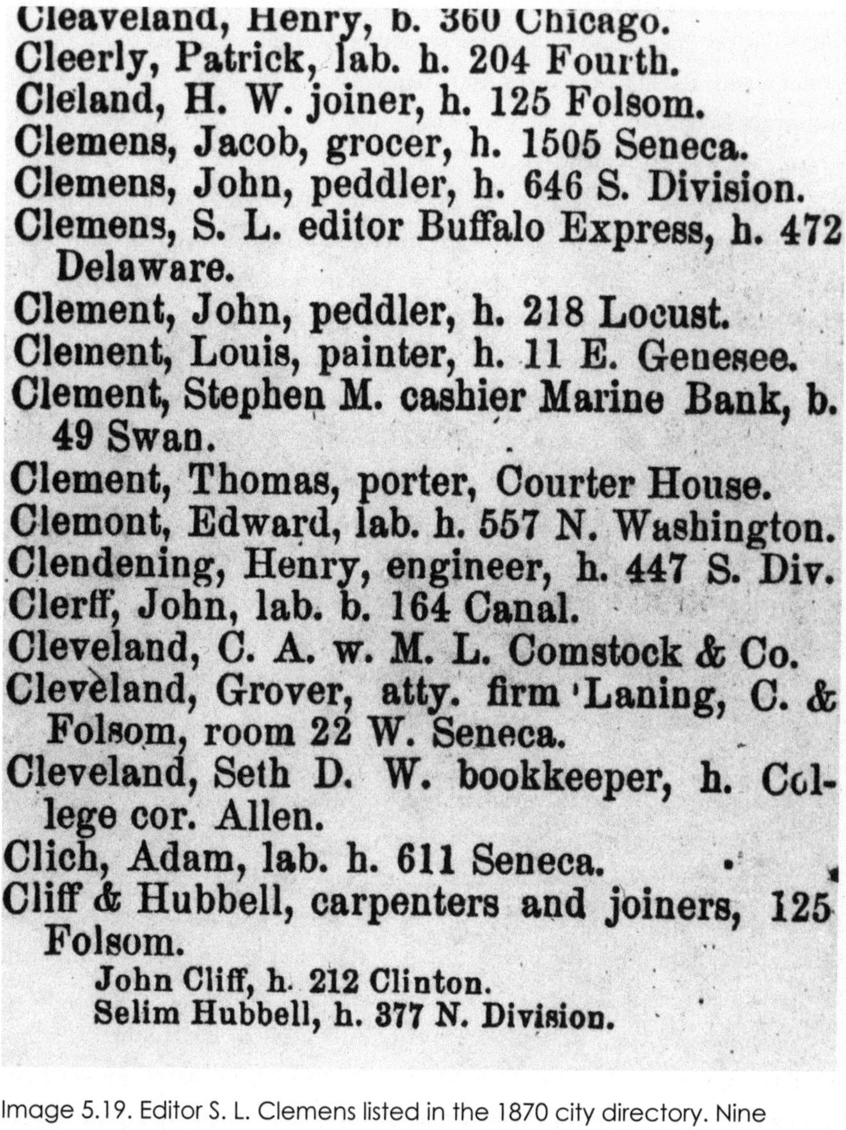

Cleaveland, Henry, b. 360 Chicago.
Cleerly, Patrick, lab. h. 204 Fourth.
Cleland, H. W. joiner, h. 125 Folsom.
Clemens, Jacob, grocer, h. 1505 Seneca.
Clemens, John, peddler, h. 646 S. Division.
Clemens, S. L. editor Buffalo Express, h. 472
    Delaware.
Clement, John, peddler, h. 218 Locust.
Clement, Louis, painter, h. 11 E. Genesee.
Clement, Stephen M. cashier Marine Bank, b.
    49 Swan.
Clement, Thomas, porter, Courter House.
Clemont, Edward, lab. h. 557 N. Washington.
Clendening, Henry, engineer, h. 447 S. Div.
Clerff, John, lab. b. 164 Canal.
Cleveland, C. A. w. M. L. Comstock & Co.
Cleveland, Grover, atty. firm 'Laning, C. &
    Folsom, room 22 W. Seneca.
Cleveland, Seth D. W. bookkeeper, h. Col-
    lege cor. Allen.
Clich, Adam, lab. h. 611 Seneca.
Cliff & Hubbell, carpenters and joiners, 125
    Folsom.
        John Cliff, h. 212 Clinton.
        Selim Hubbell, h. 377 N. Division.

Image 5.19. Editor S. L. Clemens listed in the 1870 city directory. Nine
entries below that is attorney Grover Cleveland, who was elected sheriff
of Erie County in 1870. In 1884, Twain called on Cleveland in his office
as governor of New York. Cleveland remembered often seeing Twain
in Buffalo, but Twain had no such recollection of him. (Image from the
Buffalo City Directory, published 1870 by Warren, Johnson, and Company.)

On the domestic side, the tranquil idyll at 472 Delaware Street was dreamlike for Twain and Olivia. They planned autumn vacations in Europe or London with the Langdons, August to September vacations for six weeks in the Adirondacks with the Twichells and Grays, and a tentative trip to California the next spring with the Fairbankses.

Olivia wrote Alice Hooker Day that she and Twain were the happiest people on earth. She invited Day and her husband to come and stay, envisioning the four of them sitting by the fireplace grate in the library and gazing at the Madonna painting, the wedding gift from the Days that hung over the mantel.[68] For his part, Twain referred to life at home as a comforting blur of days that "swing by with a whir & a flash, & are gone. . . . To me, passing time is a dream."[69] And Twain wrote the Langdons that 472 Delaware Street was an "unsurfeiting feast for the eye & the soul, . . . a constant delight . . . a poem, it is music—& it speaks & sings to us all the day long."[70] In a letter to the Howlands, Twain described his marital bliss with characteristic comic hyperbole, relying on his standard "infancy" gag: "If all of one's married days are as happy as these new ones have been to me, I have deliberately fooled away 30 years of my life. If it were to do over again I would marry in early infancy instead of wasting my time cutting teeth & breaking crockery."[71] Their early weeks together purred with a pleasing predictability. In bed for the night at ten and a wake-up call at six, with meals at regular times: breakfast at ten, lunch at one, and dinner at five. Of course, Twain put an amusing spin on their daily agenda: "The reason we get up at 6 in the morning is because we want to see what time it is. . . . We then go back to bed, & get up finally at half past 9."[72] Most evenings were spent together in the library, with Twain reading poetry aloud. Twain managed to wring humor out of that ritual, too. In doing so, he evoked one of his favorite targets of satire in *The Innocents Abroad*, which was sentimentalism. He described to the Langdons a typical nightly poetry reading as one in which Olivia "shatters" his aesthetic overemoting about a poem with a practical household budget question: "Every now & then I come to a passage that brings tears to my eyes, & I look up to her for loving sympathy, & she inquires whether they sell sirloin steaks by the pound or by the yard."[73]

As much as Twain adored his ideal domestic situation, he was content to let Olivia manage the housekeeping duties. He looked on with bemused detachment, except when it came to dealing with servants. Twain wanted nothing to do with supervising the help. When Olivia let Harriet go and hired a German girl in her place in mid-April 1870, Twain was happy to leave the decision up to her: "I had rather discharge a perilous and unsound cannon than the soundest servant girl that ever was."[74] Yet, for the more mundane, day-to-day matters, Twain tended to sit back and make light of Olivia's inexperience at running a household. According to Twain, she balanced three sets of books and was particularly conscious of using royalties from *The Innocents Abroad* to pay off the *Express* loan. After finding a barrel of rotting apples in the cellar late in February, Olivia hired carpenters and plumbers to move the laundry tubs and remedy the dampness there. Twain viewed the expenses as unnecessary and playfully mocked Olivia, saying she might as well move the tubs into the woodhouse, the wood into the stable, and the horse into the laundry while she was at it. Jervis Langdon joined in on the fun, writing Twain that, as master of the house, he had the right to institute further housekeeping alterations by putting the carriage in the cellar, the horse in the drawing room, and Ellen the cook in the stable.[75] Twain also poked fun at Olivia's unsteady judgment with menus, fibbing to the Langdons that she ordered fricasseed mackerel with pork and oysters for breakfast. In the same letter, he did not exempt himself from good-hearted ridicule, saying that he squeamishly donned glove stretchers in order to remove stuffing from a chicken.[76]

The newly married couple even did some shopping together downtown. They almost certainly bought their merchandise at either W. H. Glenny, Son, and Company at 204 Main Street or Flint and Kent dry goods store at 261 Main Street. The Flint and Kent store was where members of Buffalo's upper crust did their shopping because it "had attractive things in it; all our ribbons and ginghams for summer dresses came from there, and when people bought some new furniture coverings or things for their houses they bought them upstairs in that store."[77] The other stores farther north on Main Street, such as Adams and Meldrum, were for lower-class rabble, were "unpleasant stores to go to," and emitted a "disagreeable common smell," as Delaware Avenue resident Mabel Dodge Luhan reminisced (the grand boulevard had been renamed from "street" to "avenue" around 1879).

Just a few days after settling in at 472 Delaware, Twain and Olivia noticed some ink spots spilled onto the bright-scarlet table cover in the library. At first they simply set the inkstand over the stain, but soon they searched for a more permanent solution. They took the carriage downtown and bought two large sheets of blotting paper, one was to lie under the inkstands in the library, the other in Twain's upstairs study. On another shopping trip in early February, Olivia purchased a clothes bar, a breadbox, a flatiron stand, and a flower stand. In May, Olivia bought a "beautiful plated syrup cup"[78] because Twain felt that the Japanese pitcher they had been using was inappropriate. In June, Olivia went downtown to purchase a spring lounge and mattress for the library. One item they could not find at any store in Buffalo was a polishing and fluting iron preferred by Twain for servants to polish his starched shirtfronts, collars, and cuffs. They ended up ordering it from a hardware store in Elmira co-owned by Olivia's brother, Charley.

Elmira, in fact, provided a constant stream of household needs—large or small—for inexperienced homeowners Olivia and Twain. Luckily for them, the Langdon munificence was unbounded. In February, Olivia asked her parents to send some old tablecloths to wrap bread in and a sprig of ivy so that she could begin to grow a train of it at the dining-room window. She also asked them to send her hand mirror along with porcelain pictures of themselves, which would be framed in blue for the master-bedroom mantelpiece. The Langdons also sent an exquisite serving fork and napkin ring and oversized pillowcases. Then when they discovered that a wedding gift of a statuette called *Peace* from Elmirans Alexander and Amanda Diven had been damaged in shipment—its head and an arm had broken off—the Langdons generously bought a replacement. Olivia had temporarily placed the broken headpiece on top of the blue enameled clock in the drawing room. But when the surprise replacement gift arrived in early March, Twain sneaked into the dining room, spread the scarlet-red-fringed dining tablecloth over the big rocking chair, and set the new *Peace* on it. When he led Olivia in from the drawing room, she "went into convulsions of delight" at the sight of the unexpected restored wedding gift provided by her parents.[79]

Once April warmth struck in Buffalo, Jervis Langdon paid for a landscaping overhaul outside 472 Delaware. The crew, supervised by Langdon's right-hand man in Buffalo, Slee, planted shrubbery, pansies, moss-rose bushes, and Irish juniper. Once again mocking his lack of homeowner skills, Twain joked to

Langdon that he and Olivia were unsure if the flowers were to be planted with the roots pointed upward, or in the more "conventional" way. Later in June, Twain asked Langdon to inform Slee—who had moved to Elmira to become a partner in the Langdon coal company—that the juniper was looking more like a "fox-squirrel's tail" than an evergreen.[80] Langdon also paid to have Twain's sister Pamela's house in Fredonia attractively landscaped that spring. Still another example of the Langdons' stunning magnanimity was when Olivia and Twain opened an envelope on Friday, May 13, and found a check for $1,000 inside.

Twain's apparent enchantment with the marital scene at 472 Delaware Street set the stage for one of his most celebrated personal letters. On a snowy afternoon early in February, the first Sunday spent in his wedding-gift house, Twain found himself alone in the library. Olivia was napping upstairs. He sat down and wrote seven letters. The longest turned out to be a remarkable reply to his Hannibal, Missouri, childhood pal Will Bowen. One-half of the letter extols Olivia and the miraculous wedding presents from the Langdons. The other half documents an epiphany that secured Buffalo's role forever as the place where he mined his creative mother lode, "the Matter of Hannibal, the childhood memories that were to provide the vocabulary of images he would use in *Tom Sawyer* and *Huckleberry Finn*."[81] In three sentences, the last one a whopping 450 words long (in Twain's typical run-on fashion, clauses linked by semicolons and dashes), Twain records a sweeping set of Hannibal reminiscences in stream-of-consciousness style. He names people, places, and events. Of the seventeen Hannibal townspeople he spills out onto the page, James Finn becomes the model for Huck Finn's father, two Hannibal murderers are the basis of the Sherburn-Boggs case in *Huckleberry Finn*, and Bowen himself is one of the models for Tom Sawyer. Holliday's Hill, cited by Twain in the cascading memory sweep, becomes Cardiff Hill in *Tom Sawyer*. Twain snaps out of his reverie when he recalls his childhood sweetheart, Laura Hawkins, whom he eventually recast as Becky Thatcher in *Tom Sawyer* and *Huckleberry Finn*. On that same Sunday in Buffalo, Twain sent a wedding notice to Laura, care of her parents in Hannibal.

The Bowen letter was not the first time that a Western New York incident inspired Twain to unlock key memories of his Hannibal childhood. A year earlier, while in Lockport, just north of Buffalo, during the blizzard, he conjured up similar flashbacks of the old days, a kind of rehearsal for his fuller, richer Bowen epiphany. He was called on by Rev. Joseph L. Bennett, a Lockport resident who had been the pastor of the Clemens family's Presbyterian church in Hannibal during the late 1840s and early 1850s. Twain wrote Olivia that Bennett's visit "filled my brain with trooping phantoms of the past—of dead faces & forgotten forms—of scenes that are faded—of old familiar voices that are silent forever, & old songs that are only a memory now."[82]

Despite such emotive moments of dreamy domesticity and other declarations of absolute homey bliss, we can safely assume that at times Twain doubted his ability to head so large a household and may even have mildly resented being thrust into homeownership so unexpectedly. His housekeeping angst is reflected in two unpublished, handwritten sketches of about 160 words each, which he wrote, presumably, in February of 1870. The sketches appear to express Twain's private insecurities about his new homeowner responsibilities. The chief sources of self-doubt in these sketches stem from his utter lack of preparedness and his shaky self-image as master of the house. Even though Twain was thirty-four years old when he and Olivia moved into their Delaware Street wedding palace, he had theretofore lived a transient bachelor life, barely unpacking his suitcase in a series of mining camps, ship and train compartments, hotel rooms, and boardinghouse apartments.

Both of the sketches allude to Twain's previous gypsylike lifestyle as an excuse for functioning as an incompetent lord of the manor. There is almost a sense that Twain is yearning for the simplicity of his former existence, as if he would be happier living with Olivia back at Mrs. Randall's Swan Street boardinghouse. One sketch begins with a tongue-in-cheek statement on how pleasant it is to keep a house, contradicted immediately when Twain admits to lacking the proper skills because he has been boarding since he was thirteen years old. In the second sketch, Twain also attributes his housekeeping ineptitude to the comic distortion that he has boarded all his life. In the first sketch, Twain describes the pressure of maintaining a "solemn farce of being perfectly acquainted" with housekeeping[83] in front of the servants. He includes Olivia as his partner in homeowner inadequacy by repeating the same joke he used in the early-February letter to the Langdons about Olivia telling the cook to order beefsteak by the yard. Twain may not have shared the sketch with Olivia because, in it, he also criticizes her air of false confidence that does not fool the house servants. The second sketch comments, too, on the domestic help's uncanny ability to occasionally detect uncertainty in an order issued by inexperienced masters.

Twain further reflects publicly on the harrows of being a new homeowner in a *Galaxy* magazine story that appeared in September of 1870. He draws upon his customary fictional Mark Twain character as inspired idiot to dramatize his new real-life role as misfit, easily duped homeowner. In the *Galaxy*'s "Political Economy," Twain reaches back to the tried-and-true comic technique of "climactic arrangement," in which the narrator is victimized by an increasingly humiliating series of catastrophes. In "Political Economy," Twain is a serious writer driven from his domestic writer's den by a persistent and sly door-to-door salesman of lightning rods. By the tale's end, the Twain character is an object of ridicule—a self-inflated author and a gullible homeowner, easy prey to a traveling huckster. The homeowner comes across as hapless due to the snowballing calamities he invites upon himself, much like the "climactic arrangement" framework in Twain's earlier *Express* feature stories on Niagara Falls and "Journalism in Tennessee," and like other *Express* stories later in his tenure at the newspaper. Two comic situations are juxtaposed in "Political Economy": the humor of disturbing the tranquility of an author's private writing space at home and the humor of a naïve homeowner hoodwinked by a slick salesman.

The Twain character is rousted from his writer's desk at home, where he is lovingly laboring over a long-winded political treatise, to answer the doorbell. He is so upset at being interrupted that he wants to dump the visitor "in the bottom of the canal with a cargo of wheat on top of him." In fact, Twain's home at Delaware Street near Virginia was within a quick one-mile walk west, down Virginia Street, of the bustling Erie Canal, Buffalo's commercial lifeblood.[84] In the story, Twain once again relied on his boardinghouse gag. An overconfident Twain informs the salesman, who is eager to peddle lightning rods, that while "[I am] new to housekeeping, have been used to hotels and boarding-houses all my life," he nevertheless knows everything about lightning rods and will purchase "six or eight."[85] The salesman quickly recognizes an easy mark. No sooner does Twain settle back in to write than the salesman is back, intensifying his pitch, persuading Twain to buy more rods and offering a dizzying array of choices—plain, coppered, zinc plated, or spiral twisted. At one point, Twain notices that the persistent canvasser is standing "like the Colussus of Rhodes," trampling his new flowerbed "with one foot on my infant tuberose and the other among my pansies," seemingly the very spring plantings that Jervis Langdon had recently subsidized to spruce up the grounds outside the 472 Delaware Street home.

With each new installation of superfluous and costly lightning rods, the salesman is at the door again with further recommendations, taking Twain from his precious writing project. One chimney alone now is burdened with a ridiculous eight new lightning rods, a lovely "natural sight" to the innocent victim Twain, "almost equal to Niagara Falls in beauty." The other chimneys soon receive similar treatment. Finally, Twain retreats to his writing den but takes an hour just to recapture his writing rhythm. Suddenly the salesman is at the door urging Twain to add more rods to ensure full protection against a thunderstorm. A thoroughly frustrated Twain explodes that the salesman can add rods to the kitchen and on the cow. Twain manages to write for three hours until he is presented with an outrageous bill for $900. He also spies a crowd of amused gawkers on the street pointing at his house, now gaudily bedecked with an enormous number and assortment of lightning rods. "Political Economy" closes with a scene three days later, when a severe thunderstorm activates the multitude of lightning rods, transforming the house into a "pyrotechnic display" as lightning strikes the house 764 times in forty minutes. The witless Twain character, butt of a joke in his own home, hires a crew to remove the new rods, except for three on the house and one each on the kitchen and carriage house. He sells the stripped lightning-rod materials at bargain rates and never does finish his esoteric essay.

"Political Economy" is humorous, but it might also be read as a veiled expression of Twain's disenchantment with his new challenges of maintaining a house, handling door-to-door canvassers, and trying to accomplish professional writing at home. Indeed, over the first few months of wedded life at 472 Delaware, the initial perfect luster of the lamp illuminating Twain's Aladdin's palace was showing signs of fading into a dull reality. However, this domestic slippage from ideal to mundane pales in comparison to the dramatic disillusionment Twain was undergoing with the world of newspaper work. He was approaching a professional crossroad. Yet, as one career door was closing, another was about to open.

6

WRITING FOR ENJOYMENT, AS WELL AS PROFIT

Mark Twain was frustrated, not unlike a caged animal. For hours on end over several days in February of 1870, he paced back and forth, cooped up in his scarlet-appointed upstairs writing den, stymied by writer's block. One week into his honeymoon at 472 Delaware Street, he confided to the Langdons that his heart was not in the subjects of his *Buffalo Express* assignments and that he was abandoning "the newspaper scribblings for to-day."[1] Four days later he shared his continuing writing disability with Mary Fairbanks: "Every day I nerve myself, & sieze [*sic*] my pen, & dispose my paper, & prepare to buckle on the harness & *work*! And then I pace the floor—back & forth, back & forth, with vacuous mind—& finally I lay down the pen & confess that my time is not come—that I am utterly empty."[2]

His last contribution to the *Express* had been on January 29, one of only five stories (one of which was just a brief about Harriet Beecher Stowe) to appear the entire month. Such a reduced output was understandable given the closing out of his lecture obligations, participation in wedding festivities, and settling in at his new Buffalo dwelling. However, once he returned to Buffalo, Twain's writing drought extended an uncharacteristic three weeks. Even then he barely eked out a one-paragraph unsigned review of "Petroleum Nasby's" (David Ross Locke's) Buffalo lecture for the February 19 *Express*, and six days later, a eulogy for his friend and mentor Anson Burlingame. It wasn't until the final day of February

149

that Twain seemed to recapture his voice and caustic wit in a commentary titled "The Blondes."

Occasional signs of a creeping disgruntlement with journalism may have been simmering between the lines if careful readers of Twain had noticed. Throughout his initial autumn 1869 stint with the *Express*, Twain had mocked how newspapers stoked the sensationalism of the Stowe-Byron controversy. In "Journalism in Tennessee," published in the September 4 *Express*, Twain again ridiculed sensationalistic journalism. In that story, a reporter and editor are gradually maimed and the newspaper office systematically destroyed. In hindsight, the mayhem inflicted might be symbolic of Twain's eventual rejection of the newspaper profession. Two weeks later, in "The Wild Man Interviewed," Twain satirically indicted fellow reporters who are more interested in selling newspapers than in publishing facts.

Back in Buffalo in February, living in style, he avoided the *Express* by stretching out his honeymoon and bragging that he planned to contribute only one or two stories per month. Twain also boasted to his publisher, Elisha Bliss, that he showed up at his *Express* office only a couple of hours each week.[3] In addition to limiting his face time at work, Twain shirked his editing duties and ignored the innovations he had previously instituted. The police blotter and People and Things departments he had enlivened in autumn had reverted to their former dull formats during his absence. Twain, now disinterested, left those columns to languish.

Two more nails hammered into the coffin of Twain's journalistic career were additional handwritten private jottings, apparently written in early March of 1870. These unpublished sketches point to his ennui with journalism. In "A Wail," Twain complains about being undervalued at the *Express*. He is tired of shouldering blame for distorted local columns, even though he did not author them. In language echoing the hyperbole of physical violence in "Journalism in Tennessee" six months earlier, Twain complains that as editor he endures the wrath of unhappy readers by "getting waylaid, & bruised, & knocked down, & shot at, by parties whom the reporters have told unpleasant truths about."[4] Twain describes dealing with absurd gripes from an ignorant, irate public about a wide range of *Express* lapses from proofreading to ad placement and typesetting. In "A Protest," Twain continues his mild diatribe over unwanted responsibility for the editorial product of the *Express*. Again he cites hate mail from a reader whining about "brash" local items and threatening to watch over Twain's work with a critical microscope. Twain insists that he does not write the local columns that offend "this sensitive vermin."[5] He closes "A Protest" by quoting a letter praising two sentimental poems by Twain that had been printed in the *Express*. Twain disavows authorship of such "dreary blank verse" and promises that he would have killed off the sappy heroes in each poem if he had been the poet. These two unpublished musings suggest that Twain was weary of his newspaper editing duties, of perceived sloppy practices by his staff, and of overreactions by the *Express* readership.

Even though "A Wail" and "A Protest" were private expressions of frustration, Twain's absence from the *Express* office and pages spurred local rumors that he was leaving the paper. He published the same denial four times in March, stressing that he was a "permanency" in Buffalo and was "in a state of tranquil satisfaction" at the *Express*.[6]

The notorious Blondes incident in Chicago finally roused Twain from his journalistic stupor. Twain first arrived in Buffalo in mid-August of 1869 at the same time that Lydia Thompson and her British Blondes burlesque troupe were booked for several sold-out shows in the city. Their highly anticipated appearance at Buffalo's Academy of Music was so successful that special evening-excursion trains shuttled theatergoers back and forth to Niagara Falls and Lockport, well north of Buffalo. Tickets ranging from one-dollar "parquette-circle" seats to the prime eight-dollar private boxes could be purchased in advance at Cottier and Denton's music store. The British Blondes opened in Buffalo on Monday night, August 16. In "Sinbad the Sailor," Thompson played Sinbad, and Eliza Weathersby was Koh-i-moor. Other performers included Rose Massey, Bessie Power, Harry Beckett, and J. W. Cahill. The next day, Twain published "Removal of the Capital" and an amusing People and Things column in the *Express*. He may have even contributed a light observation in the City Notes department: "A great number of blondes made their appearance on the street yesterday." However, a glowing, unsigned review of the Lydia Thompson troupe was written by another *Express* reporter, possibly Earl D. Berry or Josephus N. Larned. Larned regularly supplied book reviews.

The August *Express* review of the British Blondes ignored any hint of impropriety in the show and instead focused on its artistry. The reviewer described how the audience "fairly bubbled over with applause."[7] The "fair Lydia" performed with "an original style of action, a dash and *abandon* in her manner, that makes her such an agreeable and vivacious actress as is wanted to keep the spirits of the spectators fully alive." The *Express* reviewer saw nothing unduly bawdy or distasteful about the Blondes' performance.

Six months later, the British Blondes became enmeshed in a headline-grabbing episode in Chicago. Twain's follow-up attack on the Blondes incident would be at odds with the favorable opinion voiced by his *Express* colleague in August. Perhaps Twain felt obligated as Olivia's husband of barely four weeks to uphold Victorian moral standards. Perhaps he felt obligated to defend a fellow journalist. Perhaps he was just plain tickled to glom onto a meaty, sensational event and write passionately about it. During their February run in Chicago, the Blondes had been strongly criticized by Wilbur Storey of the *Chicago Times* for their lewd exhibitions and use of degrading language. The outraged troupe said Storey's comments were slanderous. On Thursday, February 24, 1870, Storey was confronted on the street outside his Chicago home by Thompson, her manager/husband named Alexander Henderson, Blondes member Pauline Markham, and publicist Archie Gordon. While the men held Storey at gunpoint, the women took turns horsewhipping him.[8]

The resulting arrest, trial, and fine were sensational news nationwide. Twain noticed and quickly weighed in on the issue, writing "The Blondes" for the *Express* of February 28 with an energy and voice he had not shown in weeks. Twain used his skills to verbally horsewhip Thompson and Markham for being thin-skinned low-life types who physically ambushed an innocent professional critic honestly practicing his writing craft. Throughout the rest of "The Blondes," Twain critiques the Thompson troupe's act with such specificity that one wonders if he was not in the audience while still a bachelor when they played Buffalo. Twain viciously judges their stage presence as harlot-like: "They come on stage naked, to all intents and purposes; padded; painted; powdered; oiled; enameled; and glorified with false hair."[9] And contrary to the delighted reception that had greeted the Blondes in Buffalo, Twain imagines silent, stunned audiences horrified by witnessing a nearly pornographic, talentless, washed-up, ragtag group of performers: "They dance dismal dances, assisted by a melancholy rabble of painted, tinseled, gamey old skeletons, who spin on one toe and display their relics beseechingly to dull

pitlings who refuse to hunger for them and will not applaud." Twain goes on to
rage at particularly tasteless and obscene jokes in an "auction scene," which again
begs the question of whether Twain's familiarity with the Blondes' show might
have been firsthand. In the end, Twain's forceful "The Blondes" commentary casts
him as the arbiter of high moral values and the defender of freedom of the press.
He had gotten his journalistic groove back, at least for the time being.

Nevertheless, Twain's output at the *Express* over the next few months was
paltry compared to his busy initial spurt in August and September of 1869.
During that productive six-week span, he generated nearly thirty stories, editorials, and squibs while assembling regular People and Things columns. In the
first six *months* after his return to Buffalo as a married man, he published a mere
twenty-three pieces in the *Express*. However, several stories were inspired by
people and events connected to his Delaware Street community. It is no wonder
that Twain cultivated his neighborhood for subject matter, since he seldom ventured far from his home. For most of the first six months after his return to
the *Express*, he conducted business—writing and editorial, layout, and story-
selection decisions—out of his upstairs den at 472 Delaware.

Just six weeks after establishing residence at 472 Delaware Street, Twain
published "A Mysterious Visit" in the *Express*. The comical story is based on a
real visit in February by an agent of the Internal Revenue Service who was following up on recent public disclosures of Twain's income from *The Innocents
Abroad* royalties and lecturing, and of the value of Twain's opulent new Buffalo
house. The IRS district collector who called on Twain may have been Adrian R.
Root, who three months later surrendered his position to George R. Kibbee.[10]
In "A Mysterious Visit," which Twain alluded to in a letter as "the Revenue
article,"[11] the Twain narrator is duped by a federal tax assessor into bragging
about his earnings. While entertaining his guest in the parlor ("We talked, and
talked, and talked—at least I did. And we laughed, and laughed, and laughed—
at least I did"[12]) Twain is easily tricked into boasting that "two hundred and
fourteen thousand, cash, is my income for this year." After the IRS agent leaves,
the Twain character realizes he has been victimized and has made "an ass of
myself." Panicky, he consults a neighbor who suggests claiming several dubious
deductions that drastically reduce his earned income to an absurd "one thousand two hundred and fifty dollars and forty cents." In the end, the narrator

beats the system and by law is required to pay income tax on only $250. The story was soon reprinted for its entertainment value in the *Revenue Record*, the official publication of the Internal Revenue Service. Twain also included it in his 1875 collection, *Sketches New and Old*, although he changed the name *Buffalo Express* to *Daily Warhoop*.

In the spring of 1870, Twain made another entertaining *Express* contribution with a homegrown connection. It was the two-part article called "A Curious Dream. Containing a Moral," and it appeared on April 30 and May 7. In it, a Twain-type narrator is sitting on his front stoop at midnight when a parade of skeletons with coffins slung over their shoulders begins trooping by. One of them, John Baxter Copmanhurst, dead since 1839, stops to chat. He tells how "residents" are fleeing a nearby cemetery because its condition has deteriorated. Originally an idyllic, well-maintained graveyard, it is now an undesirable "neighborhood." "Low rent" families are now allowed to be buried there, graves leak so badly in the rain that the corpses have to hang their shrouds on tree limbs to dry, and there are petty thefts around the grounds. The best old families are abandoning the cemetery because the city is allowing tombstones to tip over and grass and weeds to grow unchecked. Copmanhurst shows the narrator his own disgraceful, beaten-up coffin: "Look at my coffin—in its day it was a piece of furniture that would have attracted attention in any drawing room in the city."[13] It is commonly believed that Twain's satire was a bit of social activism prompted by the deplorable, neglected state of old North Street Cemetery just two blocks north of Twain's house.[14] It was a five-acre private burying ground bound at its southwest corner by North Street and Delaware Street, and extending westward to Bowery Street (now Irving Place). At the time of Twain's writing, the cemetery was largely ignored. His story may have hastened transfer of the property to the Forest Lawn Association, after which remains were reinterred at Forest Lawn Cemetery, and the North Street Cemetery closed.

Later in May, Twain simply gazed out his Delaware Street window again to gather writing material. Another sarcastic *Express* piece led to a charming encounter with a young neighbor.

It was twilight in Buffalo on Memorial Day 1870. Jane Meade Welch, sixteen, lay stretched out after supper, with a book propped open at one elbow, on her bed upstairs in her sprawling, two-story country-style home at 514 Delaware

Street. Even though exams and graduation from the First Academic Department at Buffalo Female Academy were just days away, she couldn't focus on her textbook, Richard Parker's *Natural Philosophy*. Instead, Jane looked wistfully out her bedroom window at her lovely neighborhood. Her favorite sight was the long walkway from the street to her front entrance, bordered by luxurious, colorful gardens of poppies and fruit trees. Jane dreamily watched the last few stragglers passing by on foot and in horse-drawn buggies headed back and forth from North Street Cemetery in order to decorate gravesites. Suddenly a call from her mother from downstairs interrupted her daydream. Jane bounded down the stairs and into the back parlor only to stop short at the sight of a surprise guest wearing a big grin—Samuel L. Clemens, whom she also knew as Mark Twain. That morning, Jane had read a humorous but mean-spirited letter that Twain had published in the *Buffalo Express*, which he signed only as "472 Delaware." Twain, anticipating the increased traffic past his house on Delaware Street over the holiday weekend to lay wreaths and plant flags on graves at the North Street Cemetery, had criticized the city street-sprinkling crew in advance for not keeping the dust down in front of his house. Twain relied on a favorite comic tool—"infants"—to ridicule Streets Commissioner George W. Gillespie and his crew, whose horse-drawn water tanks equipped with spigots patrolled Buffalo's dirt streets during the summer: "A crippled infant with a garden squirt could do it better."[15]

Image 6.1. Miss Jane Meade Welch, who was a sixteen-year-old Delaware Street neighbor of Twain's, responded to his *Express* editorial and organized a water-can gang to dampen the dirt road in front of his house. Welch joined the *Express* in 1874, launching her pioneering career in journalism. (Image from *American Women's Illustrated World*, October 7, 1893.)

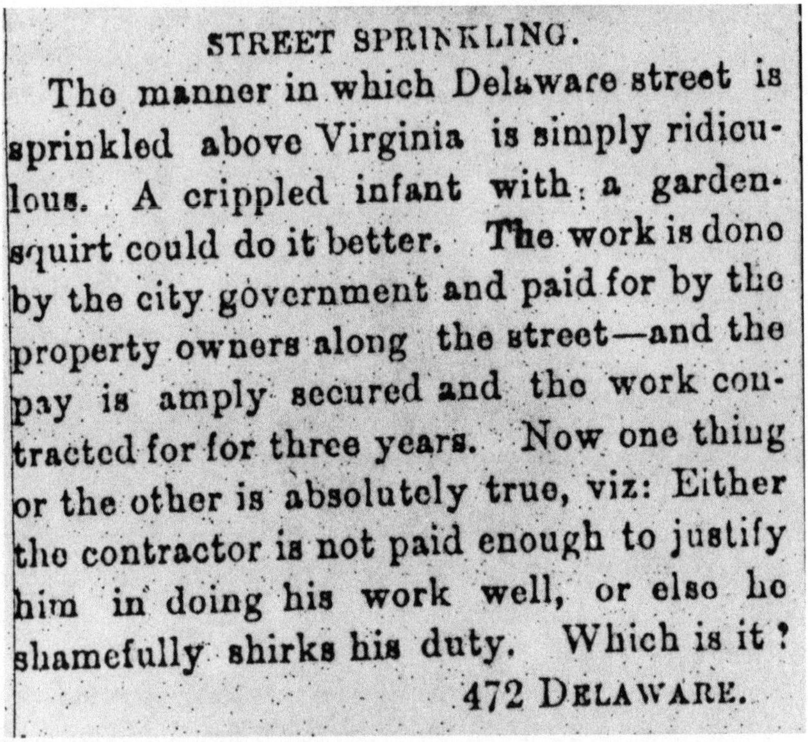

STREET SPRINKLING.

The manner in which Delaware street is sprinkled above Virginia is simply ridiculous. A crippled infant with a garden-squirt could do it better. The work is done by the city government and paid for by the property owners along the street—and the pay is amply secured and the work contracted for for three years. Now one thing or the other is absolutely true, viz: Either the contractor is not paid enough to justify him in doing his work well, or else he shamefully shirks his duty. Which is it?

472 DELAWARE.

Image 6.2. Twain's unsigned editorial, "Street Sprinkling," in the May 27, 1870, *Express* criticized Buffalo's streets commissioner and his street-sprinkling crews. (Image from the *Buffalo Express*, May 27, 1870.)

Jane, who lived just four doors north of Twain, read his letter and had a brainstorm. She mobilized her brother, Tom, and a few young friends to fill watering cans and douse the unpaved section of Delaware in front of her famous neighbor's home. And now here was the great man sitting in her own parlor, in a chair by the mahogany table with the evening lamp lighted, smiling at her, shaking her hand, saying: "I hear you are the little girl who organized the watering-can brigade, and I want to thank you for laying the dust before my premises, and to say that I think it was mighty clever of you all."[16] Jane lingered in the parlor that night and listened as Twain chatted with her mother and exchanged theories with her grandmother on how the embargo had affected New England during the War of 1812.

In recent days, Twain had already used the pages of the *Express* to engage in a public feud with John J. Burke, accusing the city coroner of greed. Now he took on another official, labeling Buffalo's streets commissioner as incompetent (Twain had also facetiously targeted ancient Pompeii's streets commissioner as corrupt in chapter 31 of *The Innocents Abroad*). Shortly after Twain's satirical "Street Sprinkling" letter was published, the *Express* carried two brief retractions. One praised Commissioner Gillespie's "commendable forethought and energy securing a sufficient number of street sprinklers to thoroughly sprinkle Delaware street and the roads in the cemetery, previous to the procession to-day."[17] Another note the next day in the *Express* thanked Gillespie for his "thoughtful consideration" that rendered Delaware Street "by means of street sprinklers comparatively free from dust yesterday."[18] Both apologies were likely engineered by J. N. Larned to control any political damage Twain may have caused.

Less than a week later, Twain again barely reached beyond his doorstep for an *Express* story idea. This time he looked for inspiration to one of the most adored and colorful figures in Buffalo's history, a woman who happened to live farther up Delaware Street. Mary E. Johnson Lord was more than twenty years older than Twain when they met. She was the eldest child of Buffalo's first mayor and the wife of Buffalo's best-known preacher, John Chase Lord. The Lords lived north of Twain in a well-landscaped Gothic Revival dwelling known as "Oakwood" on Delaware Street near what is now Potomac Avenue, opposite the entrance to Forest Lawn Cemetery. Twain shared Mary Lord's love of animals. In 1867 she had started the local Society for the Prevention of Cruelty to Animals, only the second branch in the state, by gathering five hundred signatures, including that of Millard Fillmore. Her zeal and grit angered teamsters, who were sometimes forced to add another horse to pull a heavy load because Mrs. Lord was protesting animal abuse by sitting in the middle of the street calmly reading the newspaper. She entertained children at her home with cookies and pony rides. She took in stray cats and dogs. Perhaps what first caught Twain's eye was the popular sight of Mrs. Ford riding down Delaware Street, wearing her ever-present bonnet, in a miniature park phaeton drawn by her beloved Shetland ponies in teams of two, four, or six, occasionally slowing down so her diminutive coachman, Joseph, could scatter seeds on the road for sparrows. The names she gave her dogs and ponies added to her reputation for endearing eccentricity: Augustus Baum, Peggoty Muggins, Cricket, and Periwinkle. Her favorite pooch, Grandfather Smallweed, lived to eighteen years of age and is memorialized sitting beside her in a stained glass portrait that once hung over the fireplace in their library.[19]

Image 6.3. Mary E. Johnson Lord, charming and eccentric friend of Twain's and fellow lover of animals. (Image used by permission of the Collection of the Buffalo and Erie County Historical Society.)

Mrs. Lord struck Twain as a kindred soul in nonconformity and they became friends. As a breeder of livestock, she asked Twain how to raise chickens.[20] At about the same time, the *Buffalo Express* editorial staff had been awarded honorary membership into the newly formed Western New York Poultry Society. A group of poultry breeders and chicken fanciers had met at the Tifft House in late March to found the society and hammer out its primary objective—"the acquisition and dissemination of knowledge relating to the breeding of poultry, birds, and other small animals, by means of correspondence, fairs, etc."[21] The combination of Mrs. Lord's offbeat inquiry and the quirky invitation resulted in

Twain's hilarious, witty story in the June 4 *Buffalo Express*, "More Distinction." Twain exaggerates the dignity of his honorary induction into the new poultry club and claims that poultry raising has intrigued him since childhood. He extends a pun on "raising" as a comic thread throughout the story. He suggests raising chickens from their nests by lighting matches under their behinds, feet, and noses (not beaks!) or by placing heated planks under them or by lifting the entire chicken coop. Presumably Mrs. Lord was entertained by Twain's response, even if her question was not answered.

The Lords were valued members of Twain's social circle in Buffalo. Rev. John C. Lord was known as "the Buffalo Thunderer" for his sermons delivered from the pulpit at the Central Presbyterian Church, an impressive structure located where Genesee and Pearl Streets intersected in downtown Buffalo. During Twain's brief bachelorhood period in Buffalo, he attended a Presbyterian church, which may have been Rev. Grosvenor Heacock's Lafayette church or Lord's Central Presbyterian—both were an easy walk from Twain's boardinghouse. Indeed, well into the twenty-first century, longtime parishioners of Central Presbyterian perpetuated church lore that Twain had been a member of their church.[22] Two accounts mention that Twain wrote about Central Presbyterian in the *Express*.[23] Central Presbyterian was massive, with walls constructed from Lockport sandstone, a pulpit made of Lisbon marble, a fine organ that cost $3,000, and an auditorium seating capacity, including a spacious gallery, for nearly two thousand attendees. A beautiful chandelier with seventy-eight burners was suspended from the center of the worship hall.[24]

Reverends Lord and Heacock were close friends. Twain's business partner at the *Buffalo Express* George Selkirk modeled a bust of Lord that had been commissioned by John C. Graves. Twain undoubtedly saw the bust when he visited Lord's extensive library at Oakwood. Lord bequeathed his collection of over ten thousand books and pamphlets to the Buffalo and Erie County Historical Society. Twain coveted one particularly rare volume of *Gentleman's Magazine and Historical Chronicle*, which contained the original music of the British national anthem. "Mark Twain has expressed repeatedly a wish to pilfer from the Lord library this quaint representative of early magazine literature. Its title page is dated MDCCXLV."[25]

Image 6.4. Rev. John C. Lord, pastor of Buffalo's Central Presbyterian Church. Twain admired his library. This bust was modeled by George Selkirk, one of Twain's *Express* partners, before he entered the newspaper trade. (Image used by permission of the Collection of the Buffalo and Erie County Historical Society.)

Later in June of 1870, Twain completed his batch of *Express* stories based on local issues. This time, he shifted his attention in the other compass direction from his home, a few blocks south toward the campus of the Buffalo Female Academy. The school included the Cottage, which faced Delaware Street, and Goodell Hall, the classroom building behind it on Johnson Park. In May, Twain and one of his friends, *Daily Courier* editor David Gray, were asked by the Buffalo Female Academy to judge the student writing and to award a winning piece, which would be read at commencement. The principal, Rev. Albert T. Chester, a relative of an associate editor of the *Courier*, may have used his family connection to approach Gray. Perhaps one of the academy's trustees, attorney Dennis Bowen of Bowen and Rogers, who had recently handled a $3,000 loan from Twain to J. N. Larned, asked Twain to read the essays. Whatever the circumstances, Twain and Gray fulfilled their duties with gusto. Twain would write their rationale and Gray would deliver it at commencement, a perfect division of labor, since Twain was unexpectedly called to Elmira the day before graduation.

Judging schoolgirl essays provided an opportunity for Twain to reflect on what constitutes good writing and to ridicule the state of writing instruction in

America's schools. In all, Twain and Gray read eighteen beautifully handwritten compositions and picked winners from the Collegiate and the Graduating Classes.[26] By 1870, the Buffalo Female Academy was a well-established private women's school, and this was a year in which over two hundred girls in total were enrolled in the five departments. On Thursday evening, June 23, students (including Twain's young neighbor Jane Meade Welch) marched in formal academic procession from the academy grounds southward to Reverend Lord's Central Presbyterian Church. Exercises commenced at 7:30 p.m. After hymn singing, prayers, separate reports read aloud about each department—Primary, Third Academic, Second Academic, First Academic, and Collegiate—and additional reports read about Latin, French, penmanship, music, reading and recitation (interrupted by the student chorus singing "The Song of Spring"), it was finally time for David Gray to stride to the platform that had been erected in front of the pulpit. He then read the report composed by Twain, explaining their collaborative effort to pick the first-place winners.

In the first half of his report, Twain announces the essay winners and explains why the top picks stood out. The report begins a bit defensively and in typical Twain fashion, using exaggeration as a comic device to defuse potential backlash against their judgments. Twain takes great pains ensuring the academy audience that he and Gray were scrupulously objective when deliberating. By overstating the case for their meticulously mutual honesty, Twain mildly mocks the solemnity of the process of judging contests. In the opening paragraph of the report, Twain inserts a variety of similar disclaimers: "We have done our work carefully and conscientiously"; "We have determined the degrees of literary excellence displayed, with pitiless honesty"; "We feel it is necessary to say a word or two in vindication of our verdict"; "We have judged these compositions by the strict rules of literary criticism."[27] Such somber overstatement adds a humorous element. Twain goes on to describe their criteria. The winning essayists are the "least showy," the "least artificial," and the "least labored," yet represent the "clearest," "shapeliest," and "best carried out" writing. Of all the entries, Twain and Gray found Lillie W. Powell's "The Golden Treasure at the End of the Rainbow" by far the superior work. Twain says "Golden Rainbow" is unique for its "unpretentious language," its description of a simple incident without overemphasizing a moral, its "rare merit" of exiting gracefully (*"stopping when it is finished*"), its "high gift" of using the right word, and its economical phrasing. Perhaps mindful of his role as editor at the *Express*, Twain adds an aside about the tendency by unskilled writers to be verbose and add clutter to their sentences: "And let us remark instructively, in passing, that one can seldom run his pen through an adjective without improving the manuscript."

Twain and Gray selected "A Little Fish" by Lillie Kelsey as the best composition in the collegiate class. In his report, Twain again extols the student's light-handed treatment of a moral, "compressed into a single sentence," and expresses delight at the essay's vibrant simplicity, "told with a breezy dash, and with nothing grand or overpowering about it." Kelsey's composition is an imaginative one. It is a light, bright fiction about a family of fish on a Great Lakes outing. They misplace their little one, and the narrator finds the tiny fish swimming alone in a pitcher of water. After studying the lost fish, wondering about its future, and vowing to free it and reunite it with its family, the narrator steps away from the pitcher momentarily. The essay concludes with her surprise at finding the pitcher empty and the fish gone when she returns. The final line moralistically urges the reader to act rather than to think: "I was left to know that if I had spent less time in thinking of him and more in helping him, it would have been better for the fish and just as well for me."[28] Twain loved the closing for its succinct, powerful punch, a "nub" that "is a jewel of a price" for the essay.

Twain's Female Academy report then takes an abrupt turn. He removes his essay-judge cap and adopts the pose of education reformer.[29] The second half of the report, approximately seven hundred words, is a minirant by Twain against the traditional, formulas-driven method of teaching writing in American schools. He compliments the two Female Academy essay winners for taking risks and breaking the molds of accepted composition writing that have been handed down for generations in America's classrooms, resulting in a distressing sameness and staleness in academic essays. Twain lambastes the standard school texts of his time, Webster's spellers and McGuffey's readers, for publishing "unspeakably execrable models which young people are defrauded into accepting as fine literary composition." Twain's report appeared in the *Buffalo Express* and in the *Buffalo Daily Courier* on June 24, 1870.

Despite having reestablished a somewhat halting rhythm to accomplish his scaled-down *Buffalo Express* writing tasks—the community-focused stories and others on broader topics like mining and the insanity plea—Twain was still seldom seen at the *Express* office. He wrote at home and had editorial directives written on his personal stationery delivered to the *Express* staff by hand. One such message was sent by courier to his trusted young colleague Earl Berry. Twain requested that Berry give ample publicity to a charity concert for orphans of soldiers and sailors.[30] Berry followed Twain's orders to the letter. A lengthy item under the City and Vicinity column announcing details of the benefit concert appeared in the *Express* six days before the event. In the ensuing days, three more reminders of the concert were published, one of which advertised that Rev. Grosvenor Heacock would make an address before the concert. Finally, the *Express* commented that the concert had been a "decided success" before a "well-filled house" in a review the day after the concert.[31] With a talented, enthusiastic city editor like Berry, Twain must have felt secure about conducting his *Express* business from home.

Twain's self-imposed exile and diminishing role at the *Express* signaled a sea change in his aspirations as a professional writer. Early in 1870 he was poised to take a significant step away from the daily grind of journalism toward becoming a man of letters. He was tired of the mechanical writing dictated by newspapers. He sought something loftier, a higher calling. He wanted to experience writing not as labor but as art. He wanted to escape the relentlessness of newspaper deadlines and write with literary panache at a more leisurely pace. Twain was ready to move on. Just three weeks into his marriage, he was hatching a plan to elevate his writing status with a wistful statement to his book publisher, Elisha Bliss, about having "a strong notion to write a _____"[32] Twain broke off the sentence, explaining to Bliss that he would fill him in later. Twain was likely about to tell Bliss that he hoped to sign a contract with *Galaxy* magazine.

Two weeks later, Twain had successfully negotiated a regular department for himself with coeditors Francis and William Church at the monthly *Galaxy*. He agreed to edit a humorous section called Memoranda, consisting of ten pages of copy each month at a rate of $200 per month, or $2,400 a year. Writing for *Galaxy* was an important step up in Twain's eyes, providing an outlet for work too good to appear in the *Express*. His *Galaxy* exposure represented another rung in his climb up the literary ladder, a chance to strut his writing stuff before a highbrow reading public in "a first-class New York magazine."[33] He wrote

Mary Fairbanks that he would save "fine-spun stuff" for the magazine, publishing items in *Galaxy* that were not "entirely suited to either a daily, Weekly, or any kind of newspaper."[34] Twain expected to write for the *Express* less often, not even every week, because those "who write every week *write themselves out*, and tire the public, too, before very long." In the letter to Fairbanks he summarized his epiphany and impending transformation from journalistic hack to author: "I just came to the conclusion that I would quit turning my attention to making money especially & go to writing for enjoyment as well as profit." Twain reinforced his sense of artistic liberation by describing to Mr. and Mrs. Langdon how *Galaxy* writing allowed him "to write what I please, not what I must."[35] Furthermore, Twain had felt a kind of doomed constraint in writing just for the *Express*, as if he "would have been tied hand & foot here & forever & ever."

Twain announced his arrangement with *Galaxy* in the April 12 *Express*. His first Memoranda installment appeared in the May 1870 *Galaxy* and continued monthly until the following April, with the exception of the March 1871 issue. Eighteen *Galaxy* items were also published in the *Express*; only seven of them appeared in the newspaper first. Twain had a notion to bundle his *Galaxy* contributions into book form, but the scheme never panned out.

By the end of May 1870, he was delighted with his *Galaxy* maneuver. He again expressed to Mary Fairbanks his preference for magazine writing over newspaper work, stressing slick appearance and sophisticated audience as huge *Galaxy* plusses: "Do you know, Madam, that I would rather write for a magazine for $2 a page than for a newspaper at $10? I *would*. One takes more pains, the *truck* looks nicer in print & one has a pleasanter audience."[36] In a prophetic personal death knell ringing out his disenchantment with the newspaper industry, Twain closed with a metaphor derived from his experiences on the lecture circuit. He compared the *Express* and *Galaxy* writing universes to the contrast between addressing crowds in rough-hewn frontier territories versus speaking to cultivated audiences in civilized settings: "It is the difference between lecturing in 'The States' & doing the same thing in delectable Nevada." Following a lifelong pattern governed by his volatile personality, however, the prestige offered to Twain by *Galaxy* was destined to be quicksilver. Where *Galaxy* replaced the *Express*, a book project soon supplanted *Galaxy* writing in Twain's quick march toward literary respectability. In late March 1870, Twain's mother had, at his request, shipped a carton of his newspaper clippings from the Virginia City, Nevada, *Territorial Enterprise*. And in July, his brother Orion sent his personal journals from their "plains" trip. Twain had in mind a "mighty starchy" book about his time out west in the 1860s.[37] He had already rehearsed elements of his western reminiscences in several *Express* letters for the Around the World series and in his April 2 *Express* story "The Facts in the Great Land Slide Case."

In mid-July, Twain met his publisher, Elisha Bliss, in Elmira and signed a contract for a large book with many illustrations to be submitted by January 1, 1871. The book was eventually titled *Roughing It*. He would miss the deadline by more than seven months. The continuum of his rapidly changing writing priorities, from the *Express* to *Galaxy* to *Roughing It*, was played out in a letter in which he described gradients of writing time that he intended for each writing task. Predictably, time spent on stories for the *Express* got the shortest shrift, a similarly minimal amount of time was set aside for *Galaxy* work, and his book project was allocated the most writing time: "I shall write one or two sketches a month for the Express, & have an idea that for a good while I shall do nothing else on the paper. Thus the Galaxy & the Express together will give me fully six days' work every month, & I positively need the rest of the time to admire the house in. Need it, too, to write a book in."[38]

By early 1871, Twain was as eager to shed himself of *Galaxy* responsibilities as eagerly as he had once been to sever ties with the *Express*. In January of 1871, he wanted to stop contributing to *Galaxy*; in March, he referred to his monthly magazine obligation as "harassment" that "cheapened himself" as a writer.[39] In the same letter to Orion, Twain impugned the character of his *Galaxy* editors and benefactors, the Church brothers, calling them "those shuffling gentlemen," though he crossed it out. In May of 1870, Twain had likewise backstabbed his friend and *Express* partner George Selkirk. He wrote Jervis Langdon that recent moves—discontinuing the evening edition and subletting the printing-job office department—were long-overdue, cost-cutting acts that exposed Selkirk's incompetence: "The Evening paper & the job office were *leaks* from the start, & these boys did not know it. That is the sort of business man Selkirk is."[40] In the *Express* of June 25, 1870, Twain took a slap at newsroom colleagues in his story "The Editorial Office Bore."[41] The editor/narrator criticizes lazy journalists lolling around the newspaper editorial room, smoking, yakking, sleeping, avoiding writing, and interfering with the editor's job. These newsmen are always just hanging around. Only a bomb would disturb them. The editor silently invokes a string of curses upon the "bores" and suggests that being burdened with such lazy coworkers is worse torture than hanging. It is likely that Twain was targeting the work ethic of his *Express* staff. Earl Berry recalls Twain's dissatisfaction with the habits of some slothful *Express* workers: "No man detested loafers more than Mr. Clemens, and assuredly no man could be more pitiless in his treatment of bores. He was vigorous in his denunciation of that class of people who aimlessly and impudently intrude their constant presence in an editorial room."[42] Mark Twain had arrived at a pivotal point in his development as a writer. He rejected whatever conviviality newspaper workplaces once offered him, and he distrusted supervision of his writing. He wanted to make a living as an author and do it on his terms.

While the arc of Twain's literary ambition was rising through the spring and summer of 1870, the social life that had started so promisingly for him and Olivia was flatlining. Prolonged absences from their "delightful nest"[43] between May and August made it hard to nurture many of their newly forged friendships in Buffalo. However, some degree of domestic normalcy did exist at 472 Delaware. They regularly exchanged visits with the Grays. *Express* staff artist John Harrison Mills stopped by to paint a portrait of Twain.[44] In June, Olivia managed to can eleven containers of strawberries and six of pineapple. That same month, Mrs. White, "the pleasantest neighbor we have,"[45] wife of Henry G. White, who lived on the same block catty-corner across the street at 523 Delaware, sent over an ample dish of large homegrown strawberries. The timing was perfect. Twain and Olivia had just finished dinner, so the fresh strawberry dessert caused them to be "in a surfeit, now, from an overdose of them."[46] White, a painter of houses, steamboats, and signs, once described his own unique dwelling as a "queer looking house in the style of the time of Queen Elizabeth."[47]

Twain and Olivia enthusiastically planned various vacation trips to the Adirondack Mountains, Paris, and California—pleasure excursions that were soon canceled. A trip that Twain did take was to Washington, DC, for five or six days in July. He was there to lobby on Jervis Langdon's behalf in support of legislation that would guarantee payment owed him for a street-paving job in Memphis, Tennessee. On July 8, Twain posed for a photo portrait in the

Washington, DC, studio of famed Civil War photographer Mathew B. Brady at 625–627 Pennsylvania Avenue, NW. Twain also had an opportunity to meet President Ulysses S. Grant while he was in Washington.

Olivia desperately wanted her parents to come to Buffalo from Elmira for an extended stay. They had not visited 472 Delaware since the day after the wedding in early February. Over four months later, she was still pleading with them: *"Be sure to come to us. Don't fail us."*[48] Unfortunately, her father's health had become a serious concern. Jervis Langdon's chronic indigestion, or dyspepsia, was getting worse. In early April of 1870, Langdon and his wife had taken a convalescent trip to the South accompanied by his friend and physician, Henry Sayles, and Mrs. Sayles. The trip did not restore Langdon's health. He wrote from Richmond, Virginia, that his organs were failing. His liver was sluggish. His digestive system functioned on and off, sometimes allowing him to eat and retain food, which was then followed by constipation and vomiting. By the time the Langdon party returned to Elmira at the end of April, Jervis Langdon had lost thirty pounds and was tired and in pain. He was diagnosed with stomach cancer.

Facing mortality, Langdon quickly took care of business. He restructured his Elmira coal company. J. Langdon and Company added as partners Jervis Langdon's son, Charley, his son-in-law Theodore Crane, and John D. F. Slee, the trustworthy head of his Buffalo office. In May 1870, Slee moved his family to Elmira. Late in May, Langdon wrote his son, who was still traveling around the world with Professor Ford, that he had better not extend his tour beyond the scheduled year's duration, because his father's "health is not good."[49] Three weeks later, Charley received an urgent summons in Bavaria to return home immediately. On June 25, in Elmira, Langdon executed his will, appointing Twain, Slee, Charley Langdon, Theodore Crane, and his wife as executors. On that same day, Twain ordered a book on child rearing. Olivia was three months pregnant.

Thus began a Buffalo–Elmira shuttle for Twain and Olivia during May, June, July, and August. Twain and Olivia memorized the Erie Railway schedule connecting Elmira and Buffalo, a trip of four and a half hours. What little time they spent at home in Buffalo during those months was occupied with high anxiety as they waited for the next emergency telegram calling them back to Elmira to help nurse Olivia's father. Langdon would rally, then fall deathly ill again. In May, Olivia and Twain were away from 472 Delaware for ten days in order to tend to Langdon's needs. They spent four more days in Elmira in early June. Before leaving for Buffalo, Twain sent word to his chief housekeeper, Ellen White, to have their coachman, Patrick McAleer, meet them with the carriage at Buffalo's Erie Depot at 11:30 p.m. on June 11. Twain and Olivia departed Elmira at 7:07 a.m. on the Erie Railway day express.[50] On June 22, another telegram brought them back to Elmira, where they remained for the next two months, with the exception of Twain's brief sojourn to Washington, DC, in July.

Image 6.5. Jervis Langdon, coal magnate from Elmira, Twain's father-in-law and friend. (Image courtesy of the Mark Twain Archive, Elmira College.)

On July 18 and 25, under the heading "Personal," the *Buffalo Express* published notes written by J. N. Larned, based on information sent by Twain, that Langdon was improving and that a full recovery was expected. But the grim vigil in the Langdon mansion continued. The house was kept quiet; blinds were shut. Twain described the pervasive heart-wrenching atmosphere to Mary Fairbanks: "The gloom in the hearts of the household finds its type in the somberness of hall & chamber."[51] For days and weeks, emotions swung back and forth between hope and despair. Twain, Olivia, and her sister, Susan Crane, sat in shifts at Langdon's bedside. The family had decided to dispense with nurses since medicine was no longer a factor. Twain took his turns in the middle of the day and from midnight to four in the morning. Olivia and Susan split the remaining, longer shifts. Each caregiver waved a palm leaf back and forth over Langdon's bed to provide him relief from the scorching summer heat. Years later, Twain would recall how slowly time passed during his early-morning shifts and how much he grew to despise the torturous predawn "lamentings" of the same bird who chirped every morning outside Langdon's window.[52]

On August 5, Twain wrote Elisha Bliss that Langdon's condition was "utterly hopeless," that the family was "shrouded in gloom, awaiting the end."[53] Twenty-four hours later, around five o'clock in the afternoon, it was over. Jervis Langdon, Mark Twain's defender, benefactor, friend, and surrogate father, was dead at sixty-one, leaving an estate reportedly close to one million dollars. Twain wrote and sent a tribute to the *Express*, which incorporated the tribute into a eulogy published on August 8. Writing to Bliss five days later, Twain referred to the Langdon mansion as a "house of mourning."[54] He described Olivia as so grief stricken that she was "nearly broken down."

Twain could not know that unimaginable sorrow, illness, and heartache would follow them back to Buffalo.

7

TOPPLING PYRAMIDS

On Thursday, October 20, 1870, an earthquake struck Buffalo. It was nothing compared to the tremors that had been shaking the Twain household at 472 Delaware Street the previous few weeks. The quake hit around five o'clock in the afternoon and lasted only thirty or forty seconds. Church steeples and chandeliers swayed. Walls of buildings shook, windows shattered, and furniture moved across floors. In the upper-floor offices of the *Buffalo Daily Commercial Advertiser* on Washington Street, the editorial staff felt the building tremble and watched "gas-burners vibrating to and fro as if struck with a stick."[1] A *Commercial Advertiser* wag joked about the difficulty in reading proof while the building rattled.

Despite the quake, *Commercial Advertiser* proprietors James N. Matthews and James D. Warren were relieved. That morning, a jury had acquitted them in a celebrated libel case, a decision that had sent its own shockwaves across Buffalo. Businessman David S. Bennett had lost his high-profile $100,000 slander suit against the newspaper, despite an eloquent four-hour closing speech by his attorney, William Dorsheimer. Twain's commentary in the October 21 *Express* criticized his rival newspaper for abusing freedom of the press and hiding behind "walls of an unassailable fortification" in order to print "venom" that impugned Bennett's character.[2] Twain's moralistic scolding of the *Commercial Advertiser* is odd, given his dubious use of the *Express* to advocate for the coal monopoly and his vilification of the Blondes troupe for defending themselves from newspaper defamation.

David Gray's *Buffalo Daily Courier* offered further tidbits on the earthquake's curious effects on people. The *Courier* described a "goodly number of people" who were terrified and a local teacher who ran out of his school in a totally disoriented state.[3] The *Courier* told of quake victims shaken with "the terrible sensation which belongs to sea-sickness" and others suffering as if "they had been attacked with palsy." The earthquake must have been particularly upsetting to Twain's wife. Since their return to Buffalo after Jervis Langdon's death in Elmira, Olivia's health had been frail. After the October earthquake, she would be subjected to quotidian aftershocks of sickness and sorrow that would not let up during their remaining five months in Buffalo.

Twain and Olivia had lingered in Elmira for two weeks after Langdon's passing, returning to Buffalo on August 22, a day after Rev. Thomas Beecher conducted a memorial tribute for Langdon in Elmira's Opera House. Olivia's heart was so broken with grief that Twain was afraid she "would never smile again."[4] Olivia's mother accompanied them to Buffalo and helped transform 472 Delaware Street into a house of mourning. Etiquette dictated that children of a deceased parent remain secluded for some weeks and months, clad in black in a household where curtains were mostly drawn and items such as urns were draped. Years later, Twain recalled the harsh mourning custom: "In accordance with the hard terms of that fearful law—the year of mourning—which deprives the mourner of the society and comradeship of his race when he most needs it, we shut ourselves up in the house and became recluses, visiting no one and receiving visits from no one."[5] Twain remembered that David and Mattie Gray managed to regularly penetrate the shroud covering 472 Delaware. But even so stalwart a friend as John D. F. Slee apologized profusely for barging in on Twain unexpectedly. The promising social life that brightened Twain and Olivia's first months of married life in Buffalo had sputtered during the summer of 1870 and ground to a halt by the fall. Olivia was given opiates to help her sleep and to reduce stress.[6] Compounding the stifling mourning rituals and the mental suffering from bereavement, Olivia's second trimester of pregnancy was not going well. Then a dear friend came to Buffalo to comfort Olivia.

By the end of August, Emma Nye was staying at 472 Delaware to help care for Olivia. Nye was a close childhood friend from Elmira. Since Buffalo was on the route back to her teaching position in Michigan, she offered to assist Olivia until the school year started. (Two years earlier, at Olivia's behest, Twain had called on Nye while he was lecturing in Detroit.) On September 2, shortly after Nye arrived in Buffalo, Twain reported to Mary Fairbanks that Nye was visiting and had become so ill that her travel onward to Detroit would be delayed.[7] Five days later, Nye showed signs of typhoid fever and was moved from the guest room to the master bedroom. Olivia, weak herself, watched over Nye around the clock, as did a nurse and Dr. Andrew R. Wright: "Poor little Emma Nye lies in our bed-chamber fighting wordy battles with the phantoms of delirium. Livy & a hired nurse watch her without ceasing, night & day. It is not necessary to tell you that Livy sleeps as little as nurse or patient, & sees little but that bed & its occupant. The disease is a consuming fever—of a typhoid type—& also the lungs seem stricken with disease. The poor girl is dangerously ill. Ours is an excellent physician, & we have full confidence in him."[8] Within a week, Nye's condition had deteriorated to the point where she was dying. Twain wrote his brother on a sheet of Nye's stationery that "the premises are full of nurses & doctors & we are all fagged out."[9] Perhaps two of the additional attendants now at 472 Delaware were the Spaulding sisters, longtime friends of Nye and Olivia from Elmira.

Nye soon succumbed to the disease, dying in Twain's blue satin bed on the morning of September 29. She was twenty-four years old. That evening, her body was taken back to Elmira to the Spaulding house (Nye's parents had moved to South Carolina), and she was buried the following day in the Second Street Cemetery.[10] Twain and Olivia did not attend the funeral. Olivia was physically and emotionally exhausted.

Olivia, who had felt a sense of loss when the Nyes moved to South Carolina, now plummeted into "a deep depression" over her friend's passing.[11] Four months later, she was still suffering remorse and disbelief over the back-to-back deaths of Jervis Langdon and Emma Nye: "Can you realize that dear Emma Nye has gone from us? I feel often, in thinking of both Father and Emma, as if I would write them of this and that."[12]

Amid the turmoil swirling within 472 Delaware during Nye's tragic sickness, a moment of dark comedy occurred. An old Clemens family friend and nemesis from Hannibal, Missouri—unaware of the mourning and illness impacting the household—pulled up uninvited at Twain's address. Twain intercepted the notorious freeloader, Melicent S. Holliday, before she even exited her carriage. He gave her fifty dollars and dispatched her to Fredonia, but not before sending a warning telegram to his mother and sister there.[13]

During the hectic month of September, Twain also contacted attorney Franklin D. Locke, of the firm Bowen and Rogers, whom Twain employed in Buffalo, asking that Locke finalize Twain's power of attorney over Olivia's financial affairs without requiring Olivia to take an unnecessary carriage ride and face "the terrors of the law in your awe-inspiring den,"[14] which was located at 28 Erie Street.

Twain later referred to the final days of Nye's fatal illness as "among the blackest, the gloomiest, the most wretched of my long life."[15] Yet, Twain made progress that month on the book that became *Roughing It*. He also somehow summoned up the wherewithal to produce humorous material for the *Express*.

In 1906, Twain categorized his wild mood swings, those "periodical and sudden changes of mood in me, from deep melancholy to half insane tempests and cyclones of humor," as "among the curiosities of my life."[16] It has been suggested that Twain's mood swings might be attributed to manic-depressive illness.[17] Like other writers, artists, and composers who suffered from manic depression, Twain's cycling from depression to mania may explain his periods of writer's block followed by stretches of radically increased writing productivity. No matter what, his *Express* entry "The Fortifications of Paris" created a spectacularly comic splash in September despite his personal circumstances of "a heavy heart, and in a house of lamentation."[18]

Six days after France declared war on Prussia, Twain signed a satirical piece in the *Express* mocking the lack of active warfare and the confused state of loyalties in Europe. The piece pokes fun at the incompetent armies on both sides.[19] Almost immediately, though, Twain allied himself with the Prussians (he had a history of ridiculing the French anyway). Buffalo had a huge German American population; by 1855, 39 percent of heads of households in Buffalo were from German states.[20] In the 1869 city directory, there were ten pages with 432 names beginning with the ethnic German suffix *Sch-*, from Schaad to Schwitzer. Germans operated the majority of Buffalo's breweries. Year-round beer halls and summertime beer gardens were plentiful on Buffalo's German east side. When visitors toured Buffalo, carriage drivers routinely pointed out Albert Ziegele's lovely beer garden. During the summer that Twain first arrived in Buffalo, the *Niagara Falls Gazette* carried two briefs celebrating the ethnic stereotype of jovial, beer-swilling

Germans. One cited a large excursion of Germans from Buffalo who were accompanied by a band and a wagon full of lager.[21] In the same month, another brief told of two Germans who engaged in a drinking contest; after the eighteenth glass of lager, the loser paid for the drinks. "Female Help Wanted" ads in the *Express* sought "German or American" or "German preferred," "good Protestant girls" to cook or to do housework.[22] Olivia dreamed of hiring a German servant girl for the Buffalo home,[23] and in honor of the preponderance of Germans in Buffalo, one of the cats owned by Twain and Olivia at 472 Delaware Street was named Fraulein.[24] Twain's next salvo on the evolving Franco-Prussian conflict was delivered in the *Express* of September 7 in the form of an amusing City and Vicinity brief. Twain described a waterfront brawl between German and Irish grain shovelers (the Irish were French sympathizers) on Buffalo's Ohio Street. Of course, the German gang prevailed.[25] This item was a warm-up for "The Fortifications of Paris," which appeared ten days later and was probably the most famous humorous work Twain ever produced while at the *Buffalo Morning Express*.

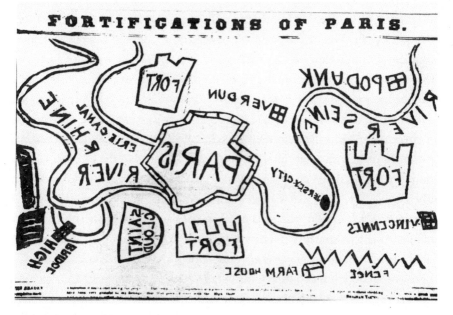

Image 7.1. Twain's mock map, "Fortifications of Paris," appeared in the *Buffalo Express* of September 17, 1870, and created a sensation across the country. (Image from the *Buffalo Express*, September 17, 1870.)

By mid-September, Twain had encountered in newspaper exchanges countless maps of Franco-Prussian War battlefield tactics and accounts of the progress of Prussia's invasion. Seizing the opportunity to escape the dismal, suffocating atmosphere at 472 Delaware Street and pursue a comic brainstorm, he made a rare appearance at his *Express* office. He asked one of the pressmen or compositors for a large wooden block. Armed with either a penknife or a jackknife, he sat at his desk whittling away on his satirical depiction of the siege of Paris. His coeditor, Josephus N. Larned, witnessed Twain's laughter as he carved the map. Accounts of the incident vary. One claims it took Twain a half day to complete the map; another, two days.[26] He personally supervised the page proofs at midnight, and the engraving and text of "Fortifications of Paris" were published on the political page of the *Express* that morning, Saturday, September 17.

Twain's zany illustration of the Paris defense system contained an absurd, incongruous collection of place names and drawings like Omaha, Jersey City, and the Erie Canal, all written backward, as Twain intended, using his typesetting expertise. The accompanying narrative listed hilarious fake testimonials by Brigham Young, Napoleon, and others. The Saturday issue of the *Express* sold out quickly. The Wednesday *Weekly Buffalo Express* reprinted as an insert a fourteen-and-a-half-by-eleven-inch broadside version of "Fortifications of Paris." By that time, "Fortifications" had been picked up by newspaper exchanges and was a nationwide sensation. The *Express* carried a funny exchange item lifted from the *Cleveland Herald*, whose staff joked about attempting to duplicate the map "by having chickens 'draw' it with their scratchings."[27] The map of Paris and original narrative, along with a new introduction, were published in the October *Galaxy* magazine as "Mark Twain's Map of Paris," guaranteeing an even wider audience. The *Buffalo Express* carried Twain's *Galaxy* introduction on October 15. In his *Autobiography*, Twain says that the map was circulated in Berlin beer halls, entertaining American students and bewildering German soldiers.[28] His parting shot on the Franco-Prussian War was a bizarre, somewhat maudlin satire two months later, one of his last half dozen contributions to the *Express*, fantasizing about a blockaded Parisian populace resorting to raiding their public zoo for food.[29]

"Fortifications of Paris" appeared twelve days after Canisius College first opened its doors on Ellicott Street, east of Main Street. The college's founding German Jesuits likely were amused by Twain's satirical attack on the French military. The establishment of Canisius College was one of many noticeable advances in Buffalo since Twain had first taken over the editorial reins at the *Express* one year earlier. The city had continued its boom. Since August of 1869, the population had grown by another four thousand people. A second institution of higher learning, the Buffalo Normal School, on the city's west side at Jersey and Thirteenth Streets, was preparing to open. Work had begun on Delaware Park, the jewel in Frederick Law Olmsted's park system. The Democratic nominee—and ultimate winner—for new sheriff of Erie County was Grover Cleveland. The new Republican mayor, Alexander Brush, so popular he would be elected three times, earned a salary of $2,000. Seven new businesses had started up: a florist, a ship chandler, a roofing company, a civil engineer, a processor of wools and hides, a jewelry store, and a coffee merchant.[30] Because he and his family were virtually sequestered by mourning conventions, it is unlikely that Twain enjoyed Buffalo's pervasive economic and cultural surge. However, he surely was aware of two well-established and thriving companies located across the street from his house. They stood as anomalies in the otherwise exclusive Delaware Street promenade.

At the end of a row of lovely mansions on the east side of Delaware in the lower-500 block, situated diagonally to the north across a grassy median from Twain's house, sat C. S. Cooper Marble Works. On that site, Cooper manufactured marble furniture tops and fireplace mantelpieces of Italian marble, some of which may have been installed in Twain's house when it was first built. The Cooper Works also produced marble monuments, bases, headstones, posts, and parlor grates and fenders in styles varying from plain to trimmed in gilt and silver. The most grievous industrial intruder, however, occupied most of the block, more than two acres, running from Cooper's Marble Works south on Delaware to the corner of Virginia Street, which was directly across from 472 Delaware, called Cornell Lead Works. The business had been there since 1865.[31] Those at Cornell Lead Works factory tried cosmetics to fit into the upscale residential neighborhood, erecting a high board fence along the Delaware Street side of their property and planting a row of trees on the Virginia Street side. However, they could not hide the tall end-to-end chimneys that belched coal smoke and other toxic chemical elements—such as arsenic—necessary to manufacture their flourishing line of lead products. The Cornell plant specialized in white lead and lead pipe, sheet, and bar lead "free from all flaws and seams."[32]

The factory's capacity was five tons of white lead a day and an equal amount of pipe, sheet, and bar lead. During the worst of times for Twain and Olivia in October of 1870, the Cornell Lead Works turned out a coil of lead pipe for a company in Corning, New York, reported as the longest ever—two inches in diameter, 110 feet long, and 549 pounds.[33] Henry G. White, a neighbor of Twain, called the Cornell factory "a nuisance to all who desire to have Delaware *The Avenue*."[34] And Twain's young neighbor, Jane Meade Welch, later recalled "the ugly lines" of the Cornell white lead works.[35] In addition to marring the aesthetics of Delaware's streetscape, the constant racket, stench, and polluted emissions emanating from Cornell must have made it a very unwelcome neighbor indeed. In nineteenth-century industrial American urban scenarios like this, "not uncommonly, houses stood right up against gasworks, rolling mills, and paint factories, exposed to round-the-clock noise and poisonous discharges."[36] One can only speculate about the perilous health effects on Olivia's difficult pregnancy as daily westerly breezes wafted hazardous particles from the smokestacks of Cornell Lead Works just thirty or forty yards directly across to 472 Delaware Street into Twain's open windows. The unfortunate, family-unfriendly setting of 472 Delaware might explain its availability on the real estate market in November of 1869 when Jervis Langdon was house shopping.

Image 7.2. The Cornell Lead Works at Delaware and Virginia, opposite the Twain house. (Image courtesy of the Buffalo State College Archives, *Courier-Express* Collection.)

As October of 1870 dragged on, woes at 472 Delaware Street intensified. Olivia began her eighth month of pregnancy in a very fragile state. She was fatigued, experienced headaches, was depressed, and had no appetite. Twain made sure she took a narcotic every night so that she could rest. Most days, Olivia was bedridden and tended to by her mother, nurses, physicians, Twain's sister Pamela, and later in the month, Olivia's sister, Susan. Even though the baby was not due until the first week of December, Olivia nearly suffered a miscarriage on October 19, the day before the earthquake hit Buffalo. Two and a half weeks later, still almost a month prematurely, Dr. Wright delivered a son, Langdon Clemens, at eleven in the morning. The baby weighed only four and a half pounds. Twain wrote a humorous letter to Joe and Harmony Twichell in Langdon's voice, saying that his birth had been "staved off two weeks, & by jings I missed the earthquake."[37]

Image 7.3. Baby Langdon, Twain and Olivia's firstborn, who would not survive infancy. (Image courtesy of the Mark Twain Archive, Elmira College.)

Sometime between late October and the baby's birth, Mary Fairbanks arrived from Cleveland to help for several days. Even though Olivia was virtually an invalid, she insisted on accompanying Fairbanks to the Buffalo train depot when Fairbanks headed back to Cleveland just a couple of days before Langdon was delivered. In his memoirs, Twain said he believed that Olivia's carriage ride in a rush over rough Buffalo streets further jeopardized her already perilous pregnancy:

> We had a visitor in the house and when she was leaving she wanted Mrs. Clemens to go to the station with her. I objected. But this was a visitor whose desire Mrs. Clemens regarded as law. The visitor wasted so much precious time in taking her leave that Patrick had to drive in a gallop to get to the station in time. In those days the streets of Buffalo were not the model streets which they afterward became. They were paved with large cobblestones, and had not been repaired since Columbus's time. Therefore the journey to the station was like the Channel passage in a storm. The result to Mrs. Clemens was a premature confinement, followed by a dangerous illness.[38]

In fact, a few days before baby Langdon's birth, Olivia and her bed were moved downstairs to the library. She slept there for her remaining four months in Buffalo. The library was kept so dark that she could not even read there during daylight hours. As sick as Olivia was, the baby was in critical condition. Four days after he was born, Twain wrote his brother Orion that he did not expect the child to live another five days.[39] So many servants, medical personnel, friends, and relatives bustled throughout the house at 472 Delaware Street that Twain insisted that his brother, and his brother-in-law Charley stay away. By the end of November, Twain counted eleven people residing in his home. Auntie Smith served as nursemaid, and Mrs. Brown, a wet nurse, fed baby Langdon in the kitchen with her own recently delivered baby in tow. Olivia's mother sent a silver set for a baby gift and soon shipped a carton of apples; Charley Langdon and his new wife sent a pair of baby shoes. With holidays approaching, Twain begged Olivia's mother to ease Olivia's loneliness and rejoin them for Thanksgiving Day. On the Sunday after Thanksgiving, Olivia celebrated her twenty-fifth birthday, her first birthday as a wife and mother. Twain presented her with a copy of John Greenleaf Whittier's *Snowbound. A Winter Idyl.*[40] Three days later, Twain turned thirty-five, dreaming of a book collaboration on African diamond mines with his old pal John Henry Riley.

Given his somber domestic circumstances, Twain exhibited moments of playfulness. He seemed delighted to be a father. In addition to the letter to the Twichells, Twain wrote another charming letter from the baby's point of view to Olivia's grandmother, Eunice Ford. "Baby Langdon" complained about ill-fitting clothes, overmedication, and lousy food. He called the intrusive Dr. Wright "the meanest looking white man I ever saw," and in contrast to the family pet, the baby felt abused by an unfair number of baths: "I never see them wash the cat."[41] Twain declined invitations to lecture, saying he was too busy singing lullabies. He announced that baby Langdon would soon begin the lecture circuit, speaking on "Milk."[42] Twain referred to himself as a wet nurse and sent two pencil drawings to Susan Crane of the baby sleeping. He joked to Joe Twichell that sometimes when he held young Langdon, he worried that "his loose head [would] fall off."[43] Twain looked forward to the only Christmas he would ever spend in Buffalo. He basked in the glow of his newly expanded family and called the Buffalo Christmas one of "unexampled magnificence."[44]

Oddly, though, if Twain had written a personalized Christmas card, his seasonal slogan might have read "Business First." That is exactly how Twain began a letter to a former publisher at the end of November, peevishly asking for the $400 royalty due him for his first book of stories, *The Celebrated Jumping Frog of Calaveras County*, and negotiating a buyback of the original set of printing plates.[45] He then turned right around and pestered Elisha Bliss to release a fresh volume of the same collection. Twain's dizzying array of business interests during the holiday time of 1870 spotlighted his skill at self-invention and marketing. He continued his futile effort to complete the California book (*Roughing It*) by the contractual deadline, routinely writing in his upstairs den from eleven in the morning until three in the afternoon, and averaging ten to twelve manuscript pages per day.

Twain even left his ailing wife and frail newborn son for a weeklong business trip to New York City in December. He met with another publisher to pitch his latest brainstorm, a whimsical pamphlet called *Mark Twain's (Burlesque) Autobiography and First Romance*. While in New York, he also got together with Charles Henry Webb to buy back the rights to *The Celebrated Jumping*

Frog of Calaveras County, saw Riley, and stopped by the *New York Tribune* to chat with old friends Whitelaw Reid and John Hay. Barely back in Buffalo, five days before Christmas, Twain signed a contract to write the book about a South Africa diamond mine rush. Twain insisted that the book proposal be kept secret because the unique literary venture was guaranteed to become a huge success. A day or two before Christmas, Twain endorsed a publisher's advance check for $1,500 to Riley and mailed it to him. He dreamed of producing two six-hundred-page books derived from Riley's diamond-mine adventures. Twain's euphoria about the deal died when Riley perished from blood poisoning in 1872. Twain's Scrooge-like, mercantilistic mindset in Buffalo during his family's troubled times at Christmas concocted one more book scheme, a collection of his sketches. This project, too, would be shelved.

Twain felt under pressure. He half-heartedly fulfilled his diminishing newspaper and magazine writing obligations. He dearly wanted to continue his big step toward becoming a full-time man of letters by completing the California book draft. He was bubbling over with schemes for other books. These career aspirations clashed with the dire health issues at home. He began to feel as if his ideal professional and private universes were collapsing. In December, using a metaphor borrowed from his disappointment when viewing Egypt's iconic treasures close up, Twain wrote journalist Warren Brigham that "work is piled on me in toppling pyramids now."[46] From October onward, most of his stories served double duty, appearing in both the *Express* and the *Galaxy*. His final contribution to the *Express* was published in January of 1871, six weeks before he left the city. Twain skipped his March 1871 Memoranda column in *Galaxy*, blaming "serious illness in the editor's family."[47] His final column in April announced his withdrawal from the magazine because for "the last eight months, with hardly an interval, I have had for my fellows and comrades, night and day, doctors and watchers of the sick," making humorous writing a "grisly grotesqueness."[48]

Twain was closing the door on this chapter of his writing career. In early December, the *Express* carried a poem called "Three Aces," by a Carl Byng, igniting a mild controversy. Thomas Bailey Aldrich of *Every Saturday* soon accused Twain of being the author and of plagiarizing Bret Harte. Ironically, Twain had recently chatted with John Hay about charges that Hay's first installment in his poetry collection *Pike County Ballads* was an imitation of Harte. In

January, Twain categorically denied writing "Three Aces." He maintained that the *Express* work of Carl Byng and another *Express* freelancer (who was writing under the pseudonym "Hy Slocum") had improperly been attributed to him.[49] A few years later, the man behind the Carl Byng pseudonym was revealed to be Frank M. Thorn, a writer, lawyer, and farmer from Orchard Park, New York, just south of Buffalo. Thorn also adopted the pen name "Frank Clive" and may well have been Hy Slocum, too.[50]

Another of Twain's last *Express* stories aimed yet again at a local public official, in this case, Buffalo's postmaster. His "Dogberry in Washington" compares the postmaster with Shakespeare's hapless civil servant in *Much Ado about Nothing*.[51] Twain objects to a new postal policy that significantly increased the cost of mailing "author's manuscripts," print-ready proof sheets. Twain criticized the Buffalo postmaster's strict interpretation of the ruling, which hiked Twain's mailing of *Galaxy* manuscripts to first class, which was a considerably higher fee. "Dogberry in Washington," apparently based on an actual conversation Twain had with Buffalo's postmaster, calls the postmaster a "well intending but misguided officer." Twain promises not to harass him or attack him physically, since Buffalo is too cultured and civilized a place for such behavior. Twain's animosity might have begun several days earlier, when his letter to Olivia's grandmother using baby Langdon's persona was temporarily lost and he contacted the postmaster about the problem. "Dogberry in Washington" was another mild revenge editorial on inept public employees, similar to his carping about Buffalo's streets commissioner in "Street Sprinkling" and his series of briefs mocking the city coroner. Most of Twain's remaining *Express* and *Galaxy* pieces were formulaic and unremarkable. "Running for Governor" and "My Watch—An Instructive Little Tale," in November and "The Facts in the Case of George Fisher, Deceased," in December are well-crafted humorous tales, but all are built on Twain's stale "climactic arrangement" comic framework. He faded away from the pages of the *Express* on January 29, 1871, with the uninspired "The Danger of Lying in Bed," which addresses the relative safety of rail travel, especially the record of the Erie Railroad, compared to domestic accidents. Twain did not bother to write a valedictory or formal goodbye to his loyal *Buffalo Express* readers.

By the start of 1871, the situation at home was worsening, if that was possible. Baby Langdon's health remained uncertain, and he cried constantly. For six days at the end of January, Olivia and a nurse took the baby to a wet nurse at Buffalo General Hospital, located a half mile away at Main and High Streets. It was founded in 1855 and had been designated as a US Army hospital during the Civil War, treating 864 sick and wounded Union soldiers over a two-year period.[52] Buffalo's Hospital of the Sisters of Charity was a stone's throw away from 472 Delaware, at the corner of Franklin and Virginia Streets. But Twain and Olivia may have balked at taking their infant to a Catholic institution. And their neighbor, Dr. Cornelius Cox Wyckoff, was a member of Buffalo General's medical staff. While sitting in a hospital waiting room as baby Langdon was fed, Olivia wrote a letter in pencil to her friend Alice Hooker Day. She described her frustration at not being up to nursing Langdon herself and his inability to accept baby food, which resulted in Dr. Wright's recommending a schedule of six daily trips to Buffalo General until the newly hired wet nurse could report to 472 Delaware for feedings. The days were long, with Olivia, the nurse, and the baby not returning home from the hospital until nighttime. Olivia wrote Day that Buffalo General was "about the forlornest place that ever you saw."[53] The baby's physical development was not encouraging: in addition to the crying, his muscle tone was unusually flaccid, his forehead was markedly narrow, high, and bony, and when he demanded to be picked up, he reached out with palms turned inward rather than outward.[54]

In early February, a weakened Olivia began running a fever and showing rose spots on her stomach. Dr. Wright recognized the symptoms as early signs of typhoid. Olivia experienced delirium, and Dr. Rachel Gleason from the Elmira Water Cure joined the cadre of physicians at 472 Delaware Street, staying for several weeks, as Twain and his wife began losing confidence in Dr. Wright.

One bright light was an agreement Twain struck with Olivia permitting him to smoke for two hours on Sunday afternoons—during his New York City trip, Twain had bragged of smoking "a week, day and night."[55] Another happy development was Olivia's sudden fondness for ale—as a tonic. Twain described her one afternoon as being "tight as a brick" and "unendurably slangy" in her speech.[56] Twain continued his isolation as "a bachelor up stairs"[57] in his den and left the administering of Olivia's "soothing-syrup" to the houseful of care-givers downstairs. Twain did, however, spend time with Olivia in her make-shift library bedroom playing cribbage and cutthroat euchre. During these dark times, a *Buffalo Express* office boy, James Brennan, recalled straw being spread on the street in front of Twain's house "to lessen the noises of passing vehicles."[58] Commissioner Doyle promised neighbors that police would enforce the driving speed on Delaware Street to a "moderate trot."[59]

Image 7.4. Buffalo General Hospital at Main and High Streets, circa 1858, where Olivia took baby Langdon to a wet nurse during January of 1871. (Image courtesy of Buffalo General Hospital/Kaleida Health.)

Twain sneaked away for a few days in January to attend the wedding of Mary Fairbanks's daughter in Cleveland and then again in February to Washington, DC, for a week. He lodged at the Ebbitt House with David Gray of the *Buffalo Daily Courier* and *Express* colleague J. N. Larned. On February 7, Twain posed for another photo portrait with Gray and George Alfred Townsend, a journalist, in Mathew B. Brady's studio.

In March, Twain admitted to Elisha Bliss that he had hardly written a page on his big California book in three months. Yet he told Orion that he still hoped to crank out two hundred manuscript pages a week and finish the book in the spring. However, anxiety over the baby and Olivia prevented Twain from

Image 7.5. A photograph of Twain with David Gray of Buffalo (*right*) and journalist George Alfred Townsend (*left*), taken in Mathew B. Brady's Washington, DC, studio in February 1871. (Image courtesy of the Buffalo State College Archives, *Courier-Express* Collection.)

concentrating on work. Instead, he focused on moving his family from Buffalo. Although Olivia was still "dangerously ill with typhoid fever,"[60] her delirium was decreasing, and by mid-March she had recovered her appetite. She was now able to leave bed for the short walk to a chair, where she could sit up for two hours at a time.[61] Encouraged by Olivia's progress, Twain put their wedding-gift house at 472 Delaware Street on the real-estate market and arranged to sell his one-third share of the *Express*. Twain, Olivia, the baby, and half their servants would move to Elmira for the rest of the spring and summer. Beginning with March 3 and continuing through the end of June, house-sale ads appeared in the *Express* and the *Daily Courier*. Twain insisted on an asking price of $25,000, which was $5,000 more than his father-in-law had paid. Instead, on September 23, they settled for a loss of $1,000, with Olivia holding a second mortgage for the buyer, Mary L. Smith. The *Express* sellout was even less favorable; Twain lost $10,000 in his sale to partner George Selkirk. Twain described his unpleasant final weeks of life in Buffalo as a "state of absolute frenzy," as being for weeks "buried under beetling Alps of trouble," and of feeling "half-crazy."[62] He wrote Bliss, confessing he was so stressed that "if that baby goes on crying 3 more hours this way I will butt my frantic brains out."[63] Years later, Twain recalled desperately seeking a change from the "horrors and distress" that had saturated their experience in Buffalo.[64]

FOR SALE—HOUSES.

472 DELAWARE AVENUE (THE RESI-
dence of S. L. Clemens, Esq.,) for sale, by
HUME & SANFORD, 16 West Swan st.   c3

Image 7.6. This house-sale ad was printed in the *Express* and *Buffalo Daily Courier* several times between March and June of 1871. Twain finally sold 472 Delaware in September, at a loss. (Image from the *Buffalo Express* and *Buffalo Daily Courier*, March–June 1871.)

Still, a pair of intriguing incongruities suggest that Twain was not quite ready to abandon social climbing in the city of Buffalo or his newspaper career. The first is that on January 7, 1871, he was elected to membership in the elite

Buffalo Club at the northeast corner of Chippewa and Delaware Streets, yet another social organization that Twain belonged to (along with the Young Men's Association and the Nameless Club). William G. Fargo, a close friend of David Gray, was the president of the Buffalo Club in 1871. Twain resigned his membership two months after leaving Buffalo.[65] The second odd indicator hints that Twain entertained a last-ditch rescue of his journalistic career in Buffalo. In January of 1871, he either invited John Hay to collaborate with him and David Gray to start up a new Buffalo newspaper, or he proposed that Hay help him reenergize the *Express* by joining him as a partner.[66] Hay was a close friend of both Twain and Gray—they "were as inseparable as the romantic Three Musketeers of Dumas"[67]—but he declined Twain's offer.

With Olivia and her bookkeeping skills temporarily out of commission, Twain sat down in early March to fill out their 1870 income tax forms on a worksheet to be filed before they left Buffalo. Using two colors of ink, he entered dollar amounts and crossed out others, claiming a salary of $1,200 with an additional income of $8,200, and a tax of $77.55 after deductions.[68] Before departing, they paid a modest city tax bill of $222.25. Nevertheless, Twain worked himself into a lather, using Western New York's "ruinous" tax structure as another reason to flee the area. He raged to Orion that "they would scorch us if we staid [*sic*] here."[69] Twain and Olivia hired a replacement wet nurse, their third, and started packing for Elmira. On Saturday, March 18, Olivia was carried out of 472 Delaware Street on a mattress and taken to Buffalo's train depot. By the end of the day, the family was settled in at the Langdon mansion in Elmira.

In little more than a year, 472 Delaware Street had transformed from palace to fortress to hospital ward. More importantly, Twain had transitioned from journalist to literary author. All he wanted to do was finish his California book in peace and quiet at Quarry Farm, his sister-in-law's country estate high above the city of Elmira: "I am going to shut myself up in a farm-house alone, on top of an Elmira hill, & write—on my book."[70] Twain's bitterness over the series of tragedies that befell his family was deflected onto Buffalo for the time being. Two weeks before moving, he wrote Riley that he had grown "at last to loathe Buffalo."[71]

Twain had no idea how connected to Buffalo he would be for the rest of his life.

EPILOGUE

THIS RENEWAL OF THE OLD TIMES

Mark Twain's first glimpse of Buffalo, New York, was in August of 1853 as a seventeen-year-old. His last visit to Buffalo was in July of 1895, when he was in his sixtieth year. In between, he was in the city on business or pleasure over a dozen times. And during the final fifteen years of his life, he remained tethered to Buffalo socially and as a property owner. Twain turned down several formal requests to speak in Buffalo over the years, accepting only one lecture invitation and delivering an impromptu public talk on another occasion. Many of the friendships he made when he lived and worked in Buffalo endured for his entire life. Twain also showed a knack for connecting with members of Buffalo's influential, moneyed class in the years after he moved from the city.

One would think that Twain's stopover in Buffalo in 1895 would have represented the triumphal return of America's literary lion. By this time in his career, he had achieved the goal he had set for himself as a young newspaper editor in Buffalo twenty-five years earlier—to become a highly respected author and literary figure. He was beloved around the world as a novelist and a speaker. *Roughing It*, *The Adventures of Tom Sawyer*, *Adventures of Huckleberry Finn*, *The Prince and the Pauper*, and *A Connecticut Yankee in King Arthur's Court* were well on their way to becoming classic works of literature. Unfortunately, upon his return, Twain literally and figuratively limped into town on Monday, July 15, 1895.

He had accumulated a staggering personal debt in the range of $100,000. Just a couple of days before Twain arrived in Buffalo, the *New York Times* had published a humiliating account, reprinted in the *Buffalo Express*, of a hearing in New York City in which lawyers examined a hefty debt to a printing company owed by Twain's failed publishing firm. The subheadline scornfully called the famed humorist "a big, overgrown boy in matters of business," and the story depicted him as ailing and slightly dotty.[1] Twain's reputation was not the only thing taking a beating. He was suffering from an attack of gout and a nasty carbuncle. Nevertheless, he, Olivia, and their daughter Clara took a train from Elmira to Buffalo. After a layover of a few hours, they were to connect with a train to Cleveland, where they would board a ship across the Great Lakes that would launch a yearlong worldwide speaking tour aimed (successfully, as it turned out) at digging the family out of debt.

Twain spent his few hours in Buffalo profitably. His old Buffalo friend Charles M. Underhill met him at the Buffalo train depot in a carriage probably supplied by Norwood stables. By 1895, Underhill was the western sales agent for the J. Langdon and Company coal business. He dropped Olivia and Clara at his 849 Delaware Avenue (by this time, the name had changed to Delaware Avenue) home for a reunion with his wife, Anna. En route, they likely made a bittersweet pass by the old Twain homestead on Delaware, which once again had served as a wedding gift—this time for Samuel S. Spaulding and his wife (in a twist of fate, their daughter Charlotte, who grew up at 472 Delaware, later married Langdon Albright, the son of Olivia's cousin Hattie, a Buffalo resident). Twain was just a few weeks too late to see his old *Express* building; it had been demolished in May, along with all the other buildings on the block, to make way for construction of the modern Ellicott Square Building. The *Express* offices had moved from East Swan to 179 Washington Street in 1879 anyway. Twain's former *Express* partners were likely unavailable for a pop-in chat. Colonel George Selkirk was now treasurer of Buffalo's Park Department. Josephus N. Larned had become superintendent of the Buffalo Library. Twain's other ex-newspaper chum, David Gray of the *Buffalo Daily Courier*, had been dead for seven years. Twain and Underhill killed time together with a quiet drive through Forest Lawn Cemetery. Twain had asked Underhill to take him to the Blocher family memorial, an ornate monument installed in 1888 and made out of 150 tons of stone at a cost of $100,000, with three life-sized white marble figures of the John Blocher family enclosed in glass. Although thousands of visitors were attracted annually to the Blocher monument, Twain was disappointed. Underhill later recalled that Twain had hoped to use the famous memorial site for an article in his correspondence, but the Blocher monument "did not stir him."[2] On that note, Twain ended his last visit to Buffalo.

Charles M. Underhill and his family were among Twain's dearest friends. Twain's playful nickname for Underhill was "Dombrowski," stemming from an incident in the early 1870s. In New York together for a coal meeting that was delayed, Twain, Underhill, and John D. F. Slee passed the time by playing cards. Twain suggested a game known as "sixty-six," and prepared to play "Wild West" style by taking off his shoes and socks. After hours of watching Underhill win hands, Twain inelegantly called him the worst name he could think of: "You're a—Dombrowski!" Jan Dabrowski was a Polish general who organized the Polish legions in the French army to serve Napoleon, and Twain had a long-standing dislike of the French.[3]

When nearby, Twain would stop in at the Underhills in Buffalo, and Twain sometimes combined social calls to Buffalo with business. Sometime around 1889, Underhill accompanied Twain across the border to Niagara Falls, Canada, in order to confirm that Twain was properly on British soil in securing a legal British copyright for *A Connecticut Yankee in King Arthur's Court*.[4] Another visit was in June of 1886 when Twain, Olivia, their three daughters, and their governess were headed to Duluth, Minnesota, on a five-day Great Lakes plea-sure voyage. They registered at the Cataract House in Niagara Falls and dined at the Underhill home along with David and Mattie Gray.[5] On Tuesday, June 22, when Twain and his family sailed from Buffalo for Duluth on the steamer *India*, many friends—the Underhills undoubtedly among them—were at the dock to wish them bon voyage. Twain lit up a cigar and could not resist a crack right out of *The Innocents Abroad*: "Mr. Clemens said as he saw no signs of "Keep off the grass" or "No smoking," on board that he was certain of a good time."[6]

Twain also became close with Underhill's son, Irving, who was only four years old when Twain lived in Buffalo. As young Irving grew into adulthood, he felt comfortable about approaching Twain in 1893 with an idea he had to publish a collection of stories about Niagara Falls. For a fee of $1,000, Twain agreed to contribute a manuscript he happened to be working on, "Extracts from Adam's Diary," by promising to insert new paragraphs that would locate the Garden of Eden in Niagara Falls. Twain sent the manuscript to Irving in Buffalo, care of Charles Underhill, with this humorous address scrawled on a large blue envelope.

For

Mr. C. M. Underhill, who is in the coal business in one of those streets there, & is very respectably connected, both by marriage and general descent, & is a tall man & old but without any gray hair & used to be handsome.

Buffalo, N.Y.

P.S. — A little bald on top of his head.

From Mark Twain.[7]

Image E.1. The 849 Delaware home of Charles M. Underhill and his wife, Anna. Twain and Olivia stayed there overnight and visited there a few times on return visits to Buffalo. (Image courtesy of the Buffalo State College Archives, *Courier-Express* Collection.)

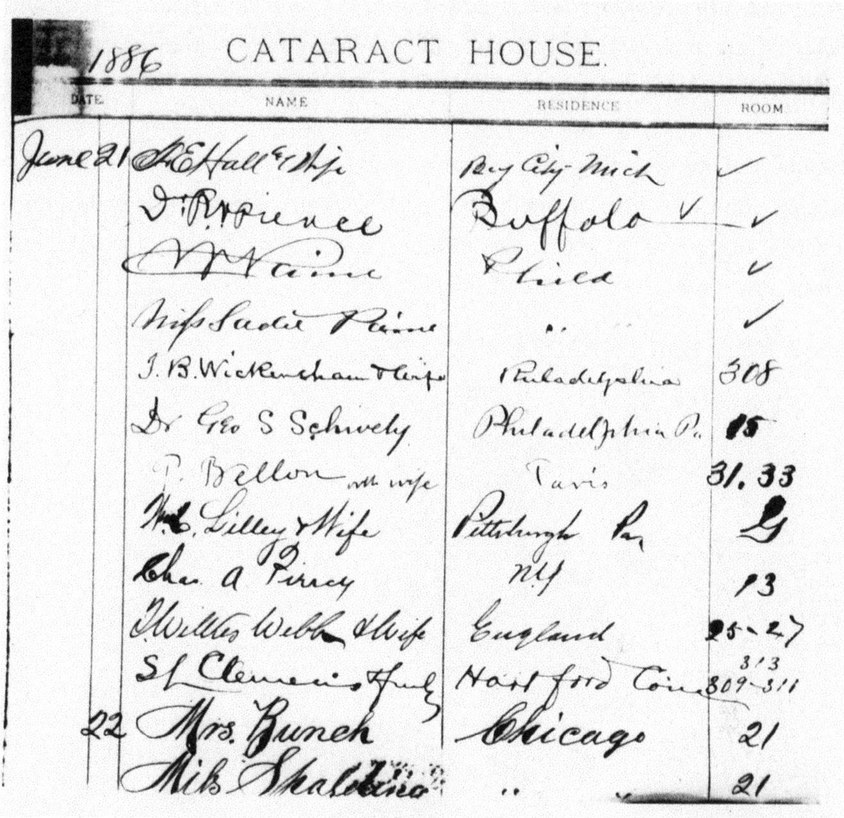

Image E.2. Register for the Cataract House Hotel in Niagara Falls, NY, where Twain signed in his family as "S. L. Clemens & Family" during a visit to Buffalo on June 21, 1886. (Image courtesy of the Local History Department, Niagara Falls (NY) Public Library.)

Twain also sent a separate letter to Charles M. Underhill, addressing it "Dear Dombrowski," informing him that he had forwarded the story, asking that his son, Irving, send the check to Elmira, and offering to "reteach" him "the uncertain game of Sixty-six" sometime soon.[8] Irving Underhill sent Twain $500 when he received "Adam's Diary." The story, eventually titled "Extracts from Adam's Diary Translated from the Original MS. By Mark Twain, the First Authentic Mention of Niagara Falls," appeared in young Underhill's *The Niagara Book* in 1893. Intended as a souvenir book promoting Niagara Falls to tourists, *The Niagara Book* included essays by William Dean Howells and Peter Porter. But Twain's charming tale was the centerpiece. In it, Eve puts a damper on Adam's fun by halting his joy rides over the Falls and his bathing in the rapids because they damage his fig-leaf suit. *The Niagara Book* was a commercial failure, selling only four thousand of the twenty-five thousand first-edition copies. In May of 1900, Twain and Irving Underhill met in London, where Irving agonized over his remaining $500 debt to Twain. A sympathetic Twain graciously absolved him of the payment.[9]

Image E.3. Irving S. Underhill, son of Charles M. Underhill. In 1893, Twain contributed a story for Irving's book about Niagara Falls. (Image courtesy of Charles S. Underhill.)

Buffalo's Pan-American Exposition of 1901 breathed new life into *The Niagara Book*. Doubleday, Page and Company reissued the book in 1901 with new wrinkles aimed at the Pan-Am market. Irving Underhill retained the copyright for the new edition and corresponded with Twain about it. Twain made minor revisions to the 1893 version of "Adam's Diary"—adding three words and deleting sixty-two from the original—and sought reassurance that Doubleday would send him the proofs to read. The new *Niagara Book* was released in time for the exposition. It also featured an additional section written by Irving Underhill describing the city of Buffalo and the exposition attractions.[10]

As much as Twain valued his continued friendship with Charles M. Underhill of Buffalo, David Gray of the *Buffalo Daily Courier* remained his treasured soul mate. Twain was close to Gray when the former lived in Buffalo and ever afterward. Twain appreciated Gray's feedback on the beginning phases of *Roughing It*, and in August of 1875, Gray commented favorably on Twain's early experiments with the vernacular fictional voice of his Huckleberry Finn character.[11] Gray also wrote Twain that he enjoyed reading the privately circulated *1601*. Twain dined with Gray or stayed overnight at his Buffalo homes on Mohawk Street, West Utica Street, or 77 Park Place (parallel to Delaware Avenue, one block west of Twain's former address) frequently in the 1870s and 1880s. And in August of 1876, Gray and Mattie visited Twain and Olivia in Elmira. Gray was on Twain's list to receive complimentary copies of *The Prince and the Pauper* and *Adventures of Huckleberry Finn* when they were first released. In 1880, Twain once again assisted a charitable function sponsored by Mattie Gray (in 1870 he had lectured in Buffalo at her request to benefit the Grand Army of the Republic [GAR]) by contributing a sketch, "A Tale: For Struggling Young Poets," to *Bazaar Bulletin*, a publication edited by Mrs. Gray and Mrs. J. B. Parke for the Buffalo Homeopathic Fair.[12] After Gray's death in 1888 at the age of fifty-one, Charles M. Underhill wrote Twain about J. N. Larned's plans to publish Gray's biography and collected works in two volumes. Twain sent Underhill a check to help underwrite that effort, and Underhill delivered the check to Larned.[13] Gray's volumes were part of Twain's personal library, inscribed by Twain in 1888.[14] In a mystery story, "A Murder, A Mystery, and A Marriage," conceived by Twain in 1876 but not published until 2001, Twain used Gray's name as an inside joke. The character "David Gray" was mean, whereas the real-life David Gray was kind and sweet natured.

In 1906, Twain bumped into Gray's son, David Jr., at a dinner party in New York City. The encounter brought to mind pleasant memories with the elder Gray during Twain's Buffalo period—such as imbibing together at local saloons and their mutual friendship with John Hay. However, when Twain reflected on

Gray's newspaper career, he grieved over Gray's "wasted" life as a poet imprisoned by the demands of newspaper work. It was as though Twain's moving epitaph for Gray could have been applied to Twain himself. Had Twain not made the fateful, transformative escape from the cage of journalism while in Buffalo, he, too, may have been doomed to suffer the same fate as David Gray Jr.'s father: "His father was a poet, but was doomed to grind out his living in a most uncongenial occupation—the editing of a daily political newspaper. He was a singing bird in a menagerie of monkeys, macaws, and hyenas. His life was wasted."[15]

While in town to give the only public lecture he ever delivered in Buffalo after he had moved away, Twain lunched with David Gray Sr. before the evening's talk. He enjoyed Gray's company, but not the lunch. He was in town in 1884 as part of his "Twins of Genius" lecture tour with Southern writer George Washington Cable. Ticket sales at Kuhn and Company music store were brisk, and the joint readings in December at Buffalo's Concert Hall on Main Street at the corner of Edward Street, went well despite the banging steam pipes.[16] Twain told the crowd that he planned to tell a ghost story, but not the one about Buffalo's old North Street Cemetery (the one published in the *Express* in 1870 as "A Curious Dream") that had been advertised that day in the *Buffalo Times*.[17] He also detoured from his prepared talk on Huck Finn to share memories of living in Buffalo. He told the audience about his surprise wedding-gift house. Then he scanned the delighted audience in vain for missing Buffalo friends before assuming that they "had gone, gone to the tomb, to the gallows, or to the White House."[18] But the noon lunch engagement with Cable and Gray went badly. Twain had to send his undercooked beefsteak back. While famished and awaiting the recooked meat entree, Twain drank two cups of strong coffee that gave him acid indigestion and interfered with his prelecture nap back at the hotel room. Twain's rare public event in Buffalo ended unpleasantly, too, with one of his nightmarish on-the-road postlecture parties hosted by an earnest local social club.

Cable and Twain had accepted an invitation by George W. Wheeler, a charter member of Buffalo's Thursday Club, to attend a soirée in their honor after their evening lectures. They expected a modest get-together of three or four gentlemen. What the thoroughly exhausted Twain and Cable got was a lavish reception taking up the massive library, dining room, and conservatory at the 506 Delaware Avenue mansion of wealthy industrialist Chelion M. Farrar. Two long tables were elaborately decorated with "pyramids of flowers and fruit with sparkling crystal."[19] In the center of the head table, where the two guests of honor sat, there was "a tall floral pyramid bearing the words 'Mark Twain and Cable' in crimson immortelles against a background of white carnations, above which were spiral wreaths of white roses, geraniums, chrysanthemums and mignonette."[20] Although Farrar had spared no expense to entertain his famous literary guests, Twain was tired and cranky. The gentlemanly Cable wrote his wife that he and Twain had "accepted too much pleasant attention in Buffalo."[21] But the ever-irascible Twain sneered to Olivia that they had suffered a reception by "the Hartford Club of Buffalo (so to speak) 25 gentlemen & half a dozen ladies."[22] Twain griped about the "clatter" and told Olivia that he refused to eat during "2 of the infernalest weariest hours that ever fell my lot." His rude behavior did not go unnoticed. One Thursday Club member, George W. Benson, remembered that Twain, decked out in a white suit, "never cracked a joke" and made dull conversation, talking "about rather commonplace things in an ordinary way."[23] Interestingly, a year earlier, in 1883, without knowing anything about the Thursday Club, Twain had declined Benson's invitation to speak at the group's banquet in Buffalo celebrating the one hundredth anniversary of Washington Irving's birth. Twain sent a handwritten regret to Benson from his home in Hartford, saying that he had "a house full of sick people, & must put in all my time as a nurse."[24]

Twain was in town in September of 1874 for the debut of his stage version of *The Gilded Age*, the popular novel he had written with his Hartford neighbor Charles Dudley Warner. It opened with a two-night engagement in Buffalo before moving on to New York City. The production premiered with Buffalo-born actor John T. Raymond as Colonel Sellers at Buffalo's Academy of Music, located at 245–249 Main Street. Twain sat in a private box enjoying the audience's enthusiastic response. After the fourth act, Twain was coaxed to stand up and address the crowd. When he seemed to choke up, the audience applauded. Twain then continued to joke about the challenge of being present at the debut of one's own play: "I sincerely hope none of you will ever write a play to be produced on the opening night. When a play is produced upon the opening night, the effect upon the author is almost too much for him to stand; on any other night he can bear it much more easily and comfortably."[25] Twain's impromptu speech was punctuated by laughter and applause.

Image E.4. The Chelion M. Farrar mansion at 506 Delaware Avenue, where Twain and George Washington Cable endured a postlecture reception in December of 1884 sponsored by Buffalo's Thursday Club. (Image by Lucas Reigstad.)

Twain's lecture with Cable in Buffalo and his brief public talk at *The Gilded Age* were exceptions. His 1883 rejection of Benson's lecture invitation was the rule. Six months after moving from Buffalo, Twain vehemently insisted that his lecture agent, James Redpath, release him from a GAR-sponsored lecture date in Buffalo for the 1871–1872 season. Twain's friend and former *Express* partner J. N. Larned probably held the rejection record, though. In the 1870s, Twain twice said no to lecture invitations by Larned on behalf of the Young Men's Association (of which Twain was a former member). And in 1900, Twain again turned down a request by Larned, this time representing the Buffalo Public Library (as the Buffalo Library came to be known), to lecture there. Twain's reply was collegial, remembering Larned affectionately after all those years and expressing delight at rekindling fond memories of their tenure together in Buffalo at the *Express*: "It has been a real pleasure to me to have this renewal of the old times with you."[26] In

1902, Twain logged a recent gift added to his personal library—that is, Larned's newly published mouthful, *The Literature of American History: A Bibliographical Guide, in Which the Scope, Character, and Comparative Worth of Books in Selected Lists Are Set Forth in Brief Notes by Critics of Authority*.[27]

Larned's friendship was instrumental in Twain's decision to donate his handwritten manuscript of *Adventures of Huckleberry Finn* to the Buffalo Library in 1885. It also provided an opportunity for Twain to cultivate a relationship with one of Buffalo's up-and-coming power brokers. On November 7, 1885, James Fraser Gluck wrote a two-and-a-half-page typed letter to Twain in Hartford; the note was written on Buffalo's Young Men's Association stationery. As a curator of the association, Gluck requested that Twain present an original manuscript or two to the association's library as part of a growing collection of author manuscripts they were amassing. He dropped Larned's name to personalize his appeal. Gluck, who belonged to a prominent Niagara Falls family, had graduated at the top of his class at Cornell University in 1874 and was ten years later a brilliant attorney and partner with the Buffalo firm of Greene, McMillan, and Gluck, specializing in big-name railroad-corporation cases. One week after his request, Gluck thanked Twain for sending the holograph manuscript of *Adventures of Huckleberry Finn* for permanent public display in Buffalo's library, a condition which lasts to this day.[28]

Other ties that Twain forged with Buffalo's late nineteenth-century titans of industry after moving from the city were related to Olivia's wealthy cousins. In 1874, Twain and Phineas T. Barnum cooked up a publicity stunt to capitalize on America's fascination with the spectacular comet Coy Coggia, whose brilliance was lighting up the summer skies. In a joint venture, Twain and Barnum purported to have "chartered" the comet for a pleasure trip to Mars and the constellations at the reasonable passenger rate of two dollars per every 50 million miles. Twain announced his fantasy excursion in early July in the *New York Sun*. He promised to give New York and federal government officials extra time to inspect Saturn's rings. The whimsical story also appeared in the *Buffalo Morning Express* and the *Buffalo Daily Courier*.

Shortly afterward, Twain wrote an engaging letter to Joseph J. Albright, a coal baron from Scranton, Pennsylvania, guaranteeing a round-trip ticket on the comet as a special offer to eliminate competition with his wife's coal business.[29] Albright was the father-in-law of Harriet "Hattie" M. Langdon Albright, Olivia's first cousin, who had married Albright's son John J. Albright in 1872. Presumably, Twain met the Albrights at Langdon family functions. After moving to Buffalo in 1883, the younger Albright became one of the city's most prominent industrialists and philanthropists, known chiefly for donating over $1,000,000 to build what is now the Albright-Knox Art Gallery. Albright was in the coal and iron businesses but also invested in a Washington, DC, asphalt firm owned by the husband of his wife's sister, Julia Langdon Barber (also Olivia's cousin). By 1896, Barber Asphalt Paving Company was credited with laying half the pavement in the United States. It is no coincidence that Buffalo was the second city after Washington to have its streets paved with asphalt.[30] Early in his career, John J. Albright had partnered with Hattie's brother, Andrew Langdon, in the coal and iron industries. Langdon, too, through his coal interests, became one of Buffalo's most wealthy men and a leader in banking, philanthropy, and civic affairs. For reasons still unclear, Twain bitterly attacked Andrew Langdon in a story, "Letter from the Recording Angel," written around 1887 but not published until 1946. Twain's letter is a savage satire accusing Langdon of being a miserly, cold-hearted, hypocritical capitalist from Buffalo.[31] Twain describes Langdon as an evil coal merchant who prays publicly for a mild winter that would reduce heating bills for poor Buffalonians, but who privately hopes for harsh weather so he can hike coal costs. When Twain's son, Langdon, was first born in Buffalo in 1870, he had jokingly used the baby's voice to criticize the attending physician as "the meanest looking white man I ever saw."[32] But in "Recording Angel," Twain used the same phrase caustically, saying that Buffalo's Andrew Langdon wielded "the greedy grip of the meanest white man that ever lived on the face of the earth."[33] Almost certainly, neither Olivia nor her cousin Andrew was ever aware of Twain's private rant on the Langdon family's coal wealth (though Andrew Langdon's business was a separate enterprise from the J. Langdon and Company firm). In fact, Twain wrote two cordial letters to Andrew Langdon in the early 1900s.

Another Buffalo coal magnate with whom Twain continued to keep in touch was one of his first friends when he came to Buffalo, John J. "Mac" McWilliams. Mac had come a long way since he and his wife boarded with Twain in 1869 when he was just a clerk in Jervis Langdon's Buffalo coal company office. By the

1890s, McWilliams was a prosperous western sales agent for the D. L. and W. Railroad Company coal department. On behalf of his company, he donated ten tons of coal to Buffalo's poor in 1894.[34] He was a member of Buffalo's powerful Grade Crossing Commission, and he served as director of the Buffalo Historical Society and as president of the Chamber of Commerce. After retiring from his railroad-coal post, McWilliams was president of Niagara Lithograph Company. At the time of his death in 1912, he was considered "one of Buffalo's leading businessmen."[35] One indication of Twain's high regard for McWilliams is that upon the death of Olivia's mother in 1891, the eulogy delivered by Rev. Thomas Beecher in Elmira's Park Church was transmitted by an experimental technological device through long distance directly to the telephone at the home of the McWilliamses on Buffalo's fashionable Linwood Avenue.[36] And just as he had fictionalized David Gray's name, Twain used the surname of John and Esther McWilliams for his three domestic short-story comedies published in the 1870s and 1880s, "Experience of the McWilliamses with Membranous Croup," "Mrs. McWilliams and the Lightning," and "The McWilliamses and the Burglar Alarm."

Then there was Twain's close association with George Urban Jr., scion of a pioneering family in Buffalo's flour-milling industry. In 1870, Urban became a partner in his father's thriving mills, which eleven years later were the first to be electrified. Urban sponsored the installation of the first electric streetlights in Buffalo on lower Ganson Street, and he early on explored hydroelectric power at Niagara Falls. He counted as friends David Gray, Thomas Edison, President William McKinley, and Grover Cleveland. Urban had known Cleveland through the flour mills and restaurants of Buffalo's Black Rock neighborhood. It is said that Cleveland's presidential ambitions were launched during a clambake at Urban's eight-acre estate at Pine Hill just east of Buffalo's city limits.

One of Urban's avocations was botany, and his home featured hundreds of elm trees, fine shrubs, extensive flower gardens, and his famous Urban bantam corn. In the 1900s, while wintering in Bermuda along with Henry Huttleson Rogers and Twain, he spotted green roses growing on the hotel's grounds. He cut some blooms, scented them with violet perfume, and gave them to Twain. After letting a dazzled Twain show off the miraculously colored and scented roses to friends, Urban finally informed him of the hoax, whereupon "Twain was so provoked that the joke had been on him that he wanted to throw [Urban] out of the hotel."[37] On another of Urban's frequent vacations to Bermuda, he gave Twain his first long black cigar, which Twain enjoyed so much that he bought a barrelful immediately.[38]

Perhaps Twain's most poignant continuing brush with Buffalo's upper crust was sometime around 1872 after their sickly first born, Langdon, died in Hartford of diphtheria. Langdon was not quite nineteen months of age. Before his burial, a plaster death mask was cast, which Olivia kept protected secretly in a green box in the closet of their study. Sometime in late 1872, Twain and Olivia commissioned a plaster bust of Langdon to be fashioned from the death mask. They hired a renowned thirty-year-old Buffalo artist and sculptor, Augusta Caroline Moore Graves, to model Langdon's bust.[39] Graves's work was much admired by famed American sculptor Augustus Saint Gaudens. Olivia and Twain may have met Graves when they lived in Buffalo. Or Graves may have been recommended by New York City artist Joseph Graef, or Twain's former *Buffalo Express* partner George Selkirk.

As evidence of the three degrees of separation that interlocked Buffalo's high society and Twain's contacts with it, Twain's former *Buffalo Express* partner George Selkirk had sculpted a bust of Gen. John Card Graves, Augusta's husband. David Gray's son, David Jr., wrote and illustrated a poem commemorating the Graves's golden wedding anniversary. Augusta Graves sculpted a bust of George Matthews's wealthy father-in-law. When Twain first arrived in Buffalo in 1869 as a bachelor co-owner of the *Express*, George Matthews was a young clerk and acquaintance living in the same boardinghouse. He went on to acquire a multimillion-dollar fortune in Buffalo's flour-milling industry. General Graves donated Selkirk's sculpted bust of Twain's friend Rev. John C. Lord to the Buffalo Historical Society. General Graves, whose military rank came from the National Guard, accumulated his wealth through his insurance company and other ventures. He and Augusta Graves raised their family in a spectacular mansion known as "the Lilacs" on Buffalo's Chapin Parkway, where she worked in a roomy upstairs studio with a skylight.[40]

A final enduring link between Twain and Western New York was the land itself. For years, Twain frequently took the two-hour, forty-five-mile ride on the Lake Shore and Michigan Southern Railway Line southwest from Buffalo to Dunkirk, New York, and then the brief horse-car trip into Fredonia to visit his mother and sister. After his sister Pamela Moffett bought a cottage at Van Buren Point, a scenic spot outside Fredonia on the shore of Lake Erie, Twain and Olivia admired it so much that they purchased an adjoining lot in 1879 for $115. However, they never built on the site and sold the land three years later for $200.[41] While Jervis Langdon's estate was being sorted out after his death in 1870, Twain and Olivia also briefly co-owned land encompassing Hospital Street and Rock Street, in Buffalo's Black Rock district.

Twain's Buffalo experience seemed to come full circle, however, with the coal-yard property at the foot of Buffalo's Genesee Street that belonged to the Langdon coal company for more than forty years. Twain first toured the plot with his future father-in-law during their swing into Niagara Falls and Buffalo in late July of 1869. The valuable parcel faced Lake Erie and backed up toward the Erie Canal, with railroad tracks running through it and a convenient shipping slip along one side—an ideal commercial location at the hub of Buffalo's iconic waterfront. The Langdon coal company site occupied parts of outer lots twelve and fourteen in Buffalo's Eighth Ward, bounded on the northwest by Genesee Street for 210 feet, on the southwest by the Lake Erie Basin for 207½ feet, on the southeast by the Erie Slip (also known as Slip No. 2) for 258 feet, and on the northeast by land of the New York Central Railroad Company for 201¾ feet.[42] Strategically positioned as part of Buffalo's complex inland port, the Langdon land had a view of the western terminus of the Erie Canal and the confluence of the Buffalo River into the Niagara River as it merged into Lake Erie—the geographical heart of Buffalo's origin. It was a waterway that Twain had enjoyed as a swimmer and as a boater during his bachelor days editing the *Buffalo Express*. After Olivia died in June of 1904, Twain inherited her share of the old Langdon coal company real estate. By that time, the firm had dissolved its Buffalo interests and was renting the property, looking to sell. Nevertheless, for the final six years of Twain's life, he had a stake in a vital piece of Buffalo's real estate—one-third ownership of his former benefactor's valuable waterfront plot. His brother-in-law Charley handled the paperwork, sending statements, checks, and billing information to Twain's addresses in Redding, Connecticut, and in Dublin, New Hampshire, during those six years. Generally, the rental income did not equal the amount of money they paid on county and city taxes. In 1905, for example, Twain received a check for over $100 for his share of the rent, but he had to pay city and county taxes exceeding $300, a pattern that continued until Twain died in April of 1910.[43] A month later, Charley Langdon finally sold the Langdon coal company waterfront lot.

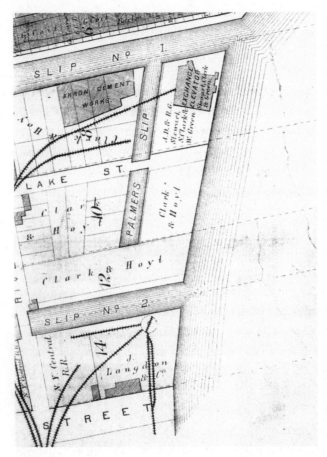

Image E.5 The property of J. Langdon and Company, the Elmira-based coal firm owned by Twain's in-laws, at the foot of Genesee Street on Buffalo's waterfront, can be seen in the left-hand quadrant of this map. Twain co-owned this land the last six years of his life, from 1904 until 1910. (Image from *Atlas of the City of Buffalo* [Philadelphia: G. M. Hopkins, 1872].)

It might be said that Twain's stewardship of valuable family land in Buffalo late in his life occasionally reminded him of the positive turn his writing career had taken in the booming city decades earlier. Although in March of 1871 he moved his family from Buffalo and abandoned journalism and the *Buffalo Express*, he did not turn his back on the city or its people. Whatever animosity Twain felt about his Buffalo experience was apparently short-lived. In opening his mail from Charley Langdon during the final six years of his life to scour account statements, sign rental checks, and respond to tax bills on the Langdon coal land that he now co-owned, Mark Twain might have at times paused to almost again feel the cool, southwesterly breezes sweeping in across the city off Lake Erie. He may have pictured the swirling snowflakes and white blanket that covered his storybook wedding house the first two months of his marriage. He might have relived the tense, overcast November skies that ushered in his first child. He may even have heard whispering from ghosts—friends and colleagues—of Buffalo's past calling to him from Forest Lawn Cemetery and other hallowed grounds. If he had these thoughts, he may have remembered Buffalo affectionately as the place where he decided to stop writing for newspapers and start writing books.

Image E.6. A view of the vicinity around J. Langdon and Company's waterfront lot, which Twain co-owned, collected rent from, and paid taxes on late in his life. The Langdon property is the strip of land toward the top right. (Image courtesy of the Lower Lakes Marine Historical Society.)

APPENDIX 1

NIAGARA FALLS GAZETTE

August 25, 1869

FOR THE *GAZETTE*

MARK TWAIN AND NIAGARA

Mark Twain hath spoken. The mountain hath heaved and opened, and the mouse hath come forth.

Mark Twain, the Great, the Wise, the Witty, has introduced himself to the people of Western New York—and the country generally by giving to us once more, in the Buffalo *Express* of last Saturday, the old, old, old worn out story, "A Visit to Niagara."

What week, or even day, can we pick up a paper without seeing a paragraph written by some ignorant penny-a-liner who, by getting a pass on the Railroad, and with hardly money enough in his pocket to get a meal at a restaurant, finds himself at Niagara. As a matter of course he must write home to let the world (which he thinks watches his every movement) know he has been to the Falls. He must know his little piece, and not having the ability to write a good and interesting description of one of the grandest and most awe-inspiring scenes on the face of the earth, he does the best his poor weak brain is capable of, and goes on to abuse the boot blacks, condemns the unfortunate hackmen who charge the (to him) enormous sum of one dollar per hour, indulges in dishwater wit at the expense of a few poor Indians, and gets off stupid jokes of which not even he himself can see the point. And, hark you! Mark Twain; there may be more truth than poetry in what you say about thriving beadwork thrown at your head. You would not be the first ninny who came to grief by insulting the squaws on Goat Island. God help thee! Poor Niagara, it is indeed hard that thou art made the butt for the namby pamby wit and spewings from the addled brain of every little newspaper scribbler who, for a short time, has escaped from his legitimate business—reporting court cases and street-rows.

B

APPENDIX 2

BUFFALO MORNING EXPRESS

August 27, 1869

IN TROUBLE

"The following telegram explains itself:

NIAGARA FALLS, Aug. 26

"To the Editor of the Express:

"I borrowed Jenkins' velocipede and tried the slack rope performance over Niagara, but it is only a partial success. I have got to the middle, two hundred and twenty feet above the river, as well as Jenkins or any other man could do it, but I cannot get any farther. I stopped like that other ass to have my picture taken, and I can't get her started again. I cannot back up or go ahead. I have been roosting between heaven and earth for a matter of eighteen hours now. My position is exceedingly ridiculous, not to say uncomfortable. Near-sighted English sportsmen are practicing on me with shot-guns and such things because they take me for some sort of a curious bird—and I am—I am a rooster. They have torn my clothes a good deal. How am I going to get out of this? I have been suspended long enough—I wish to suspend the exhibition for a while, now. But if this thing is going to be permanent, please send me an umbrella. It is warm here.

—P.S.—Does my salary go on? Because I was instructed to try this atrocious experiment by one of the EXPRESS firm. He said it would be a good card for the paper if I succeeded—but this wretched thing won't budge, you understand. I was to have been married to-day. I wish I was out of this.

"Yours, in great suspense,
"MICHAEL MURPHY,"
"Reporter, EXPRESS"

APPENDIX 3

BUFFALO MORNING EXPRESS

September 9, 1869

MARK TWAIN IN A FIX

Rochester Express says that it wasn't Michael J. Murphy, but Mark Twain himself who met with such a misadventure on Prof. Jenkins' rope at Niagara the other day. It tells the story this way:

"Twain started; he arrived at Niagara; he footed it from the depot to the American end of the tight rope; he dead-headed it as a member of the press. He went to the hotel before Jenkins crossed the rope, and took his dinner. With amazement the waiter watched him, as he sat on a chair, and dangling his legs, swung them continuously, so as to shake down and enable him to absorb a greater quantity of fodder. When Jenkins had successfully crossed on his veloci-pede, Twain watched and examined the odd-shaped machine. It seemed easy to cross, and so when the Professor left the machine upon the rope and went to the house, Twain mounted and shot out upon the tightened strand. All went on handsomely. The crowd about dispersing, reassembled, and thought they were to receive another installment of pay for the money deposited. When the centre of the rope was reached, Mark Twain was unable either to recede or advance. The rope ran up at an angle of twenty-five degrees either way, and it was abso-lutely impossible for him to move his Pegasus. The suit of the daring rider was of spotless white duck. When the crowd observed his dilemma, there was a con-

tinuous cheer and waving of handkerchiefs. Mark Twain shook his fist menac-
ingly at the vast assemblage, and again a tumultuous shout rent the very air. At
this time a very heavy thunder shower came up and drove the people to cover,
but Mark was exposed to the fury of the elements. By a frantic effort he managed
to move the machine about a foot, but tore his trousers' leg the whole length,
and blackened both of them from the tar used to promote friction between the
wheels and the rope. The wind carried away his hat, and in the war of the elements he became a pitiful object, as he desperately held on to the rope. When
the storm ceased, Professor Jenkins so contrived by sending out a rope fastened
to an iron ring, that he was drawn in."

APPENDIX 4

SIX ILLUSTRATIONS BY JOHN HARRISON MILLS

Mills created a total of six illustrations for four Saturday feature stories that would appear between August 21 and September 18, 1869. Each of the four illustrated stories was placed on the front page of the *Buffalo Morning Express*.

"GOT A MATCH?"

Image A4.1. Original caption: "Got a match?" This John Harris Mills illustration accompanied Twain's "A Day at Niagara" in the *Express* of August 21, 1869. The newspaper staff artist's signature appears in the lower right-hand corner. (Image from the *Buffalo Morning Express*, August 21, 1869.)

THE CHILD OF THE FOREST.

Image A4.2. Original caption: "The child of the forest." Another Mills illustration accompanying "A Day at Niagara." (Image from the *Buffalo Morning Express*, August 21, 1869.)

NIAGARA AS A BACKGROUND.

Image A4.3. Original caption: "Niagara as a background." A signed (lower left-hand corner) illustration by Mills accompanying the second installment of Twain's Saturday features on Niagara Falls, "English Festivities. And Minor Matters." (Image from the *Buffalo Morning Express*, August 28, 1869.)

"I THEN DESTROYED HIM."

Image A4.4. Original caption: "I then destroyed him." A second Mills illustration accompanying Twain's "English Festivities" in the *Express*, depicting the Mark Twain narrator wearing protective gear for his Cave of the Winds tour and thrashing the guide. (Image from the *Buffalo Morning Express*, August 28, 1869.)

"THAT STOVE IS UTTERLY RUINED."

Image A4.5. Original caption: "That stove is utterly ruined." Mills's signature appears in the lower left-hand corner of this illustration that accompanied Twain's "Journalism in Tennessee." (Image from the *Buffalo Morning Express*, September 4, 1869.)

Image A4.6. Original caption: "To dig up the Byron family!" With the artist's signature in the lower right-hand corner, this was the last illustration provided by Mills for a Twain *Express* story. This illustration accompanied Twain's "The 'Wild Man.' 'Interviewed.'" (Image from the *Buffalo Morning Express*, September 18, 1869.)

APPENDIX 5

POLICE COURT COLUMNS

BUFFALO MORNING EXPRESS

November 8, 1869

JUSTICE SHOP

SCENES AT THE POLICE COURT SATURDAY

Business opened briskly on Saturday, and by ten o'clock, the court room was filled with eager applicants for that ever-desirable commodity—justice. Squire Vanderpoel and his assistants for an hour or two had their hands full in attending to the demands of plaintiff and defendant. The first case was that of William Harris, whom Rebecca R. Johnson charged with having slapped her face. Harris denied this attack upon his gallantry, and without further ado the examination was deferred until Monday afternoon at two o'clock.

Edward Higgins, a sailor of extremely loose morals, went into one of those infamous saloons on Canal street Friday night with forty-two dollars and fifty cents in his pocket. He went to sleep there, and when he awoke next morning found the money gone. A female inmate of the place, Catherine Quinn by name, was accused of the theft, arrested, and enough evidence was elicited in the examination to warrant the Squire in fully committing her for trial.

John Brown, a colored man, was arraigned on a charge of assault and battery upon another African named Daniel Starks. The latter claimed that in a saloon squabble Brown stabbed him in the arm with a jack-knife, but Brown has stoutly averred that he "nebber done it, so sure as he was a hard working man." The case was put off for examination until 2 P.M.

Jane Carr and Bridget McMahon were fined $5 each for stealing and allowing their children to steal coal from Wilson's coal yard, down on the creek. Mrs. Porter, who lives in the vicinity and has been empowered by Messrs. Wilson & Co. to protect their interests, appeared as the informer and witness. It appears that six or seven families have been in the habit of helping themselves from the immense piles of coal in this yard, now and then, for the past two or three years, and it is roughly estimated that about fifty tons per annum are thus carried away. The prisoners seemed greatly incensed against Mrs. Porter, whom they claimed "was no better than she might be herself," and that they would "tend to her case bimeby."

BUFFALO MORNING EXPRESS

November 13, 1869

JUSTICE FOR ALL

POLICE JUSTICE VANDERPOEL— THE SOLON OF THE PEOPLE

The vigorous yet gallant police magistrate still holds to his memorable opinion that "under no provocation is a man justified in striking a woman." In the case of a Canal street squabble which came up Thursday, wherein a drunken man was arrested for beating several disreputable women, as he alleged in self-defense, the Squire again gave vent to his opinions on this question. "Never," said he, "strike a woman; no matter what she does to you, or how she provoked you, don't strike her. If she has a stick or weapon in her hands, take it away from her as gently as possible, but don't never lower yourself by beating her."

Now that is what may be called super-fine gallantry. Oh! If women could only vote what an immense majority Mr. Vanderpoel would have at the next election. But the true sentiment of justice is found in the conclusion of the Squire's remarks, "If any woman does you an injury, come to me, and I will punish her as the law provides, just as I would punish a man for doing a wrong to a woman." Is there ought but fairness in that?

The sessions of the Court yesterday were brief ones, the following cases being disposed of: George Kelly, for assaulting Daniel G. Pryor, the engineer of the steamer Huron, was fined ten dollars; and the same Kelly was mulcted in the sum of ten dollars more for beating a tattoo upon the head of Sherman Soule, a resident of Lockport.

Thursday was an uncommonly cold day, and the sharp, stinging air made many a poor fellow's fingers tingle. John Driscoll fully appreciated the rarity of the atmosphere, and, having no gloves of his own, stole those of a poor old negro named Samuel Beasley. He was yesterday morning brought before Squire Vanderpoel and fined ten dollars. The stolen gloves could have been bought for much less than a dollar, and as Driscoll paid his fine he was heard to mutter that "it was a deal cheaper to be honest."

BUFFALO MORNING EXPRESS

November 15, 1869

JUSTICE SHOP

AT THE POLICE COURT ON SATURDAY

Malvin Kenny, the man who bit off William Adam's forefinger in Doll's Store, on Canal street, Friday night, was arraigned in the morning on a charge of mayhem. He plead guilty, and was committed to prison to await the action of the Grand Jury. Adams, it appears, is captain of a vessel and while making some purchases in Mr. Doll's grocery, on Friday night, displayed a considerable sum of money which Kenney attempted to steal from him, but without success, whereupon the sharp toothed rascal snapped at him and bit off his forefinger near the middle joint. Kenney, it is said, has already served out two terms in the state Prison, and this is likely to send him there again.

Mary Patten plead not guilty to a charge of assault and battery preferred against her by Margaret Mahanny. After a brief preliminary examination the parties were discharged with sentence suspended.

BUFFALO MORNING EXPRESS

November 18, 1869

Justice Shop.

Rewards of Merit Dispensed by Police

JUSTICE VANDERPOEL.

Only one case was brought up before the august magistrate of the Police Court yesterday, and that one was based on a charge of assault with intent to do bodily harm. Frederick and John Storm, two young men, both about twenty years of age, were the defendants, and George Miller the plaintiff. The two brothers, it appears, were out on a spree Tuesday evening, and the "witching time of night," viz.: 12 M., found both of them pretty drunk. They went into Lagle's saloon, on Pine street between Batavia and William, about midnight, where they purchased a quantity of cigars and took drinks. From the saloon they went out in the back yard of Mr. Frederick Derr, who keeps a bake shop next door. One of the boys there commenced vomiting, when George Miller, an employee of Derr's, ordered them both out of the yard. They went out, but not until they had indulged in a deal of abusive language. Miller followed them to the gate, and stood there watching their proceedings, when suddenly John Storm turned back and struck him in the face and kicked him, and while Mr. Miller was defending himself against John, Frederick came up with a large jack-knife and stabbed him, cutting two large gashes in his right shoulder. An alarm of murder was immediately given, and the young ruffians ran away, pursued by Roundsman McCulloch and Patrolman Stendts, who happened to be near at hand. The officers followed them through an alley, over a fence and into a house in the immediate vicinity, where they arrested the brothers with the bloody knife in their possession.

At the examination the evidence proved conclusively the above facts, and Justice Vanderpoel committed the prisoners to the county jail to await trial.

Mr. Miller's injuries, although very painful, are not serious, and he will shortly be able to be about as active as ever.

BUFFALO MORNING EXPRESS

November 22, 1869

WEIGHING IT OUT

As Practiced by Judge Vanderpoel

Motto—"The scales of justice hang between
the deed unjust and the end unseen."

The illustrious beak whose exalted duty it is to dispense the blessed boon of justice to the turbulent spirits of the classic precincts, arose to his cane-seated chair of dignity early Saturday, and reaching forth his hand he drew toward him the bloody calendar of crime, and with ominous look called upon his faithful aid "Jake" to trot out the first case.

The first case aforesaid was unimportant and was discharged; the second case ditto, but the third and last case was attentively examined and brought forth all of the glaring, blood-curdling particulars of an assault and battery case. Joseph Rice had actually used muscular persuasion in a friendly argument with Jacob Rosenbaum and the heinous offense so exasperated the Court that poor Rice was subjected to the terrible torture, financially, of paying a fine of five dollars.

BUFFALO MORNING EXPRESS

November 23, 1869

METE SHOP

JUSTICE DISHED UP BY JUDGE VANDERPOEL.

The atmosphere of the court room was heavily freighted with the tragic element yesterday, and the inexorable dispenser of justice put on his severest look as the cases were arraigned one after another. An attempted murder, a highway robbery, a grand larceny, and one or two punch-one-another's-head scrapes comprised the bloody calendar.

James W. Howard and Theodore Thorn, both colored, were charged with assaulting John Denby, with intent to kill. Denby is a white man; and Saturday night he went into the negro dive on Commercial street, near the bridge. There he got into an altercation with some of the inmates, which ended by his being beaten and pushed in to the canal by Howard, Thorn and a couple of quadroons. He was rescued by the police, and the two men were arrested. Justice Vanderpoel fully committed them for trial.

Mason Hewett was examined on a charge of highway robbery preferred against him by Joseph Hallchurch, who stated that he met Mason on Fly street late Saturday night, and together they went into Peter Carr's saloon where they took a drink, and he had started to go home, when Mason sprang upon him, knocked him senseless, dragged him into an alley, and robbed him of a silver watch and chain, nine dollars in currency and several trinkets. The property was found in Mason's boots and he was fully committed for trial.

Two or three assault and battery cases were discharged and one or two more held over for further examination.

At the afternoon session of this tribunal of justice one case only was disposed of, and that one was John Ford, assault and battery on James Sheehan. The Court took into consideration the fact of Ford's youthful innocence and fined him ten dollars.

BUFFALO MORNING EXPRESS

November 26, 1869

JUSTICE SHOP

CASES BEFORE THE POLICE MAGISTRATE

The principal trial yesterday was of the patience of the Police Justice and the officers of the Court, who were forced to endure a stupidly tedious examination of witnesses in a small case of assault and battery. It may be honestly set down that there is no such thing as perversity until a Buffalo shyster has a chance to display himself.

The case of John Williams and Richard Van Valkenburg, petit larceny in stealing a pair of boots from Charles Thorn, was deferred until the afternoon session.

An assault and battery case, Philip Buck vs. Matthew Keller, was also put off for further examination.

A ragged urchin named Dennis Something-or-other was dragged before the magisterial desk this morning, and would have been sent to Father Hines this morning but for his mother, who argued strongly in his behalf, "Och! Squire; sure an' ye wouldn't sind him up?"

Squire—"Yes, I think he had better go."

Mother—"No, he hadn't. He aint no vagram chap. He's a purty little boy, and a good child."

Here the "purty little boy" dutifully wiped his nose on his mother's gown, and attempted to smile through the dirt.

Squire—"Well, then, take him away for this time, but he looks as if he needed the new clothes that he would get if he went to Father Hines."

Mother—"Thank ye, sur. Och, no, he don't want any clothes. He's a good little boy, he is. Coom, Dennis, darlint. Thank ye, Squire; I knew ye wouldn't send 'em up."

The affable Justice heaved a sigh and muttered, "So much for woman's blandishments."

BUFFALO MORNING EXPRESS

December 1, 1869

WRONGS RIGHTED.

CASES BROUGHT UP IN THE POLICE COURT

The session of the court yesterday forenoon was made unusually interesting by the development of the facts of what was at first supposed to be a case of bigamy. A young and very good looking girl named Lucy McDonald was wedded to a sailor named Peter Martin in Milwaukee, Wisconsin, about two years ago, but since their marriage she and her husband have seen but little of each other, as Peter was an ardent seaman and preferred the watery element to the company of a fond and dutiful wife. Time passed on, until their mutual cup of happiness had grown rusty from neglect. Lucy, who had assumed hymen's bonds for the sole purpose of having "some one to love and some one to caress," began to regret her choice of a mate and longed that she were again fancy free to try her fortunes once more in the matrimonial market. The dissolution came at last. Her lawful husband, who has been sailing on the schooner J. B. Martin all through the past season, was drowned (it is so reported) on Lake Huron during a terrific gale in the early part of this month. Hearing of the fact, and being satisfied in her own mind of its truthfulness, she came to Buffalo with a young man named John Gorman, for whom she had conceived a warm attachment, which was happily reciprocated, and the two were tied to each other by the connubial knot in Justice Ryan's office on Monday evening; but as the course of true love is never allowed to run smooth their bliss was somewhat marred by the appearance of an officer with a warrant for their arrest on a charge of bigamy, preferred against them by the father of the blushing bride. The upshot of the matter was that they were provided with separate apartments for the night in Police Station No. One. This morning Justice Vanderpoel examined the case, and being satisfied that the girl was a widow previous to her marriage with Gorman, discharged the parties, and they went upon their way rejoicing.

Dennis Clark wanted a room badly Monday afternoon, and Matthew

Wagner had one that he was not using, Dennis appropriated it for a while. The value of the article was fifty cents, but as rents are exorbitant, it cost Mr. Clark five dollars for what little time he used it.

APPENDIX 6

PEOPLE AND THINGS COLUMNS

BUFFALO MORNING EXPRESS

August 17, 1869

PEOPLE AND THINGS

- Mr. Geo. Peabody is no better.
- They have California honey and Chinese shoes for sale in Chicago.
- The cable brings sad news. Ms. Braddon is recovering.
- Pere L'Epingle, the king of Paris rag-pickers, is dead. Peace to his ash barrels.
- 258 marriages and 282 births last week in New York.
- Gen. Lee declines to take a hand in Virginia politics.
- The wooden toothpicks are all made in one factory near Boston.
- The great boat race comes off August 27.
- "Avitor," or air-ship stock, is in the California market at $25 a share.
- The son of the late Mr. Cornelius Grinnell, it is announced, will succeed to his father's business.
- Miss Nellie Fenton, daughter of the Senator, is shortly to marry J. N. Hegeman, of New York, druggist.
- The list of delinquent army officers who took Southern service in 1861 comprises the names of forty-seven Generals.

- Russia has purchased the ancient and famous Greek Bible from the convent on Mount Sinai.
- Chang and Eng, the Siamese twins, have an aggregate of seventeen children, but most of them belong to Chang, because Eng was absent part of the time.
- M. de Lamester's new French dictionary just issued in Paris defines virtue as "A woman who has only one lover and don't steal."
- London gives £4,000,000 annually to the poor through her charitable associations alone. And yet it is still considered a hardship to be poor in London.
- Our Southern brethren have not forgotten their old tricks; 100 postoffices in that section have been closed because the P.M.'s neglected to make returns.
- The marriage robe worn by the Princess Louisa of Sweden at her recent marriage to the Prince Royal of Denmark was manufactured at Berlin and cost $24,000.
- Simmons, the Hercules of the Harvard crew, is a third cousin of Ralph Waldo Emerson. He lives at Hawthorne's "Old Manse."
- The river Nile is lower than it has been for 150 years. This news will be chiefly interesting to parties who remember the former occasion.
- "Moral Mush Osgood" is the *World's* irreverent name for the divine whose resignation of his pulpit in New York caused so much newspaper regret some time ago.
- In England, Judah P. Benjamin, an impecunious relic of the late rebellion, has been appointed a Queen's counsel for the Lancaster circuit.
- The railroad is gradually causing Chicago people and papers to speak of the once far distant Pacific coast as of a next door neighbor.
- The Chicago *Post* says there are two kinds of Republicans in the South—genuine and counterfeit, and it takes an uncommonly good judge to tell which is which.
- Commodore Jarvis, of the United States navy, died at Geneva, Mo., on Thursday, aged seventy-four. He entered the navy in 1812, and has been on the retired list for many years.
- The *World* says: Will not the Humboldt committee accept the City

Hall Park statue of Washington as possibly looking like the author of "Cosmos"? It resembles no American, "be he alive or be he dead."

- His Reverence the Bishop of Toronto was charged at the Guild Hall Police Court in London the other day with being drunk and assaulting policemen in the discharge of their duty.

- In three Virginia districts, the tobacco revenue for five months ending August 1st, exceeds that for the same period under Johnsonian administration last year, $1,184,588.

- The 14th of September will be the first centennial anniversary of the birth of the renowned Baron Von Humboldt. St. Louis proposes to erect a "Physical Observatory"—whatever that may be—in his honor.

- Weston, who would have been an enormous success if he had lived in Jupiter, where the days contain 30 hours instead of 24, has subsided. Joliet, Ill., is his haven of rest.

- Gen. Grant, it is said, thinks something of boring for oil while he is out there in Pennsylvania. Why don't he get some of those button-holing office-seekers to do it for him? They are used to it.

- The Chicago *Journal's* London correspondent wonders where Jefferson Davis gets the money to enable him to travel with a retinue in Scotland, since the British press describe him as being without means.

- A young lady of St. Louis, aged 24, just deceased, leaves property valued at $200,000. A clause in her will sets apart "a sum not exceeding two dollars for pious and charitable purposes." Munificence after death is well, but why do not deceased parties follow the example of Mr. Peabody, and enjoy the luxury of giving before they die?

- They have a young lady clairvoyant at LaSalle, Ill., who "with eyes closed, describes with minute accuracy the contents of pockets in coats hanging in distant rooms, and even to a degree surpassing the knowledge of the owners." It is entertaining to contemplate so dangerous a talent at a liberal distance, but we had rather observe it through a smoked glass as we do other wonders, latterly, than have it imported and exercised among our Buffalo families. Seeing through a man's pocket is harmless, but she might want to "go through" it next.

BUFFALO MORNING EXPRESS

August 19, 1869

PEOPLE AND THINGS

- The complaint of the coal mines—colliery—*Boston Post*.
- The reception of the Governor-General of Canada at Prince Edward Island was very cordial.
- The Aldermen and members of the Board of Health, of Milwaukee, have had a sort of family swimming match. The doctors won—The Aldermen got aground.
- Philadelphia is almost out of water to drink, because of the exceeding low stage of the Schuylkill river. Considerable distress has resulted.
- Redpath's Lyceum Bureau, Boston, has on its list one hundred and fifty lecturers and readers, whose services are available for the forthcoming season.
- Sir Hildebrand, of Missouri, has emigrated. He had thinned out the population until further amusement was too difficult to obtain to make it worth a man's while.
- Frederick Wermicke, a soldier of the First Empire, aged 87 years, was arrested in Madison county, Missouri, recently for some offense against the revenue laws. The old gentleman's eldest son is 60 years of age and his youngest two.
- One of those venerable parties, a pre-Adamite man, has been dug up from a depth of ninety-eight feet, in Alabama. He was of prodigious stature, and is supposed by savans to have existed twelve thousand years ago. Life was entirely extinct when they got him out.
- Another Colfax party has gone to the Pacific, viz: Geo. Mathews and wife, the mother and step-father of the Vice-President, their daughter Carrie and James M. Mathews, brother of George, his wife and daughter, Lucy. They expect to be absent about three months.
- Miss Carrie A. Benning, a young lady of Harris county, Georgia, who was reduced by the war from wealth to poverty, has in cultivation a five

acre field of cotton, which is said to be the best in the neighborhood. She planted and worked it herself, with no assistance except in one plowing.

- Lord Taunton, better known formerly as Henry Labouchere, paid back £100,000 compensation money which the Bristol and Exeter Railroad Company had paid his father for cutting through his lands. He saw that his estates were enhanced in value by far more than the ordinary price of the land taken from him.

- An Alexandria (Egypt) merchant, ruined by the Viceroy's heavy taxes, recently sold his son to a slave dealer to obtain yet another 900 piastres for the tax gatherer. It would have been far better to have sold him short for double the amount, and then run off before he was worth it.

- *Figaro* says "While London raised a monument to the wealthy American, Mr. Peabody, the Pope has ordered a bust to the Yankee so universally honored. On his voyage to Rome, Mr. Peabody presented to the treasury of Pope Pius IX, for his poor, $1,000,000. A fact curious to note is that Mr. Peabody is a Protestant."

- A man in Maine has been digging for Captain Kidd's treasures for a year past under the guidance of the spirits. He is very enviably fixed, because, from present appearances, his job will afford him steady employment as long as he may want it. There would also seem to be work enough to even justify him in hiring some outsiders to help him.

- The Newport lady with the ring "cut out of a solid diamond" is still going the rounds of the press with undiminished ferocity. Those things are common in Pennsylvania. The species is the "black" diamond, and this Newport lady's experiment has lately raised its price several dollars a ton, and brought sorrow to many a struggling family. Let her have her share of the abuse.

- Kalloch, of Kansas, and formerly of Boston, is summering in Maine. His talents are unimpaired.

- Choy-Chow and Sing-Man, the distinguished Chinamen, have started on their return to California:

California's dull,
For she's lost her Moguls,
And don't know where for to find them;
But let them alone
And they'l waggle home,
And carry their tails behind them.

- The Hartford's *Post*'s inextinguishable "old man" has turned up again. He is only sixty-five, this time, but makes up for it in the liveliness of his experiences and the amount of things he can do. He is Cornelius Snyder, of Spencer, Ky., upon this occasion, and has "been twice married—eighteen children by his first wife. He has walked fifty-four miles in seven hours, and is to-day perhaps, one of the best walkers of the State." Weston is young yet—let him be encouraged. There is no telling what he may be able to do when he has had sixty-five years' practice.
- The Brown family are assembling in convention at Simpson's Corners, R.I., to form a plan of action with regard to their immense estates in England. So the telegram is worded. This is bad enough as it is—but will it stop here? Those Smiths will be at it next. It would be more generous in these two families to club themselves together in a joint convention and hire one of those ample western deserts to hold it in, and not be discommoding a helpless little State like Rhode Island which has never done them any harm.
- A correspondent of the Cleveland *Herald* reports that a Mrs. Birney, 62 years of age, living near Tippecanoe, Harrison county, Ohio, has for twenty years been in the habit of falling into a state of unconsciousness at about ten o'clock on Sunday mornings, during which she delivers ungrammatical religious discourses. Of course, when a woman does anything remarkable, it must be published far and wide, but acres and acres of poor clergymen can go on doing such things all their lives and a subsidized press takes no notice of it. A mean partiality ill becomes journalism.
- "For many years the most wonderful comet the world has ever seen" has been advertised to appear and remain visible during the months of July and August and September of this year, and grow constantly brighter until it has finished its engagement, when it will depart in the direction of Saturn

to play an engagement in the provinces. The journalists of Wisconsin are observing it now, though why a comet should visit Wisconsin before it visits New York is another of those astronomical mysteries. It appears after eleven at night, and is thenceforth visible until nearly daylight. It is described as being "many thousand times larger than the earth, and is a solid mass of fire with a tail that would reach around the earth more than a hundred times." We feel compelled to throw cold water on this comet—not in the hope of putting it out, but simply because comets, as a general rule, ought not to be encouraged, and more especially because Wisconsin journalists are too far from good points of observation to see correctly and have no business meddling with astronomy anyhow. Their comet bears marks of human manipulation, for Providence never makes these sort of things out of "solid masses of fire." We do not approve of criticising comets, especially with asperity, but this one has too short a tail for the amount of style it appears to be putting on. We never had any opinion of short-tailed comets.

BUFFALO MORNING EXPRESS

August 21, 1869

PEOPLE AND THINGS

- *Did* Garrison try to shoot Vanderbilt? That is the undying topic, now.
- Mme Ristori is in Brazil, where she has had an enthusiastic reception.
- Elise Holt has made a very decided failure in California.
- A work called the Hoosac Tunnel is being constructed in Massachusetts.
- Miss Ada Webb, the well-known actress, was married the other day to a gentleman from New Orleans—a Mr. Connor.
- Fifty-four teachers are employed in the public schools of Elmira, at an annual cost of $31,000.
- What goes with the worn-out bank notes, if there be such things, and what becomes of the dead mules, if any?

- Judge Dent is mixing his war-paint, now, for a raid on Creswell. Bonner has missed a chance in not securing him to write for the *Ledger*.
- The high price of milk is exasperating Syracuse just now, and the people are holding public meetings about it. They refuse to pay more than six cents a quart.
- Fisk is spoken of for Mayor of New York. In the language of Artemus Ward, this is the feather that breaks the last camel's back.
- The King of Prussia had, the other day, a bad fall from his horse. He came near breaking his wrist. The horse he fell from was the one on which he pursued the Austrians after the battle of Sadowa.
- The national subscription for the benefit of the Russian peasant with an unpronounceable name, who saved the Emperor from assassination, has reached a figure about equal to $100,000.
- Our gratitude in learning that Saint Beuve is recovering is only equalled by our ignorance in not knowing that he had been sick, and our entire indifference about the matter anyway.
- The king of Italy has added three dollars and a half a year to the pay of his soldiers. They only got seven dollars a year before this. But will they really be any happier now than they were when they were poor?
- Atlanta is called the Chicago of the South. It is a stirring business community. Its population has increased from 20,000 to 35,000 in the last two years, and is still augmenting.
- The saddest theatrical news is that the Florences have arrived from Europe again—and, not only that, but have brought some new plays with them. The increasing safety of travel by the ocean steamer is becoming a crying evil.
- Some of the great moneyed people of New York are not admirers of gay and gorgeous "turn-outs." The Astors ride in very shabby vehicles, as also do the Livingstones and the Roosvelts, if they ride at all. The Goelets pay a tax on three million dollars' worth of real estate in New York, but none on carriages.
- The Fat Men's annual clam-bake came off at Gregory's Point, Conn., yesterday. Nobody was allowed to participate who could not turn the scale of 200 pounds. Scant-weights were given a year to make up their deficiency in.

- The boring of the ancient and incorrigible artesian well at St. Louis has again been stopped, after reaching a depth of 3843 feet. Why do not they go around and try at the other end awhile? There is water there somewhere.
- Two travelers, stopping at a Des Moines hotel, came near losing their lives last week, by blowing out the gas on retiring to bed. One of them, when asked if he smelt anything wrong, said yes, but he thought it was the other fellow's breath.
- Ms. Clair De Evere lectured at Cape May a few evenings since. The *Revolution* says that she is "a handsome young lady of about twenty-one years, was beautifully attired in a rich black silk with a white satin surplice, and if the lecture she delivered at the Cape is a fair sample of her intellectual powers, she is on the way to being the brightest ornament on the platform of human rights that we have on this continent."
- Edward Denny, late of the British Royal Navy, son of the venerable archdeacon of Ardfert, and grandson of Sir Edward Denny, Baronet, Tralee Castle, Ireland, was married Sunday to Florence Annette, daughter of Charles Condell, of Kensington, England. The event took place at the residence, in Brooklyn, of Captain Mayne Reid, the well-known author. The ceremony was a strictly private one, only the distinguished young soldier-author, his charming lady and a few family friends being present on the occasion.
- The Los Angeles (Cal.) *News* tells an incredible story, and vouches for its truth, of a shower of meat, blood and hair which fell on the farm of a Mr. Hudson at that place. The meat, which fell on an area of two acres, was in pieces ranging from fine particles to strips six or eight inches long, and had the appearances of being freshly torn from animals. The blood that lodged upon the corn blades and grass was mixed with a short fine hair resembling the outer coats of furred animals. All that worry over a little more than ordinarily emphasized cat fight?
- During the stay of Bailey's Circus in Aurora, Ill., last week, Squire Van Nortwick united in bonds matrimonial one of the Albino boys, Amos Rockman, weight about one hundred and twenty pounds, and the "fat girl," Julia Hutleston, whose weight is four hundred and ninety-five

pounds. This is well. What the country has long needed is a monster pleasantly combining albino hideousness and imbecility with fatty vastness and skeleton deformity. We shall await the advent of the fruit of this marriage with frenzied impatience.

- Mark Twain estimates the distance by rail from San Francisco to New York at 211 games of euchre, 173 drinks and 117 cigars, which shows him to be a very slow euchre player or a very rapid drinker and smoker. —*Newark, N.J., Advertiser.*

- Inasmuch as the person mentioned above smokes 117 cigars a day, and does not drink at all, there is unquestionably some mistake about the authorship of that estimate. And would a man be likely to throw away time computing distances on the Pacific Railroad by euchre games, when he could do it so much easier by keeping account of how many times he "wished he was there?"

- Ik. Marvel having spoken disrespectfully of the New York & New Haven Railroad in *The Hearth and Home*, that paper is banished from the trains and stations on that line. The paper that would deliberately speak respectfully of that road ought to be banished from the earth. They always charge you for a seat, but if you are not good at scrambling you will not get one. The peddler-boys begin to infest you as soon as you sit down, and they never cease to harass you with pea-nuts, magic keys, sour oranges, flash newspapers, confessions of hangmen, old doughnuts and last year's pies, until you get to the end of the journey. But as no money can be got out of water, they keep no tanks or coolers on the cars. A small boy passes through the train every two hours and a half with a three-quart tin tea-kettle and saves many precious human lives. The smoking car is just as decent as a cell in a city prison, and no more. Here and there along the route they stop five minutes for refreshments and then try to clear out before you can get your change. The company's understrappers on the cars are boorish, offensive blackguards, who have been seen to crowd their way roughly through a packed throng of gentlemen, (standing up because there were not seats), and been heard to say to each other, "Make them stand out of the way livelier—knock them down if they don't." We know this has been heard and seen because we sat in one of those cars and heard and saw it. They sell seats in their high-toned "French car" in advance, at the great stations, and then after they have got your money you can do without your seat if they happen to have sold more seats than were ever in the cars. We feel reasonably sure of this matter, too, since it was also a personal experience. Finally, it is the meanest, stingiest little up-country railroad in America, to speak figuratively, and has not a solitary thing to recommend it except that it never has any accidents.

BUFFALO MORNING EXPRESS

August 23, 1869

PEOPLE AND THINGS

- Philadelphia has shipped 15,754,470 gallons of petroleum during the present year.
- The female suffrage question is to be submitted to the Vermont Constitutional Convention next February.
- The New York Sorosis is to present to Ida Lewis a breast pin bearing the legend, "To Ida Lewis, the Heroine."
- Children in Iowa bite rattlesnakes in order to prevent the toothache. Probably the cure would be more permanent if the rattlesnakes bit the children.
- Mourning relatives visited the grave of a friend in Des Moines to find it a burrow of gophers. The mourners went for him, but instinct had suggested to those other creatures to gopher him previously.
- Lawyer O'Conor, who, it will be remembered, was divorced from Edwin Forrest many years ago, has got his alimony at last. It amounts to $60,000. But he has given it all to Mrs. Forrest but $56,000.
- It is said that "Josh Billings dresses after Greeley." This disposition ought to be curbed, while it is as yet only moderately presumptuous. He will be undressing before him, next.
- The "sleeping wonder" is kept such through the influence of animal

magnetism. This mysterious remark, which is now traversing the press, seems to be a low fling at Horace Greeley's performances in Mr. Chapin's Church.

- An English magistrate has fined a poor fellow for carrying chickens with their heads downwards. He can "get even" by carrying them by the neck hereafter, if he is smart enough to think of it, but those parties never are.

- Speaking of the great pianist's concerts in Rio Janeiro the papers say the public pay $25 premium to see Gottschalk. It is not by any means a secret that two or three exasperated fathers and brothers in San Francisco would pay more than that to see him.

- The foreign gentleman who has recently located himself on the opposite sidewalk with a hand-organ of two-tune capacity will oblige us if he will play the other tune sometimes. "Buffalo Gals" is fresh and exciting, but one notices after several days that it lacks variety. This person's organ is a greater bore than the Hoosac tunnel.

- Poor children in New York collect and sell peach kernels to the druggists at a cent a hundred. Adepts make as much as thirty cents a week at it sometimes. They are fast acquiring hurtful luxurious habits through the influence of these sudden and violent accumulations of capital.

- Mr. Eddes, an octogenarian, residing in Dover, Me., never saw but two steamboats—Fulton's original and a small one on Sebec lake. He has not been in Bangor, his nearest city, in thirty-eight years. His mind is said to be richly stored with lack of information.

- On Sunday morning last at the Episcopal Church (St. Mary's) at Peekskill, Mr. Stephen Massett delivered a sermon from the text "Nothing but Leaves," for the benefit of the funds of the church. If Massett's sermons are only as serious as his comic lectures they must be quite edifying. — *Brooklyn Eagle.*

- A correspondent of the New York *Tribune* thinks, and with a deal of reason, that murderers who are acquitted, in the prevailing fashion, on the score of insanity, are lunatics by far too dangerous to be allowed to run at large. He thinks that the plea of insanity in murder cases would lose some of its popularity if a few acquitted madmen were sentenced to the asylum for life.

- Prince Arthur, in his farewell speech at Woolwich, gave the following piece of autobiography: "It is now seven years since I commenced studying for the army. From the time I was a very young boy it was my highest ambition to become a Woolwich cadet. That hope has been fulfilled, and I have had the honor and pleasure of serving in both ordnance corps, the Royal Engineers and the Royal Artillery, and I am now bound to Canada to join another corps. My stay at this garrison will ever be associated in my mind with the most agreeable and pleasing reminiscences."

- From the recent researches of Prof. Darste, in Paris, upon the production of monstrosities in chickens, it is found by varying the application of the heat to the egg, every form of known monstrosity can be produced at will. The professor should by all means continue his "researches" and leave a suffering world to grovel in ignorance no longer. All the grandeur that may result will fall to him alone—for when he gives an account at the Last Day of how he employed the great talents that were vouchsafed him, it will afford him a sublime satisfaction to be able to walk through the pearly gates of the New Jerusalem with his basket of deformed chickens on his arm and the manipulated egg shells in his hat.

- The last gratis-advertising dodge is the announcement among the condensed paragraphs of the press that Mr. Smith, or Jones, or Brown, of So-&-So's "celebrated and popular Negro Minstrel Troupe" ("it will be remembered") was promised his bride, by her obdurate father, whenever Jones, or Brown, or Smith had amassed $50,000—and then the paragraph goes on to say that the said Jones, or Brown, or Smith "discovered last night, upon counting up the receipts, that he had secured the last $100, and immediately telegraphed the joyful intelligence to his intended father-in-law, claiming the fulfillment of the contract." And then comes the glaring part of the little game: "He intends to cling to the burnt cork until he has made enough to procure for his bride a handsome trousseau." We are afraid this ingenious method of reaching the public ear, without paying for it, will not have a long life. It is a shade too transparent.

BUFFALO MORNING EXPRESS

August 24, 1869

PEOPLE AND THINGS

- The Blondes will expose themselves in Elmira to-night.
- Anna Dickinson is lecturing with great success, to crowded houses in California.
- Caleb Cushing gets $30,000 as counsel fee in the Mexican matter.
- We understand that Caleb Cushing gets $40,000 as counsel fee in the Mexican Claims Commission.
- Prussia, of all the governments with which we have relations, is the only one that owns a house in Washington.
- J.N. Waifflin, aged sixty, and Mary Lander, aged fifteen, were married at Hopkinsville, Ky., Monday.
- Peach kernels contain hydrocyanic (or prussic) acid, and are dangerous nutriment. Fifteen hundred of them taken on an empty stomach will kill a man.
- J. Ross Browne, who arrived at San Francisco on Thursday, was naturally grieved to hear that his successor don't want the place. Browne does.
- The talk is revived of bringing to France, with great pomp, the remains of the Duke of Reichstadt, the son of the first Napoleon.
- The Russian Government is said to have offered thirty-five million francs for Prince Borghese's celebrated picture gallery of ancient masters.
- The cars on the White Mountain Railroad were delayed by snow on the 7th of August, and 150 people were compelled to pass the night on Mount Washington.
- Commodore Vanderbilt has just been married in Canada. The frisky young couple have adjourned to Saratoga for the honeymoon.
- Many of the papers berate Mrs. Stowe for resurrecting the Byron scandal when it was sleeping comfortably and giving promise of being forgotten some day. But why should we be sentimentally charitable toward the memory of a bad man at the expense of the fair memory of a good

woman? The worst feature of this rampant and growing discussion is, however, that the country journals are taking sides on it, and making a political matter of the question of whether Byron committed incest or not. The Republican papers go for universal suffrage, liquidation and Byron *did*—and the Democratic go for restricted suffrage, repudiation, and Byron *didn't*.

- Another remarkable story about Vanderbilt. He owed Morrissey forty cents. Morrissey went down to his office with a keg of powder and a match. He locked the door. He swallowed the key. He lit his match. His brow darkened. He said both should never leave that room alive again unless one was a corpse. He lit another match. He placed it close to Vanderbilt's head. He said one or the other must sit down on the keg— take your choice, Mr. V. Vanderbilt is not easily frightened, but he saw he was in a close place. He paid the forty cents. Morrissey departed with his keg. Since that time both have been better friends to each other than both of them put together ever were before. Such is the story. Can it be true? "Scasely."

- The Count d'Eu, who lately distinguished himself in the La Plata war, is a son of the Duke of Nemours, and the husband of the Imperial Princess of Brazil. On the death of her father, the present Emperor, she will succeed him as Empress, with the grandson of Louis Phillippe as her Prince Consort, whose influence is expected to overthrow the institution of slavery.

BUFFALO MORNING EXPRESS

August 25, 1869

PEOPLE AND THINGS

- "The appearance of the Prince elicited universal admiration. He bears a striking resemblance to the Prince of Wales when he was here, and the close likeness to her Majesty is so marked as to be distinguished at once.

He is tall and slender, with a fine and faultlessly combed head of brown hair, and his youthful face is ornamented with an English pattern of whiskers and mustache, highly creditable to the physical development of a young man of nineteen. The dress of Prince Arthur was that of a man of more mature years, although it became him. A neat and elegant black dress coat, closely buttoned, pants of light drab hue, a 'choker' collar of enormous size and a black silk 'tile,' were the garments most conspicuous, and each one seemed to contribute to render his appearance that of a very well dressed young man." —*N.Y. Herald*.

- John Wagner, the oldest man in Buffalo—104 years—recently walked a mile and a half in two weeks. He is as cheerful and bright as any of these other old men who charge around so in the newspapers, and is in every way as remarkable. Last November he walked five blocks in a rain storm without any shelter but an umbrella, and cast his vote for Grant, remarking that he had voted for forty-seven Presidents—which was a lie. His "second crop of rich brown hair" arrived from New York yesterday, and he has a new set of teeth coming—from Philadelphia. He is to be married next week to a girl 102 years old, who still takes in washing. They have been engaged 89 years, but their parents persistently refused their consent until three days ago. John Wagner is two years older than the Rhode Island veteran, and yet has never tasted a drop of liquor in his life, unless you count whiskey.

- Another restaurant waiter has fallen heir to a colossal fortune. How is it that waiters are so much in luck? It is not worth wile to say it is because they are willing to wait for a fortune, because any small punster could dip his ladle into his pot of seething trivialities and fish that up—but honestly, why is it? Five waiters have inherited windfalls in the last two weeks, and only one miliner. Why this disparity? The last three lucky waiters are George H. Wingate, of Missouri, $45,000; Henry L. James, of Kansas, $12,000, and Morgan Bates of New Orleans, $28,000. We have already mentioned the Brooklyn one, who inherited $30,000 from his cousin; and the Newark one, who inherited $21,000 and the cholera from his uncle, and gambled the one away and died of the other, all in the space of forty-eight hours. But the lucky-waiter crop must be about out, now—let us take up the blacksmiths or the shoemakers for a while, and see how they will hold out. Any person knowing of a lucky blacksmith, will confer a favor by leaving the name at this office. We *must* have something fresh in the windfall line—the waiters won't draw any longer.

BUFFALO MORNING EXPRESS

September 2, 1869

PEOPLE AND THINGS

- Byron collars are in vogue again.
- Sheridan is not married again yet.
- Chas. Reade has invited the Harvards to Oxford.
- The rowers of the English lion are awful just now. —*World*.
- Brigham Young has lost his family Bible, and is in trouble to find out how many children he has or what their names are.
- The nine Cincinnati "Red Stockings" are said to be worth $500,000. Cannot they afford to wear white?
- The thermometer has been holding its own pretty regularly at 92 in Chicago during last week.
- It is stated that one hour after the gas of London is lighted the air is deoxidized as much as if 500,000 people had been added to the population.
- Grant was on the summit of Mount Washington when the telegram announcing the defeat of the Harvards was handed him, and reading it he remarked, "Well, I am sorry for that."
- Chicago dealers refuse to sell less than ten cents worth of ice at a time, on the ground that people who are poor enough to need only five cents worth are poor enough to do without it altogether.
- Miss Grinnell, of New York, now at the Kearsarge House in North Conway, N. H., has become insane since hearing of the recent accidental death of her brother by falling from a window at the Isle of Wight.
- A cutter-race between sailors belonging to a British and American man-

of-war took place the other day in Japanese waters. Distance five miles. The Americans were beaten four minutes and a half.

- The wonderful two-headed girl is still on exhibition in New England. She sings duets by herself. She has a great advantage over the rest of her sex, for she never has to stop talking to eat, and when she is not eating, she keeps both tongues going at once. She has a lover, and this lover is in a quandary, because at one and the same moment she accepted him with one mouth and rejected him with the other. He does not know which to believe. He wishes to sue for breach of promise, but this is a hopeless experiment, because only half of the girl has been guilty of the breach. This girl has two heads, four arms, and four legs, but only one body, and she (or they) is (or are) seventeen years old. Now is she her own sister? Is she twins? Or, having but one body, (and consequently but one heart), is she strictly but one person? If the above named young man marries her will he be guilty of bigamy? This double girl has only one name, and passes for one girl— but when she talks back and forth at herself with her two mouths, is she soliloquising? Does she expect to have one vote, or two? Has she the same opinions as herself in all subjects, or does she differ sometimes? Would she feel insulted if she were to spit in her own face? Just at this point we feel compelled to drop this investigation, for it is rather too tangled for us.

- A week ago in Farrish & Co.'s Monumental gold quartz mine, Sierra county, Cal., was found the largest nugget of gold ever unearthed in America. It weighed 100 pounds and is worth $25,000. On the same day, in the same mine, was found a beautiful cake of fine gold weighing 1180 ounces and also 37 ounces in nuggets worth from $400 to $1600 each. All this exciting and delightful work was done in one day by two men, and it was a comfortable day's work, too, since these several values, duly figured up, amount to a fraction over fifty-six thousand dollars in gold, or about seventy thousand or such a matter in greenbacks. The largest gold nugget known to history was one found in Australia years ago, which was as large as a tolerably good-sized valise, weighed 278 pounds, and was worth seventy thousand dollars, gold. The finder, a hungry and penniless wanderer, sat down on it to rest while he bewailed his hard luck, and got up presently to do some ground and lofty tumbling, out of pure joy. In the

Farrish mine, before spoken of, there is another fifty-six thousand dollar day's work in sight, and they are only sorry the sun did not wait for them to get it all out in one day. In nine weeks previously the two men had only taken out $3000.

BUFFALO MORNING EXPRESS

September 3, 1869

PEOPLE AND THINGS

- Mrs. Stowe has found a champion in John Neal, of Portland, Me., who has, it is said, facts in his possession to corroborate her statements.
- Dexter recently trotted a mile in 2:21¾ to a road wagon at Prospect Park grounds. He was driven by Bonner himself.
- The Livingston County Agricultural Society's ninth annual cattle show and fair will open at Geneseo, Sept. 29th. Preparations are being made to make it in all respects a creditable affair.
- The Hon. W. H. Seward reached Portland, Oregon, on Monday and was received by the municipal authorities. Mr. Seward is enthusiastic regarding the future of Alaska.
- The late Andrew Johnson has gone to Red Sulphur Springs, Tenn., for his health. Why does he not try the Arkansas Hot Springs? From all accounts they would help his peculiar complaint.
- Nine thousand Chinese laborers have already been contracted for in South Carolina. One thousand are to be employed on the Selma, Rome & Dalton Railroad, and another thousand are to go to Columbia.
- The newspapers say that the Treasurer of the Boston and Providence Railroad found one thousand dollars under his door the other day, with a note saying that it belonged to the company. That is probably a lie.
- General Sickles has been furnished by Marshal Serrano with a small basket-carriage and a team of ponies, which he is allowed to drive in the Royal Gardens of La Granja, a privilege hitherto only accorded to persons of royal blood.

- Geo. Francis Train has ceased to be a sensation in California, and sighs for another foreign jail or some reliable way of making a fresh noise in the world. It is strange that with his fertility of invention in this respect it does not occur to him to swallow a torpedo and jump out of the window.
- The *World* says "Forney at Gettysburg admitted that Mr. Geary would be beaten by Mr. Packer in October. It is useless for Forney to deny this; for him to deny anything only shows it to be true." Is his evidence more reliable when he "privately admits" a thing than when he "denies" one?
- It is estimated that more copies of Lord Byron's works have been sold in this country within the last fifteen days than in seven years previously. And what is particularly aggravating, is, that people *read* the book now, whereas they used only to buy it for Christmas presents and centre-table ornaments.
- Bates College, in Maine, and other colleges in various parts of the country are now open to young women on the same terms as young men. If the sex continue to push their affairs with zeal, persistence and good courage, they will certainly be voting within twenty years. A constant dropping wears a stone, and a constant endeavor will accomplish any end.
- The paregoric wedding—the latest thing out—was instituted in Oswego last Thursday. It was the first anniversary of the marriage of a worthy young Oswegoan, who, meantime, has been blessed with an heir, and his friends improved the opportunity to send in liberal supplies of that indispensable medicine. The paregoric wedding now stands first on the list. —*Ex.*
- Our exchanges are surprised that such a fertile farming and grazing country as California should order "eight car loads of butter and cheese," and be expecting seventeen more. California never has made her own butter and cheese. There is no reason in the world why she should not; yet she imports it all from the Atlantic States—formerly by the isthmus but chiefly around the Horn, 16,000 miles, but now by the Pacific Railroad.
- When Mr. Lincoln and Mr. Douglas, in the Summer of 1858, made their memorable canvass of Illinois for the United States Senatorship, they frequently met on the same hustings and addressed the same audience. On one of these occasions, after Judge Douglas had made one of his most eloquent speeches, it came to Mr. Lincoln's turn. Throwing off his overcoat,

he handed it to a young man nearby and said, in his droll way, "Here, you hold my clothes while I *stone Stephen.*" —*Harper's* Magazine

- The Mayor of Cornwall, Canada, has just been through the courts, and has emerged a little the worse for wear—in a condition of general moral dilapidation, in fact, which would unsettle the reason of most men. He stands convicted of wife-beating, perjury, subornation of perjury, and also two very rare crimes, one of which cannot be mentioned to ears polite, and the other is the one which exists upon some of the statute-books under the title of "the crime *without* a name." Where is your Byron scandal, *now?*

- The Boston *Post* says that an old and infirm negro woman of Mobile was thrust out of doors by a number of negroes with whom she had been staying, and being either unable to walk or crawl, remained two days lying in the street. Though surrounded by a large number of persons of her own sex, no attention was shown her, and the woman would, in all probability have died, had it not been for the assistance of the police. Can it be possible that while she lay dying for two days in the streets, she was surrounded by any "white" persons, strictly speaking? The intended slur fits one race as neatly as the other.

BUFFALO MORNING EXPRESS

September 4, 1869

PEOPLE AND THINGS

- Bryant has finished the translation of seventeen books of the Iliad.
- Jefferson Davis is going to remain in the United Kingdom the rest of his life.
- The *Sun* calls Wilbur F. Parker the Great American Cowhider.
- Madame Anna Bishop has returned with her eternal youth unimpaired.
- Horace Greeley has been appointed Professor of Penmanship in Union College.

- The Treasurer of Hamilton county, O., receives in fees the nice little sum of $95,500 per annum.
- Oxford's stroke is Yale's stroke. Mr. Smalley is a Yale man and that explains some things. —*World*.
- John Gorbaczevski is dead. The proprietor of this formidable name was the last of the conspirators against the Czar Nicholas in 1825.
- This is Theodore Tilton's last: A lady asked a gentleman how old he was. He replied, "what you do in everything." What was his age? XL.
- The King of Denmark makes annually fifty thousand rix dollars by his beet sugar factory, the machinery of which has been designed by him, and made under his personal supervision.
- Bishop McFarland, of Hartford, and Rev. Matthew Hart, of New Haven, have sailed in the Cuba to attend the Ecumenical Council at Rome. The Bishop carries with him $10,000 as an offering to the Pope.
- Why do men swing their arms back and forth like pendulums when they walk?—and why is it that women do not do it? Answers to the above conundrums may be left at this office until called for.
- The Boston *Advertiser* says that Mrs. Stowe will not reply to the criticisms on her Byron scandal until the comments of the English press are received by mail, when she can deal with all together in one comprehensive, annihilating broadside.
- The Empress Eugenie, it is said, is going to take on board two hundred barrels at Jaffa, to be filled with Jordan water subsequently and distributed among the cathedrals of France. In her innocence is this woman going to try to go to the Jordan river by sea?
- The war between the Patt-ites and Nilssonites is raging as extensively as ever in Paris. Some of the latter are now advertising in the papers that marble busts and portraits of Adelina may be purchased at exceedingly low prices at certain places. The Patt-ites have begun to retaliate in the same manner.
- Some people seem naturally born to good luck. Persons resembling the Napoleons can hear of something to their advantage by applying at the Tuileries. Eugenie has developed a decided kindness for parties purporting to be illegitimate children of the Bonapartes, and puts them on her pension list with fond and trusting alacrity.

- The famous duel between Paul de Cassagnac and Gustave Flourens, is to have an epilogue. A Belgian fencing-master, who is an ardent Democrat, has challenged the reactionary Cassagnac to fight a duel *a mort* with him. In his letter to Cassagnac, he says he believes that the latter has at length met with a man who knows how to fence. Cassagnac has not yet replied.

- At a large mass meeting recently held in Vienna, in regard to the convent question, which has attracted so much attention in Austria, the following resolution was unanimously passed: "Whereas, Convents are neither a necessary requirement of the Christian religion, nor in keeping with the principles of the modern State, nay, are directly dangerous to the welfare of the State; Resolved, That all convents in Austria should be closed."

- Mrs. Soalfield, of Chicago, has a pearl, inherited from her German ancestors, which is so large, that jewelers tell her its value is above the means of any one in this country, and she is going to exhibit it. Can people who can afford such property as that, afford to go into the cheap show business? Could not she prop up her native dignity by selling it for a couple of hundred thousand dollars or so and dragging out the remainder of her days in unostentatious poverty?

- The little Princess Felicia, said to be the smallest girl of her age on the continent, is still the great sensation in Paris. She is only fifty centimeters high. On her arrival in Paris she was immediately taken to the Empress, who put her into her workbasket and carried her to the Emperor's room. The girl was placed on Napoleon's writing-table, on which she promenaded and danced for awhile, and closed the performance, to the great amusement of the Emperor, by turning a somersault. She is only seven years old, and the physicians who have examined her predict that she will yet grow about eight or ten centimeters, when she will be about two feet high. Such is the tantalizing newspaper account. Will somebody be so good as to state in a Christian way how high, that girl *is?*

- It must be a very unhappy thing to be a prince and have people thrust presents upon you and then turn around and blackguard you if you do not pay back value received, in strict measure. "The wolf's long howl on Oonalaska's shore" is mere foolishness compared to that far-reaching howl that Australia and Tahiti are still wafting across the billowy solitudes of the South Pacific, concerning the parsimony of Victoria's second son. It used to be a popular notion that a present was a free-will offering, and not a "swap," but they appear to see the thing in a different light out there among the soft summer lands, where the sportive kangaroo sings his songs of thankfulness and praise, and the simple cannibal eats his frugal meal of missionary in peace and is contented with the humble lot that denies him the flimsier luxuries of a pampered civilization. The wail continues. It grows longer and louder and more and more plaintive in its anguish. Is there no relief for these poor outraged foreigners?

BUFFALO MORNING EXPRESS

September 8, 1869

PEOPLE AND THINGS

- Sojourner Truth is probably dead by this time. Charlotte Cushman also.
- Rev. Father Boehm is the oldest Methodist minister in the world. His age is 95, and he still preaches, sometimes.
- A southern paper advises Mrs. Harriet Beecher Stowe to go to the "Erring Womans' Home" in Chicago.
- What was it that Archimedes said about the lever? These things escape one's memory from lack of repetition.
- We are to have the Dr. Livingston excitement all over, once more. He is not found again.
- Harriet Martineau, the ancient and reliable, comes to Mrs. Stowe's rescue on the Byron matter.
- Engine 103 drew the special Chicago Express from Syracuse to Rochester Friday evening in eighty-five minutes! Distance, *eighty-five miles.*
- San Francisco is to be the great fur market of the world. Which is true enough, but still it isn't so fur now as it was before the railroad was built.
- The new order requiring the New York policemen to wear their uniforms on all occasions, is making trouble—they do not like to sleep with their clothes on.

- McKean Buchanan and troupe are playing a week in Auburn. There goes another "Auburn, sweet village of the plain," deserted in consequence.
- The N.Y. *Mail*, being afraid to eat oysters in months that have no "r" in them, altered August to "Orgust," and enjoyed bivalves just as well as ever, during the dog days.
- Prince Napoleon has a wary eye on the throne. The Emperor is growing feeble and the other prince—the Emperor's son—may find it well to travel for his health if the father yields up the ghost.
- Even the names of the editors of some of those dreadful southern journals are shudderingly suggestive of the war-path. The name of the Vicksburg *Herald's* editor is Swords, and the publisher's name is Spears.
- Somebody has been meddling with the lock on Yerger's door and taking a wax impression of the key hole. Is it possible that there are people who fear a trial for murder in these days when "temporary insanity" is so cheap and convenient?
- The Boston Coliseum is to be put up as a gift enterprise. Three concerts are to be given in it, at a dollar a ticket, all the tickets to be blanks but one, and that one to draw the building. It is considered that the Coliseum will sell for $15,000 as old lumber.
- There has been some dispute as to the last words which Lamartine uttered on his death-bed. The last version is, that the poet, a few moments previous to his death said: "Do not disturb me!" Marshal Neil's were "*l'Armée française!*" (the French army).
- Miss Braddon, says the *Review Bibliographique*, "has taken the plot of most of her novels from French romances of an inferior character. In this point she is an almost slavish copyist. She retains even the most awkward feature of the plot, such as it was conceived by the French author."
- The Parisian duelist Cassagnac, has still another cheerful challenge from one of the St. Pelagie prisoners, who says he wants to meet him, "hand on breast, pistol at forehead, ignorant as to which has the loaded weapon." Mr. Cassagnac is thinking the thing over.
- Salem, Massachusetts, was called Nahumkeika by the red proprietors. The deed transferring the title to the pale faces, was signed by Messrs. Nonnuphannowhow, Wuttaquatinuski, Upquaakussennum, Yawataw

and Quanophhownattuttinusk. These fine old family names are all extinct now.

- The ladies of the Berlin Midnight Missions deny the report that their efforts to save fallen women are unavailing. They state that their association, in the comparatively short time since it was organized has rescued upward of two hundred, and that very few of these have relapsed into their former bad habits.

- Palmo the father of Italian opera in New York, is dead. He made his opera experiment in 1844 and it ruined him. He made several fortunes in various ways, during his residence of nearly fifty years in New York, and died at last in poverty. He was born in Italy, and came to this country when he was twenty-six years old.

- It is said that Marshal Marmont secretly went to Paris, shortly after the *coup d'etat*, and implored Louis Napoleon to give him again a command in the French army, in order to set at rest the caluminious rumors which had been circulated about him ever since the capitulation of Paris, in the year 1815. Napoleon refused to grant his request, and ordered him to leave the country immediately.

- Mr. W. H. Hurlbert, of the *World*, is now in Europe. He had been invited to go to Egypt in the suite of the Empress Eugenie, but as she is not going his plans will be changed. The Napoleon family has cherished a strong feeling of friendship for Mr. Hurlbert ever since 1859, when he advocated the cause of the French Empire with his wonted brilliancy in the columns of the New York *Times*.

- Mr. John Lester Wallack, since his return from Europe, wears on full dress occasions a blue swallow-tailed coat, with velvet collar and gilt buttons, a white vest with rich fancy buttons, black knee breeches and black silk stockings and pumps with delicate silver buckles. This is now the correct thing for full dress. As worn by Mr. Wallack it is a very elegant costume, and our dandies will imitate it of course. It is not well suited for their legs. —*New York Sun*.

- It is estimated that it would give one million birds constant employment for upwards of 7000 years to produce the 10,000,000 tons of guano which have already been exported from Chincha Islands—and there is more there yet. The estimate is seriously made, and is plausible. These 10,000,000 tons were 20,000,000, tons before the evaporation and decay took half their weight but this fact is left out of the calculation. Consequently, birds were vastly more plenty there in ancient times than they have been within the memory of man, or else the geologists are right in fixing the age of the world at a high figure. Guano now becomes an agent in the demonstration of knotty scientific problems.

- No one will more regret that the Empress Eugenie has changed her mind in regard to her Oriental journey than Madame Deschelles, who now makes the bonnets of the Empress. Madame Deschelles had got up for her Imperial Majesty a real love of a bonnet, which she called "the Oriental bonnet," and she had ordered thousands of them for the Parisian ladies, who never feel happy unless they can imitate the costume worn by the Empress. The Oriental bonnet will now be a complete failure, and Madame Deschelles will lose a large amount of money in consequence.

- Frederick William the Third, of Prussia, was in the habit of riding out in the streets of Berlin, in a very unostentatious carriage. One day his coachman drove him through a very narrow street, in the middle of which they were met by the splendid equipage of a wealthy Mecklenburg nobleman, Count Hahn. The King's coachman, of course, refused to drive aside, so as to allow the Count's carriage to pass by. The Count's coachmen who did not know who was seated in the plain little carriage before him, was equally unwilling to give way. Suddenly Count Hahn sprang to his feet, and shouted, indignantly, to the King's coachman, "Sirrah, do you not know that I am the rich Count Hahn?" Whereupon the King, on his part, rose, also, and said quietly, "And you, sir, do you not know that I am the poor King of Prussia?"

- A Boston young lady has been eloping with a negro minstrel and causing her friends much trouble. Music hath charms, and when it is coupled with a musician that hath charms also, the combination is strong. Four or five years ago a San Francisco young lady aged 18, educated, accomplished and beautiful, the pet of a father worth two millions of dollars, and whose high official position and old respectability gave his family the familiar entrée to the best society California could afford, eloped with a fat, vulgar, lubberly Italian whale who performed nightly with a troupe of negro minstrels in the metropolis of the Pacific. The fellow was forty or forty-five years old, and had the superabundant ignorance and self-conceit which are born into all professional tenor singers. He owed for his board. He had a sick wife. Yet notwithstanding these little drawbacks the young girl eloped with him and started for Australia in a sailing vessel—the minstrel leaving his sick wife behind, of course. The father chartered a steamer and gave chase, and recovered his daughter at sea and allowed her obese paramour to continue his journey alone.

BUFFALO MORNING EXPRESS

September 9, 1869

PEOPLE AND THINGS

- The Harvards will reach New York next Saturday morning.
- "Old Town Folks" has reached a sale of 25,000 copies in England.
- Two thousand correspondents thank Banting for having relieved them of an aggregate of a hundred tons of fat.
- J. C. Ayer is up for Congress in Massachusetts. Still, his highest hopes take no more definite shape than expectoral. The person who made this remark is since dead.
- Gough has quit sitting up nights on his book, and sent it to the press. It turns out to be an autobiography which he has been writing for another fellow.
- The Pacific Mail Steamship Company have reduced the sailings of their vessels to California *via* the Isthmus to two in place of three a month. The railroad is beginning to tell already.
- George Casey, colored, of New Orleans, has inherited $75,000, and is exceedingly popular as a bond and free man. This joke will be explained to the ignorant at the small charge of forty cents. Press and clergy free.
- Prof. Harkness will shortly report on the eclipse as observed by him and

the other savans at Des Moines. The news is too stale, now—this sort of promptness would have answered well enough in the canal-boating days.

- An English letter-writer mentions as a curious fact that none of the leading women's rights reformers in that country are mothers or fathers. He adds: "A few are married, but those who are married have not been blessed with children."

- Four hundred and twenty-nine Mormon converts have just arrived at New York, bound for Utah. They are chiefly from England and Wales. Polygamy is no new thing in Wales—they have it there on the liberal plan that dispenses with the marriage ceremony.

- A hat and cap manufacturer in New London, Conn., has discovered a new way of advertising. He makes his three sons go bareheaded Winter and Summer. Benevolent people buy caps for them, and they throw their custom into their father's hands. The self-same caps are purchased for them six times a week on an average.

- Since the Haarlem Lake in Holland has been drained, the average temperature of the region has been increased one degree Fahrenheit in the Summer and one degree colder in the Winter. That makes the average right and the Dutchmen are satisfied. They simply want all the weather they are entitled to, but are not particular as to how it is distributed.

- A man who owes a bill in London can now pay it in four hours by simply going to Wall street and purchasing a document known as a "cable transfer," a device born of the great Atlantic telegraph enterprise, whereby the equivalent of the money which he gives in New York will be immediately delivered to his creditor in London.

- Detectives employed by Mr. Bergh go in disguise to the New York horse market and kill glandered horses after a veterinary surgeon has examined and pronounced them unfit for use and beyond recovery. Few men could stand the abuse that Mr. Bergh gets and go courageously on with a good work. New York scoffs at him now, sometimes, but New York will build a monument to his memory some day.

- There is a veteran in Ohio 107 years old, who does not go tramping around, or chopping four cords of wood a day, or turning handsprings for exercise. And strange to say, he has not voted for more than half the Presidents, either. Moreover, instead of having a tenacious memory and an unimpaired intellect, he is a driveling old idiot. This is the most remarkable case on record. It is proposed to exhibit him.

- A star-spangled banner fish was caught at Norwich, Ct., a few days ago, and sent to Prof. Agassiz. It is diamond shaped, three inches square. From two sides of the diamond floated glutinous streamers of most delicate color, at least two feet long. Between those are smaller streamers, grid-ironed by stripes of red, white and blue. When swimming in the river the fish resembles a crystalized American flag, its sides resplendent with all the hues of the rainbow.

- The "Colfax Party" will learn with regret the singular and tragical death of one of their most hospitable California entertainers, Col. Harasthy, formerly President of the great Buena Vista Vinacultural Society of California. He had resigned that position and removed to Central America, where he had obtained from the government a valuable franchise for the manufacture of distilled liquors for twenty years, and one day he was looking for a mill site along one of the little Nicaragua water courses when he fell in the stream and was devoured by alligators.

- Dispatches from France are a little confusing. One day they say: "The Emperor is not sick—the imperial physician denies the reports to that effect." Next day they say: "The emperor is still in good health and spirits, and rested well last night—the rumors to the contrary are gotten up by enemies of the government for a purpose of their own." And the third day they say: "His Majesty was in no pain of any consequence last night, and the official paper pronounces the reports about his ill-health pure fabrications." Then a pause, and another telegram comes: "The court physician considers the Emperor out of danger now. The Oriental journey of the Empress is indefinitely postponed."

BUFFALO MORNING EXPRESS

September 10, 1869

PEOPLE AND THINGS

- Juarez will meet Mr. Seward at Acapulco.
- Harriet Martineau suffers from heart disease.
- Carlotta Patti returns to the United States with 6,000,000 francs, the receipts of her concerts in Europe.
- The Lawrence *Republican* claims that Kansas in its corn crop will this year lead every other State in the Union.
- "Well, what is it that causes the saltiness of the ocean?" inquired a teacher of a bright little boy. "Codfish," was the quick reply. —*Ex.*
- Worth, the man-milliner of Paris, is dead. It is at least a comfort to know that he cannot make any more remarks about that 800f. dress.
- Provincial papers speak of Commodore Vanderbilt's erection of a monument in his own honor, as a remarkable exhibition of personal vanity. Oh, gammon! It isn't brass; it's bronze. —*World.*
- The first historical apple that fell, revealed to Eve the attractions of dress, and the second historical apple that fell revealed to Newton the attraction of gravitation. No charge.
- The Red Stocking Base Ball Club, of Cincinnati, have accepted an invitation to visit San Francisco. They are to stay ten days, and play several match games. Their expenses are to be paid by citizens of San Francisco.
- Judge Jeremiah S. Black of Pennsylvania, has brought suit in the sum of $25,000 against the Louisville and Nashville Railroad Company, for injuries sustained some time during the early part of the summer.
- The *Sun* says that Pierre Plante, a Canadian, has just died at the age of 120. He had a fall two years ago that materially accelerated his death. Is that place convenient, so that other old prodigies can get there?
- An English writer of twenty years ago says that Byron sent a copy of his famous "Fare Thee Well" verses to Lady Byron with a butcher's bill enclosed therewith with a slip like this: "I don't think we could have had so much meat as this; please to see to it."

- Dickens says: "I have known vast quantities of nonsense talked about bad men not looking you in the face. Don't trust that conventional idea. Dishonesty will stare honesty out of countenance any day in the week, if there is anything to be got by it."
- At a Chicago fair, held by the ladies, they are voting "for the most popular editor," in order to determine who that party is. Perhaps this will account for the sudden disposition to gush, and drop into poetry, and talk glibly about Woman and her Mission, which has come over the Chicago journals within a few days.
- A boy in Portage county, O., has used tobacco since he was five months old. He was a nervous and fretful child, and a plug of tobacco was early placed in his mouth, for its soothing effects. Before he could talk plainly he was a confirmed tobacco chewer. A defender at last! This noble youth deserves the fervent gratitude of the abused and down-trodden millions whose only crime is that they feel an honorable affection for the generous, health-giving weed. See what a benefactor it was to this poor feeble, worthless child. No family should be without it.
- W. Frank Stewart, of San Jose, Cal., is still predicting earthquakes. For several years he kept a neat but not gaudy little liquor saloon in San Jose, (and doubtless keeps it yet,) and in the intervals of mixing gin-toddies and Santa Cruz punches he instructed himself in the abstruse science of earthquakes—if there be such a science, properly. He invented a machine for determining the direction of earthquake shocks. It was simply a lead pencil fastened in such a manner with its point against a sheet of white paper that it would make a mark up and down, across or zig-zag, when the house was shaken by an earthquake; and so, whenever Stewart was shaken out of his boots or his bed, he did not rush for the streets, as other citizens did, but rushed to see what the earthquake had written him as to what direction it was traveling and whither it was probably bound. The building was a small frame one, and the hogs got to scraping themselves against it for comfort; their performances were faithfully recorded by the earthquake machine, and as faithfully reported to the public by Steward, until he found out the fraud at last—and none too soon for his reputation as an earthquake expert. But Stewart is an earnest, ingenious and indus-

trious man, and he has clung to his investigations between drinks until he has gotten so now that he can swing the formidable scientific earthquake terms with the ease of a bald and venerable college professor. His latest achievement was the promising of an earthquake on a particular day, and the specification of the hour wherein it would arrive, its exact duration, and the probable amount of damage it would do. Everybody pumped up a supply of misery and consternation for the occasion, and when they were all ready, the earthquake did not come. This is an excellent lesson for little boys. This poor man was nothing but an ignorant bar-keeper at first, but by diligent attention to watering his whisky and studying Latin technicalities and such things, he has got so that he can tell within a year or two of when there will not be an earthquake. And he has grown wealthy, too, and some day when he gets a little further along, so that he can be prompt with his earthquakes and not disappoint the people, he will become great. He is getting up a prodigious earthquake for November, and will spare no pains or expense to make it everything the public can desire. Thus, by industry, enterprise and close attention to business, this humble young man has raised himself up to be a shining and useful member of society. Let us hope, for his sake, and the sake of his widowed mother, who is solely dependent upon him for support, that his earthquake will be an awful one this time.

BUFFALO MORNING EXPRESS

September 22, 1869

PEOPLE AND THINGS

- Chicago snubs the century plant.
- The California Pioneers are on their way to the Atlantic States.
- Joe Jefferson pockets $27,000 from his New York engagement.
- George Francis Train has been stricken deaf and dumb.
- Chicago has just shipped seven tons of mail matter by a single train.

- A Berlin comedian has been fined forty thalers for putting in a "gag" referring to the Cracow affair.
- Prophets are prematurely turning up who prophesied many years ago that Napoleon would die in the Autumn of 1869.
- The night trains through Pella, Iowa, now go screeching the whole length of the town, to make the citizens sick of a law which requires whistling at crossings.
- The *Post* says James Hannay is still at work on Thackeray's life. This will be news to parties who are under the impression that Thackeray is already dead.
- There is a man in Ohio who has written three thousand communications to the newspapers, not one of which has ever been published.
- The Albany Typographical Union unanimously voted $100 for the relief of the widows and orphans of the victims of the Avondale disaster.
- There is to be a grand Sir John Franklin hunt through Africa for Dr. Livingston. The party is to consist of a hundred well-armed men.
- Kate Bateman revived the Jewish drama to a riotous state of activity. "Leah" is on the boards at four different theatres in New York.
- Velez, who arranged the betrayal of Maximilian with Lopez, has been appointed Governor of the city and district of Mexico.
- The *Pall Mall Gazette* infers from the length of the patent lists in Paris for the last quarter, "that the French are becoming scarcely less inventive than the Americans."
- In England, when railway companies sell tickets and the cars are full, excluded passengers hire coaches, and make the company, by suit in court, pay the bill.
- When Sir Henry Holland arrived in New York from England, he found a cable dispatch informing him that the day after he left Southampton his son was accidentally drowned.
- After A. T. Stewart had cancelled the $3,940 worth of stamps on his deeds of the Hempsted Plains property, he discovered that he was required to use only $394 in stamps!
- The Chicago *Post* says the Wisconsin Democratic Convention substantially adopted the following resolutions: 1. Bow, wow, wow! 2. Bow! 3. Wow! 4. Wow, wow! 5. Bow! 6. Ki, yi, yi!"

- Women's rights has cropped out in France. Madame Audouard, a literary lady, has challenged the editor of *Figaro* to fight a duel with her. The offense was a newspaper article reflecting upon her.
- Two hundred and seventy-one miners were killed at the terrible coal mine disaster in the Plauensohben Grund, in Saxony. They left two hundred and nine widows and six hundred and eighty-three orphans.
- The Grand Jury of St. Clair county, Ill., have indicted Allen, Gallagher and McCoole for prize fighting, and there are strong hopes that the accused will get a term in the penitentiary. St. Louis weeps.
- The famous glen at Watkins, N.Y., near the head of Seneca Lake, has been purchased for $25,000 by E. B. Parsons, of Bradford county, Pa. who proposes to improve it as a popular summer resort.
- The manufacturers of sewing needles in Aix-da-Chapelle have received such extensive orders from Asia and America—more especially from China and Japan—that it is impossible to obtain workmen enough to execute them.
- The champion croquetist in England lately got through thirteen hoops without a break. If it was out on the croquet ground, she did well; but if it was in her dressing-room, it was nothing extraordinary.
- A child in Hartford fell out of a third-story window, and was picked up unhurt from the pavement. The next morning it fell from the bed to the floor and broke its neck. An ill-directed ambition is the saddest endowment any mortal can have.
- Two sisters, of Dubuque, rivals in a love affair, made the young man the stake of a bet on a horse race. The one winning was to marry him within four weeks, if she could, and the loser to remain single five years to give her a fair chance.
- Miss Kate Murphy, who is distinguishing herself in a certain way in Dorchester, Mass., on Thursday won $300 at a jumping match, having jumped eleven feet two and one-half inches to ten feet nine inches leaped by a young man named Michael Flynn.
- The Elmira *Gazette* still contends that the State Fair was rather a feeble affair, and its judgment is good. If it had not been for the gorilla, and the three-headed calf, and the other side shows, the State Fair would have been a dead failure.

- A friend was speaking to Thackeray of a lately deceased Bacchanalian, an ardent disciple of Barclay & Perkins. "Ah!" said the great humorist, with a twinkle in his eye, and a chuckle in his sigh, "Ah!" said he, "take him for half-and-half, we ne'er shall look upon his like again!"

- Anna Dickinson is "catching it" from the California press for saying shocking things about the morals of the California women of the early days. However, the San Francisco *Chronicle* hints that it will not be good policy to abuse Miss Anna too much, as evidence can be found wherewith she can back up her opinions.

- Happy Haymakers who are to have the honor of companionship with a scion of the house of Morrissey!—at least that person has made proclamation to that effect. The iron-clad egotism of this individual, in accepting his obscene notoriety as enviable fame, is enjoyable. He evidently feels that a club which is to have a son of Hon. John Morrissey as a member can need no further happiness here below.

- An "old miner" at Avondale proposes that hereafter all the miners give one day's pay every year towards the fund for the benefit of widows and orphans. By this means, he says, they can raise ten thousand dollars, and for himself he counts the first day's work that he has done since the catastrophe sacred for this purpose.

- The late Henry Keep's estate is valued at $4,000,000. By will he leaves all to his wife, daughter, and his and his wife's sisters. He gives $500,000 to his daughter; to his sister, Mary Kenyon, $185,000 and two farms in Jefferson county, New York; to his sister, Martha Fuller, $500,000; to his wife's sisters, Mrs. Cooper and Mrs. Munday, of Watertown, New York, Mrs. Fowler and Mrs. Lane, $100,000 each. The residue of his estate, including a Fifth avenue residence, &c., he gives to his wife, formerly Miss Woodruff, of Watertown.

- The *Gazette Musicale*, a Paris paper, that pretends to authority on questions of music, affirms that it has positive knowledge that Adelina Patti (Marquise Caux) has entered into a written agreement with Strakosch to come to the United States on the first of September, 1871, and to give during the ensuing eight months one hundred representations, for each one of which she is to receive ten thousand francs in gold, Strakosch paying also the expenses of the trip, and depositing with Messrs Rothschild five hundred thousand francs as security that he will carry out his part of the contract. The *Gazette* says that with this series of performances Patti's career as a singer will absolutely end, and that she will thereafter reside in Paris as the *Marquise*, and no longer as the *Diva*.

BUFFALO MORNING EXPRESS

September 24, 1869

PEOPLE AND THINGS

- Brigham Young's mother-in-law is dead.
- Some young Paris snobs have actually started the fashion of wearing bracelets.
- Vanderbilt has dined Jem Mace and Morrissey. Why this brutal neglect of Reddy, the blacksmith?
- A good thing is done, now, in writing autograph letters of Humboldt. They bring fifty dollars apiece in the market.
- Mrs. Stowe finds a champion in the person of Mr. George William Curtis, who sees nothing incredible in the Byron story and nothing heinous in the publication of it.
- The editor of the Louisville *Courier-Journal* informs his readers that "Twenty-one hundred and ninety-one years ago today (Thursday), our distinguished friend Demosthenes died by poison."
- Adelina Patti says she will not sing in New York any more. However, she will find that New York will have her Sing-Sing any how. The author of the above is no more.
- It is suggested that Bouccicault himself got up the newspaper tirade in England against the indecency of his new play, in order to secure an immense success for it in America.
- An Englishman has arrived at Odessa on his way from Calais to India on foot, in accordance with the terms of a wager. The other man keeps right along after him, to see that he does not "soldier."

- The body of a New Hampshire youth has been exhumed and his heart cut out and burned, from a superstition that this alone would save the life of his brother who is dying with the same disease, consumption.
- Burns' pew, once in St. Michael's, Dumfries, and bearing "R. B." cut by his hand in an idle hour and under weary sermonizing, has been put up for auction. As the bidding did not reach five pounds, the pew was bought in.
- Johnny McGrade, the "celebrated pugilist" (whom few people have ever heard of, perhaps), was shot dead in a saloon in White Pine, on Sept. 12, by a youth named Leonard, whom he had beaten with a slung shot. Will Leonard please come East?
- Milburn, the blind preacher, is back again from Europe, and will lecture, the coming season, on "What a Blind Man Saw in Paris," and "A Blind Man's Experience in Search of Light." He visited Europe to have a surgical operation performed on his eyes, but only an inferior success was the result.
- The *Tribune* avers that not more than two hundred and fifty thousand dollars of the five hundred and five thousand appropriated for the cleaning of the streets of New York are spent for that purpose by the ring holding the contract. It says the streets are in a shameful condition.

PERSONAL

Mr. Twain,:

Honored Sir—We have seen, from your pen, an article headed "Last Words of Great Men," O, thank you sir! Bless you! You've started a doubt,

> That shall grow until it puts our maligners to rout;
> For these great men were married, or some of them were,
> That's certain; and we, sir, shall beg to infer,
> Hence the probable end of a charge we have heard,
> That a man with a wife never *has a last word*.

Yours truly,

SOME OF THE LITTLE WOMEN

S'cat!—{M. T.

BUFFALO MORNING EXPRESS

September 25, 1869

PEOPLE AND THINGS

- Read "Hy. Slocum" in to-day's paper. (It is in John Phoenix's book, rather, but not in this mutilated condition.)
- Another Byron, the nephew of his own father, has transpired.
- Caleb Cushing's fee in the Mexican Claims Commission is starting around again. It has already had one good run.
- Prince Arthur has been making presents to Canadian dignitaries. More trouble brewing.
- Miss Braddon has gone deranged. In a fit of absence of mind, she dipped into one of her own novels.
- Ozias Potter, of Williamsport, Pa., who died recently, bequeathed about $70,000 to the poor of that city.
- There have been sixteen cases of suicide in Lowell, Mass., within eight months, mostly of young girls.
- John Burns, of New Hampshire, who died in 1846, aged eighty-six, had thirteen children, all twins.
- Mrs. Myra Bradwell, of Chicago, has been admitted to the bar with her husband—the mosquito bar, probably.
- Caleb Cushing's fee in the Mexican Claims Commission case is $4,000,000 in gold. Let it go at that a while.
- The Leavenworth *Commercial* says the Red Stockings passed through Omaha on Sunday last, and engaged to play the Omaha club on their return from San Francisco.
- A Mississippi steamboat recently ran half an hour without an engineer. The passengers had a chance to be safe for a little while, at any rate.
- Gardiner C. Hubbard addressed the San Francisco Chamber of Commerce on Tuesday night, on the subject of a postal telegraph.
- The annual reports of the National Grand Lodge of Odd Fellows show that 44,000 persons were initiated last year, making a total membership of 260,000.

- The Empress of Fashion and France has decreed that "long chatelaine braids" shall succeed chignons, high puffs and frisettes. We had been expecting this.
- A man in St. Joseph was lately detected trying to steal the gallows. He was probably meditating suicide, and was too poor to build one for himself in these hard times.
- The new Swiss settlement in Grundy county, Tennessee, is flourishing. The Swiss are delighted with the climate and with the land, which they bought at fifty cents an acre.
- George Peabody has just given an additional $400,000 to the Peabody Institute of Baltimore. Is it not about time he was figuring up to see what he has got left? The first thing he knows, he will have to be borrowing money to get home on.
- The following version of an ancient ditty is circulating as a means of fixing Vanderbilt in the juvenile mind:

> "This is the man the bears have torn,
> That married the maiden all forlorn,
> That took the Wall street bull by the horn,
> That tossed Jim Fisk, that worried Dan Drew,
> That loosed the rat that stole the stock,
> That lay in the house that Vander-bilt."

- The climate of Tennessee must possess remarkable sanitary qualities. Thus the *West Tennessee Whig* of last week says: "A negro man who was split open with an axe at Trenton a few weeks since is recovering, though slightly paralyzed on one side."
- The following inscription is on a tombstone in San Diego, Cal.: "This year is sacred to the memory of William Henry Shaken, who came to his death being shot with Colt's revolvers—one of the old kind, brass mounted— and of such is the kingdom of Heaven." —*Exchange*.
- The old church at Hingham, Mass., built in 1635, and the oldest in New England, if not in the country, having been thoroughly repaired and refitted, was rededicated on Wednesday. The church has had only seven pastors in the two hundred and thirty-four years of its existence.

- The Charleston (S.C.) *News* reports that a Northern man, who is extensively engaged in planting on the Sea Islands, having been struck with the remarkable speed attained by some of the negro boatmen in his employ, has determined to extend in their behalf to the rowing clubs of the world a challenge to a grand contest.
- The record of the Sir John Franklin expedition was found on the California coast by Mr. James Daly, of the firm of Daly & Rodgers, lumber merchants in San Buenaventura. Mr. Daly, walking on the beach, accidentally stumbled upon a battered leather bag, made of seal-skin and closely fastened, and in that the paper was found.
- The *Utah Daily Reporter*, alluding to the Byron scandal, says that in Utah apostles, presidents, bishops, elders, priests, and teachers, without shame or secrecy, practice worse crimes than Mrs. Stowe accuses Byron of. High officials marry nieces—their own brothers' daughters' and even two of them at once—marry half sisters, mothers, and daughters at the same time, and even sisters of the whole blood.
- The Right Rev. Dr. Lynch, Bishop of Charleston, will ordain Mr. Henry S. Lake, son of George Lake, Esq., late of the firm of Lake & McCreery, and a convert to the Catholic faith, in the Church of the Paulist Fathers, Fifty-ninth street and Ninth avenue, at eight o'clock this morning. Mr. George M. Searle, formerly Professor in the Naval School of Newport, will receive tonsure on the same occasion. —*N. Y. Sun.*
- An estrangement once took place between Senator Fessenden and a Senator not now a member of that body, on account of words spoken in debate. After a few days, the Senator sent him, from his desk, a note: "If I have offended you, I ask your forgiveness; if you have offended me, I have forgotten it." Mr. Fessenden did not keep back the tears when he crossed the Chamber to shake hands with his old friend, from whom he had been temporarily separated.
- A man, on the day he became one hundred years old, went to have a pair of shoes made, remarking that he wanted them built substantial, with plenty of hobnails. The storekeeper suggested that he might not live to wear such a pair of shoes out, when the old gentleman retorted that he commenced this one hundred years a good deal stronger than he did the last one! It is

a comfort to find some wit in one of these pestilential old prodigies, who have broken out like a rash all over the whole country lately.

- Two young men have been fighting a duel in California. One of them, James R. Smedberg, is a citizen of California, and the other, F. Gardner, is a tourist, "son of a former Governor of Massachusetts." The provocation was abusive gossip about Gardiner, circulated by Smedberg. Gardiner challenged, and Smedberg refused to notice him. Gardiner caned Smedberg and challenged again. Smedberg was now more tractable, and accepted. The parties met at three in the morning, at the place appointed, and at the second fire Gardiner shot off a couple of Smedberg's fingers. They then made friends and returned to the city. The weapons used were navy revolvers—distance ten paces. The penalty for dueling in California is "imprisonment in the penitentiary for not more than fourteen years." The California journals earnestly demand that the law be brought to bear upon these gentlemen.

BUFFALO MORNING EXPRESS

September 27, 1869

PEOPLE AND THINGS

- The son of the King of Malabar is in jail in London for swindling.
- The Pioneers have arrived in New York.
- Mrs. Lucy Morehead Porter, of Covington, has been appointed Postmistress of Louisville, Ky.
- The *Saturday Review* states that an unmarried daughter of Mrs. Augusta Leigh is still living.
- The most promising young sculptor in Paris is George Warren, the son of American parents, but born in France.
- The Prussian Court spends daily five hundred dollars for charities; the Russian Court twenty-five hundred.
- Another trunk has been found with a dissected body in it at Rochester. The owner is requested to call for his baggage.

- The Chicago Young Men's Christian Association has just received fifteen tons of tracts from Dublin.
- The San Francisco *Chronicle* is disgusted because no hatter there has been "smart enough to inaugurate a Seward hat."
- P. T. Barnum states that he once saved the life of James Gordon Bennett. He prevented a madman from throwing him overboard at sea.
- Dr. Cusco is the name of the young physician who succeeded in ascertaining that Napoleon III, had the stone after Ricord and Nelaton had failed to find it.
- A woman died in Worcester, Massachusetts, last week, who was thirty-eight years old, and the mother of nineteen children.
- The King of Greece is very fond of negro music. The royal band at Athens in consequence plays mostly Stephen Foster's melodies.
- No dispatches in cipher were allowed be sent from Paris to any part of the world during the panic which the dangerous illness of the Emperor created.
- Read "Hy. Slocum" in to-day's paper. [It is in John Phoenix's book, rather, but not in this mutilated condition.]

By a blunder in "making up" the forms for our last issue, the above unfortunate combination occurred. Such a discourtesy to "Hy Slocum" we certainly never intended. The following paragraph is the one to which that ungracious comment was meant to be attached:

The following inscription is on a tombstone in San Diego, Cal.: "This year is sacred to the memory of William Henry Shaken, who came to his death being shot with Colt's revolvers—one of the old kind, brass mounted—and of such is the kingdom of Heaven." *Exchange*.

After *this* we meant to say: ["It is in John Phoenix's book, rather, but not in this mutilated condition."] John Phoenix wrote that celebrated squib about one "Jeames Hambrick," who was shot on the plains, in the manner described. Virtue was not its own reward, this time, for in trying to save a dead humorist from wrong, we wronged a truly live one ourself. "Hy. Slocum" is not a plagiarist, but writes thoroughly original articles, and articles which are boiling over with hearty and healthy humor, too. We are sorry for that shabby mistake in the "make-up" and we hasten, now, to beg pardon.

APPENDIX 7

BUFFALO MORNING EXPRESS

September 28, 1869

ARTHUR.

We seldom have a live prince to chronicle, and though we have little to chronicle about this one that has been visiting us a moment yesterday, we calculate to make the most of him, anyhow. He is one of the sons of the Queen of England, but *which* one we cannot possibly get at. But being the son of a Queen, and especially the Queen of one of the greatest empires on earth, the *reveille* of whose military garrisons "follows the sun around the globe," and rattles and clatters on British territory all the time; and being a young personage whose ancestors have always sat on thrones, and whose crowns glitter in far-reaching procession back through history and the mists of tradition for a thousand years; whose blue imperial blood is filtered down to him in a more or less diluted state. From Plantagenets, Tudors, Stewarts, Dutchmen, Germans, and all sorts of people whose sires look out from the shadows of antiquity in questionable shapes as Scandinavian, pirates stirring up unoffending Normandy—stout old William, the Conqueror, stirring up the good Saxons eight hundred years ago—Richard of the Lion Heart doing fabulous feats of valor at the head of his crusading hosts in Holy Land—the knightly Black Prince, of romantic memory—stage-ridden Richard III, whose crime of smothering his infant nephews was insignificant compared to the misery he has doomed the world to suffer in theatres, watching

McKean Buchanan and similar artists cavort through the tragedy that bears his name—the old "original Jacobs" of the divorce policy, Henry VIII, who missed his opportunity when he was born in Windsor Castle instead of Chicago—the stately old Elizabeth, the "virgin queen" of questionable virginity—Charles the Martyr, Charles the Fop, James the Bigot, and that nice invoice of Georges, who began as semi-savages and ended mildly civilized but with crazed brain—we repeat that when we capture a youth of such illustrious antecedents as this young Prince Arthur is graced withal, we feel it a Christian duty to make the most of him.

THE PRINCE'S MOVEMENTS

But it is not possible to spread him over much ground, from the fact that he did not stay with us long, and did nothing but what any common mortal might have done, while he did stay—for he only took lunch, and then got out of the United States again, right away.

He and his party arrived in this city at one o'clock yesterday afternoon on a special train from Niagara Falls.

No notice was given of his coming, and there was but a small crowd at the depot, and that consisted in a large part of passengers who came in on the regular, one minute ahead of the extra.

On alighting from the car the Prince gave his arm to Lady Young, and the party proceeded at once to the carriages.

The first carriage was occupied by the Prince, Lady Young, Colonel Roland and Colonel Elphinstone.

In the second carriage were the Governor Genera, Sir Henry Young, Miss Bush, Colonel Turville, and Colonel McNiell.

Just as the carriages started the crowd indulged in quite a hearty cheer.

The party proceeded at once to the Tifft House for lunch.

There was no crowd about the hotel, for nobody knew so august a visitor was expected. A luncheon was set in parlors Nos. 1 and 2, at the hotel, and the party as above named partook of it, assisted by five invited guests—ex-President Fillmore, British Consul Hemans, Col. Pickard, and two ladies.

Mr. Fillmore was the most distinguished American to be had, and he was appointed to preside over the affair. A colored man in white kids stood guard at the door and kept strict blockade against reporters and other hunters after the British Lion. A dozen young misses, not old enough to marry, but plenty old enough to have a maidenly curiosity about princes, stayed around in an unintentional sort of way, and seized the occasional opportunities that offered to take a peep.

THE REST OF IT

His Highness is a slim-breasted youth of nineteen, with dainty side whiskers, very light hair parted three inches above his left ear, and with the royal nose and shelving forehead of the Georges. He made no remarks to us; did not ask us to dinner; walked right by us just the same as if he didn't see us; never inquired our opinion about any subject under the sun; and when his luncheon was over got into his carriage and drove off in the coolest way in the world without ever saying a word—and yet he could not know but that that was the last time he might ever see us. But if he can stand it, we can.

Prince Arthur looks pleasant and agreeable, however. He has a good, reliable, tenacious appetite, of about two-king capacity. He was the last man to lay down his knife and fork.

This is absolutely all that England's princely son did in Buffalo—absolutely all! We shall go on and make all the parade we can about it, but none of his acts in Buffalo were noisy enough for future historical record. It was *Veni, Vidi, Vici*, with him. He came—he saw that lunch—he conquered it.

The party took carriages and drove through Main and Ohio streets to the Niagara elevator; glanced at it, and at another; drove through half a dozen of the principal streets and out in the neighborhood of Fort Porter; drove back in front of the hotel and waited till one of the party went in for a moment—to pay the bill or make a royal present to somebody, likely; drove down and stopped a moment in front of Mr. Fillmore's; and then they rattled off to the depot, took a special train, of one Director's car, and left for the Clifton House, Niagara Falls. Time on American soil, four hours and a half—two and a half of which were spent on the sacred soil of Buffalo. The party were in something of a hurry to get away and prepare for a hunt in the vicinity of Long Point in the morning.

Prince Arthur's visit was unexpected, and his presence almost unknown while he remained. So his movements were free and unembarrassed by the throng of curious citizens that might have appeared on the streets if they had known what royal Jehu it was who was driving so furiously through our thoroughfares.

It is usual for princes to "express themselves well pleased with their visit." No doubt this one did—but not to us.

NOT COMING TO THE FAIR

His Royal Highness is invited to be present at the opening of the Fair—and if he could have accepted, he would have been cordially received and kindly welcomed. The following is the

CORRESPONDENCE:

International Industrial Exhibition,
Buffalo, September 27, 1869

To His Royal Highness Prince Arthur,

May it please your Royal Highness, on behalf of the Board of Managers and Officers of the International Industrial Exhibition, I would most respectfully and cordially invite your Royal Highness and your distinguished suite to attend the inaugural ceremonies of the Exhibition, which take place in this city on the 6th proximo. The high esteem in which the royal family you represent is held in the United States assures you of a generous welcome to the Empire State.

I am, with great respect,

Your obedient servant,

DAVID BEEL,
President International Industrial Exhibition

[REPLY]

NIAGARA, September 27, 1869

DEAR SIR: I am desired by H.R.H., Prince Arthur, to acknowledge the receipt of your letter of this date, inviting His Royal Highness to attend the inaugural ceremonies of the Industrial Exhibition, which is to be held in Buffalo on the 6th of October.

His Royal Highness fully appreciates the kindness of the invitation, but desires me to say that he regrets very much that a previous engagement at Kingston will prevent his attending this very interesting exhibition. Believe me,

Yours faithfully,

H. ELPHINSTONE
Col. R.E., Governor to His Royal Highness

APPENDIX 8

BUFFALO MORNING EXPRESS

December 20, 1869

INNOCENCE AT HOME; OR HUNTING A HERO IN WASHINGTON.

WASHINGTON, DECEMBER 15, 1869.

To the Editor of the Express:

Y ou know that Mark Twain lectured here last week. You also know most likely that he met with great success; had an audience composed entirely of the beauty and fashion of the city. I was there; some others were, too. Lincoln Hall was crowded, in fact, and he made an impression. I mean a lasting one— well, as lasting as—as an appointment in the Treasury Department. I can think of nothing more permanent just now. I was there, too, and can tell you the whole story; but if in the telling you should think you recognize some remarks as former acquaintances, don't blame me, or expect quotation marks to be put up. I shall do nothing of the kind, because I shouldn't know where to begin. I have read "The Innocents Abroad," and was a long time about it, but when I got through I wished the bowl had been stronger, so the tale might have been longer. But, since, I haven't been good for much. I haven't uttered a single original remark. I can't, when all I meant to say for the rest of my natural life has been put in a book by someone else. Really, it is not right. I don't believe in monopolies, and so I defy them and absorb them. I don't want to injure the sale of the book, but if its contents are in me I can't help bringing them out now and then. You understand how one can become imbued with the spirits of things, don't you? Well, that's what I mean. I don't know now which is Me at home and which is Me Abroad.

I always had a liking for literary people. I don't know many which may account for it. For lions in a general way, I don't particularly care, and I never could run after foreigners, and counts and things. I suppose I used to be afraid they would marry me for my money, because I once had a fine income of $75 per month, enough to tempt any impecunious immigrant, but owing to some prejudices existing in the minds of certain high officials in regard to the increase of the National debt, I was retrenched, although I did go to school with a Grant, and kept the Appointment Clerk's teapot in my own box. Before this I was afraid of these foreigners, because they do have a way of marrying girls for money, and if the girls are not willing, I suppose they do it any how, and then turn out to have been somebody's groom last year, and perhaps somebody's bridegroom day before yesterday. It is pleasant though to be no longer a prey to the mercenary, so my courage has risen of late, and when I heard Mark Twain was coming here, a native American hero, I grew bold and audacious and determined to know him. When Dickens was here I had designs on him and imagined all sorts of little things to write to him, which would inspire him with an ardent desire to know so gifted and appreciative a person. Once I was to be an invalid whose weary hours on a painful couch had been soothed by his magical art. But that was abandoned because I feared he might put me in his next book as a lazy novel-reading woman in a wrapper on a soiled chintz sofa with broken springs. Then I was to be one who had suffered all sorts of secret sorrows, the current of whose thoughts his wit and humor alone could divert. But that wouldn't work because he might have supposed himself addressed by a dyspeptic lunatic and have replied, "Madam, with the greatest possible respect for you, dam the current of your thoughts!" Finally I gave the whole thing up and was content with silent adoration. But after reading "The New Pilgrims' Progress," I was fully determined on capturing that author and having him for breakfast. He wouldn't put me in a book. He never does. Nor would he run away with me because those

officials whom I shall always regard as angels very completely disguised had provided against such a contingency. Therefore I made up my mind at once. That
process did not take me long whatever may be the case with some folks abroad,
but perhaps it was because the point to be decided did not require a prodigious
quantity of mind. I began after this fashion. I said to everyone, "I am crazy to
know Mark Twain," and some believed me and some didn't, and neither conclusion was flattering. But no one offered assistance. Then I changed my tactics
and for two whole days before the lecture went along the streets eyeing every
man I met with nothing but a moustache, in the most interrogative manner.
Little did I know I was far from the land where the young hero slept, until some
one told me he liked his natural rest, and having lectured the night before in
Philadelphia, would not arrive here until the last afternoon. It was charitable
information, because I was endangering my life by staring so persistently at all
the tall men arrayed as above, that I calmly walked over the small craft similarly
attired to their very just indignation. I had arranged in my mind that if I saw any
one resembling him I should say quite loud, to my companion of course, "I *must*
know Mark Twain, whereupon he would come up in his most gracious manner
and announce himself as the lecturer for the evening. I, with wonderful presence
of mind, would put up my eye-glass and say, "Ah! Is he—a—is he—married?"
That's the question I always ask about gentlemen. I don't care to know if they are
dead, or if their parents are living, or any other family secrets. But that romance
did not come off, simply because of the above-named natural longing for rest.
If he had been in the city I should have infallibly tried that experiment on every
moustache I met until I found the right one.

My friends were quite patient for the first million times they heard my excla-
mations; after that they said it grew monotonous, and several, at least three, said,
"Go to the _____;" (it is best not to mention names) "he is an intimate acquaintance of Mr. Twain, and can soon tranquilize you." So I went. His place of business is quite in the city, but I took a great many steps to get there. (On reading
over the last two sentences, I fear some may mistake the personage I went to see.
He's a head of the nation in all sincerity. The dash merely conceals his rank, so
all won't know which Secretary is meant.) I bought a new hat for the occasion
and dubbed it the "Mark Twain." Some one said, "Better not, it might pass for
a joke." But I said "No, I won't label it M.T., because that might be thought to

refer to the contents, which would be no joke to me. It could easily refer to my purse after the rash act, and that's no joke either."

Well, I went to the _____ and told him my business. He was not in the least surprised. One would have supposed I went on about a few thousand persons every day. Perhaps I do, but they are usually married and don't count. He said he'd drop him a line, which he did, and I withdrew in triumph. I had thought he'd ask whence this extreme anxiety about an innocent man who never troubled me, and I had studied up a pretty little speech about wanting to know the man who could make well-spelled, unitalicized jokes, and who took to water every other page, though he confesses to having the cholera generally after a bath. There are not many men who would suffer so for their principles.

I read the note. I always read notes sent by me, as a matter of course. I don't pretend to be a mail. What I got by it was to find myself put down in black and white as an "admirer." I suppose our mutual friend thought that was the correct thing to say, so he said it, though he didn't know what it meant, or words to that effect. That comes of running up tax bills. These public men are so matter-of-fact. They never deal in figures of speech, yet they do the reverse very often, for hours.

After that, much time was consumed in planning a masterly approach to my subject. With the aid of two dark conspirators, I waylaid him after the lecture and to what purpose? Merely to receiving a polite greeting in an exasperatingly cold room, and then to make way for some one else. I believe the _____ keeps lines ready to drop on the aspirants to Mark Twain's acquaintance. I had to be agonized by the sight of thousands of charming young ladies, similarly ticketed with myself, and how can I hope to be remembered among so many? Of course, too, this thing occurs every where. Why didn't I think of that before? That was all I got by it. Never a moment to ask about the Doctor or Dan, (I do love Dan), or to get Blucher's addresses, so he could quarrel with my French teacher for me. But I did get something else, too. I got a most tremendous cold, and what I have suffered since in mustard plasters and whiskey punches my feeble pen cannot portray. Moreover, as a consequence possibly of the above, I dreamed that night of dying, and leaving pathetic directions about my tombstone. I wished my friends to Mark Twain there-upon, that no one might suppose me singular.

It's likely I'll hunt a hero again.

LITTLE RED RIDING HOOD

APPENDIX 9

FROM PAGE ONE, *BUFFALO MORNING EXPRESS*

Saturday, November 13, 1869

Image A9.1. From page one of the *Buffalo Morning Express* of Saturday, November 13, 1869. In the center columns, Twain's Around the World letter, the third in the series, concerning the climate in California, can be seen. (Image from the *Buffalo Morning Express*, November 13, 1869.)

ABBREVIATIONS

BELOW IS A LIST OF ABBREVIATIONS USED IN THE NOTES AND BIBLIOGRAPHY.

AMT	*Autobiography of Mark Twain*, vol. 1
BDC	*Buffalo Daily Courier*
BDCA	*Buffalo Daily Commercial Advertiser*
BECHS	Buffalo and Erie County Historical Society
BME	*Buffalo Morning Express*
BT	*Buffalo Times*
MTL3	*Mark Twain's Letters, Volume 3: 1869*
MTL4	*Mark Twain's Letters, Volume 4: 1870–1871*
MTL5	*Mark Twain's Letters, Volume 5: 1872–1873*
MTL6	*Mark Twain's Letters, Volume 6: 1874–1875*
MTM	Mark Twain Memorial, Hartford, Connecticut
MTP	Mark Twain Project, University of California, Berkeley
OL	Olivia Langdon
OLC	Olivia Langdon Clemens
SLC	Samuel Langhorne Clemens

NOTES

Abbreviations of books, periodicals, letter collections, and personal names are used here. Full titles and names can be found in the section titled Abbreviations.

PROLOGUE

1. I owe a tremendous debt to Patrick B. Kavanagh, historian of Buffalo's Forest Lawn Cemetery, for conducting private tours of the cemetery for me in August and September of 2011, for sharing his encyclopedic knowledge of the history of Forest Lawn and of Buffalo, and for his generous gifts of archival materials.

2. Albert Bigelow Paine, *Mark Twain: A Biography*, vol. 1 (New York: Harper & Brothers, 1912), p. 413.

3. Ibid., p. 431.

4. Ibid., p. 424.

5. Delancey Ferguson, *Mark Twain: Man and Legend* (New York: Bobbs-Merrill, 1943), p. 155.

6. Ibid., p. 154.

7. E. Hudson Long, *The Mark Twain Handbook* (New York: Hendricks House, 1957), p. 90.

8. Arthur L. Scott, *Mark Twain at Large* (Chicago: Henry Regenery, 1969), p. 72.

9. Justin Kaplan, *Mr. Clemens and Mark Twain* (New York: Simon & Schuster, 1966), p. 121.

10. Ibid., p. 127.

11. Fred Kaplan, *The Singular Mark Twain* (New York: Doubleday, 2003), p. 265.

12. Jerome Loving, *Mark Twain: The Adventures of Samuel L. Clemens* (Berkeley: University of California Press, 2010), p. 170.

13. Marty O'Neill, "Mark Twain, Buffalo Editor Who Wielded a Biting Pen," *Buffalo Evening News*, November 29, 1947.

14. "Salutatory," *BME*, August 21, 1869.

INTRODUCTION

1. Twain's witty and caustic line upon entering the *Express's* editorial room for the first time has become a part of local literary lore. The anecdote, with variations, has been told and retold. John Harrison Mills, a colleague of Twain at the *Express*, reported it in 1910 ("When Mark Twain Lived in Buffalo," *Buffalo Sunday Morning News*, May 15). It appeared in the anonymous June 30, 1912, *New York Times* story "When Mark Twain Was Editor of a Buffalo Newspaper." In a 1928 reminiscence, Samuel Potter Burrill recalled working at the post-Twain *Express* and hearing staffers still talking about it: "It was the generally accepted version in the old *Express* office, when I first went to work there" ("Yesterday, Today, Tomorrow," *BT*, sec. 9, pp. 2, 7). And Marty O'Neill's retrospective in a 1947 *Buffalo Evening News* issue repeats the story ("Mark Twain, Buffalo Editor Who Wielded a Biting Pen," November 29). The original source seems to be Earl Berry, a young *Express* reporter who was likely an eyewitness in the editorial room at the time of Twain's stinging remark. According to Berry, it may have occurred shortly after Twain's first day at the *Express*. Berry recalled it as occurring after eight o'clock one night when Twain appeared in the doorway of the editorial rooms and was disgusted to see six or so local Republican loyalists lounging around, taking up all the available chairs. After Twain's sarcastic comments, the politicos, including Rodney W. Daniels, Dan Post, and DeWitt Clinton Welch, a foreman at Pierce and Company lumber, scattered ("Mark Twain as a Buffalo Editor," *Globe*, April 1873, pp. 6–7; Earl D. Berry, "In the Fenian War: Earl D. Berry Writes of the *Express* in Those Stormy Days," *BME*, January 15, 1896, p. 2).

2. Mark Twain, *AMT*, ed. Harriet Elinor Smith (Berkeley: University of California Press, 2010), p. 320.

3. Ibid., p. 364.

4. Charles Webb's preface to *The Celebrated Jumping Frog of Calaveras County* refers to Twain as the "Wild Humorist of the Pacific Slope," as related by Justin Kaplan in *Mr. Clemens and Mark Twain* (New York: Simon and Schuster, 1966), p. 32. Twain and his publicist used that label for self-promotion on lecture tours.

5. City and Vicinity, *Buffalo Express*, July 15, 1869. Opened in 1865 by George Tifft, whose dairy farm is today's Tifft Nature Preserve near Buffalo's waterfront, the posh 250-room hotel featured a long list of famous guests. In addition to Twain, opera diva Adelina Patti, comedians Weber and Fields, and boxing champions John L. Sullivan and Bob Fitzsimmons stayed there. Millard Fillmore's son and Grover Cleveland were regular patrons of a bachelor's table on the ground floor. Twain and the Tifft House intersected in other ways, as subsequent chapters in this book document.

6. Mark Twain, *The Innocents Abroad* (Hartford, CT: American Publishing Company, 1887), pp. 620–21.

7. Victor Fischer and Michael Frank, eds., *MTL4* (Berkeley, CA: University of California Press, 1995), p. 66. Letter jointly written with Olivia to her parents, February 9, 1870.

8. Ibid., p. 254. Letter to Warren L. Brigham, December 1, 1870.

1. THE BOYS OF THE *EXPRESS*

1. According to the *Statistical Abstract of the United States, 1910* (Washington, DC: Government Printing Office, 1911), the population of Buffalo in 1870 was 117,714.

2. Twain published a story about the Lydia Thompson Blondes, "The Blondes," in the *Express*, February 28, 1870. It is interesting to speculate whether Twain may have attended one of their August performances in Buffalo without leaving a record of it. He certainly would not have admitted seeing the scandalous Blondes to Olivia, to whom he had sworn strict, morally upright behavior in his remaining bachelor days. However, Twain's *Express* story is filled with authoritative details about the Blondes' stage routines, which suggests his firsthand knowledge.

3. "Four Streets Remind Buffalo of Elam R. Jewett, Publisher," *Buffalo Courier-Express*, June 22, 1941.

4. SLC to Elisha Bliss Jr., August 14 and 15, 1869, in *MTL3*, ed. Victor Fischer and Michael Frank (Berkeley: University of California Press, 1992).

5. "Jewett Homestead," *Buffalo Evening News*, June 12, 1925. This article mentions that each year, Jewett held the annual press club outing in his yard and that "Mark Twain was present and read selections from his now immortal works."

6. SLC to OL, September 3, 1869, in Fischer and Frank, *MTL3*.

7. Dennis Bowen and Sherman S. Rogers, attorneys, located on the south side of Erie Street, number 28, between Main and Pearl Streets. Bowen and Rogers had evolved from the historic firm of Fillmore, Hall, and Haven. Millard Fillmore became president of the United States, Nathan Hall became postmaster general, and Solomon G. Haven became mayor of Buffalo and was three times elected as a member of Congress. Future US president Grover Cleveland joined Bowen and Rogers in the 1850s as a clerk.

8. Buffalo's waterfront industry at the Erie Basin and beyond developed where the Erie Canal's western terminus met the Great Lakes. There was a complex of shipyards, mills, coal docks, wharves, slips, an inner harbor protected by a breakwater, and elevators (Joseph Dart invented the grain elevator in Buffalo in 1842). The center of commerce was the Central Wharf, one thousand feet of four-story brick buildings housing offices and warehouses.

9. "An Early City Editor: Some of the Experiences of Thomas Kennett," *Buffalo Express*, January 15, 1896, p. 2

10. Earl D. Berry, "In the Fenian War: Earl D. Berry Writes of the *Express* in Those Stormy Days," *BME*, January 15, 1896, p. 2.

11. Earl Berry, "Mark Twain as a Buffalo Editor," *Globe*, April 1873. When Berry left the *Buffalo Express*, he took the yellow chair with him. At the time of his death in 1919, it was "one of the prized possessions in the Berry home." ("Earl D. Berry Is Dead," *New York Times*, December 23, 1919, p. 9). While still a young reporter and editor at the *Buffalo Express*, Berry later served on the Board of Aldermen in Buffalo, led a movement in the mid-1870s to start a professional baseball franchise in the city, and had a song, "Park Lake Waltzes" by composer Louis H. Plogsted, dedicated to him.

12. "When Mark Twain Was Editor of a Buffalo Newspaper," *New York Times*, June 30, 1912.

13. Berry, "Mark Twain as a Buffalo Editor."

14. Ibid.; John Harrison Mills, "When Mark Twain Lived in Buffalo," *Buffalo Sunday News*, May 15, 1910.

15. Francis A. Crandall, "Voice of Washington," *Buffalo Express*, January 15, 1896. Twain's interest in phrenology (a belief in which personality traits can be "read" in the features of the skull) and mesmerism appear in *The Adventures of Tom Sawyer* and *Adventures of Huckleberry Finn*. In chapters 12 and 22 of *Tom Sawyer*, for example, references are made to disappointing or quack phrenologists.

16. "New Year's Presentations," *Buffalo Express*, January 3, 1870. Twain was visiting Olivia in Elmira in between lectures, but his *Express* colleagues had fun with the strange gift of a "Palestine Fox" that was accompanied by an amusing note. Earl Berry may have written the *Express* response, since he imagines Twain's yellow office chair with the swing tablet arm "thanking" the donor of the fox: "For the gift his M. T. chair places its hand (it is an arm chair) on its second back rail and bows its grateful acknowledgements." The *Express* story continues by commenting on the fox's expensive tastes—staffers must only feed it "first-chop steak."

17. SLC to OL, August 19, 1869, in Fischer and Frank, *MTL3*, p. 304.

18. My gratitude to Maryanne Reigstad for sharing her expert analysis of the look of the pre- and post-Twain *Express*.

19. Earl Berry, "Mark Twain as a Newspaperman," *Buffalo Express*, November 11, 1917.

20. Ralph Bergengren, "The Annals of Our Age-Worn World," *Boston Evening Transcript*, October 25, 1924.

21. John B. Olmsted, *Josephus Nelson Larned*, vol. 19 of *Buffalo Historical Society Publications*, ed. Frank Severance (Buffalo, NY: Buffalo Historical Society, 1915), p. 31.

22. "Col. Selkirk, Grand Old Man of Buffalo, Is Still Young Despite 90 Active Years," *Buffalo Courier*, January 25, 1925.

23. SLC to OL, September 8 and 9, 1869, in Fischer and Frank, *MTL3*.

24. Berry, "Mark Twain as a Newspaperman," p. 40.

25. SLC to OL, September 8 and 9, 1869, in Fischer and Frank, *MTL3*.

26. SLC to OL, August 21, 1869, in ibid., p. 316.

27. SLC to J. N. Larned, November 1, 1900, MTP.

28. Albert Bigelow Paine, *Mark Twain: A Biography*, vol. 1 (New York: Harper and Brothers, 1912), p. 399.

29. J. N. Larned, *Larned's History of the World* (New York: World Syndicate Company, 1915), p. 1084. In a section of volume 4 titled "Chief Characters of the Sixth Epoch," Larned lists the most influential authors of this period of history as Thackery, Scott, Balzac, Eliot, and Dickens. He lists Twain among twenty other authors "of the second rank."

30. "Colonel Selkirk," *BME*, May 19, 1925, p. 8.

31. Kate Burr, "Meet Mark Twain of Delaware Avenue," *BT*, April 12, 1931, magazine sec., p. 2.

32. "Buffalo's Grand Old Man," *Buffalo Courier*, January 25, 1925.

33. Grace Carew Sheldon, "This Day in Buffalo's History: Fifty Years Ago Today," *BT*, November 2, 1916.

34. Mills, "When Mark Twain Lived in Buffalo."

35. Paine, *Mark Twain*, p. 388.

36. Sam Welch, "Sam Welch, Reporter," *Buffalo Express*, January 15, 1896.

37. Berry, "Mark Twain as a Buffalo Editor."

38. Mark Twain, "A Letter from Mark Twain," *Globe*, May 1873.

39. Mills, "When Mark Twain Lived in Buffalo."

40. Letter from David Gray to L. B. Proctor, June 19, 1874, in *Letters, Poems and Selected Prose Writings of David Gray*, ed. J .N. Larned (Buffalo, NY: Courier Company, 1888).

41. Olmsted, *Josephus Nelson Larned*, pp. 3–33.

42. "Twain Success a Puzzle to His Old Office Boy," *Buffalo Courier-Express*, February 24, 1929, sec. S, p. 8. Apparently, squeaky shoes were a pet peeve of Twain's. Twain once testily shouted at a man attending one of his lectures to remove his creaking shoes. Fred W. Lorch, *The Trouble Begins at Eight: Mark Twain's Lecture Tours* (Ames: Iowa State University Press, 1966), p. 352.

43. "Mark Twain Years Ago," *New York Times Magazine*, April 18, 1909, p. 9.

44. Mark Twain, *AMT*, ed. Harriet Elinor Smith (Berkeley: University of California Press, 2010), p. 351.

45. "It Vanished Like a Dream," *BME*, February 2, 1870.

46. Berry, "In the Fenian War," p. 2.

47. Twain acquired a copy of this two-volume set for his personal library in 1888. In the spring of that year he sent a check care of Charles Underhill of Buffalo to Larned to help cover publishing expenses for the Gray book.

48. SLC to Elisha Bliss Jr., September 27, 1869, in Fischer and Frank, *MTL3*, p. 362. Twain referred to his band of journalistic brothers in Buffalo as "good boys."

2. I WOULD RATHER SCRIBBLE

1. SLC to OL, 1869, in *MTL3*, ed. Victor Fischer and Michael Frank (Berkeley: University of California Press, 1992), p. 317.

2. Possibly Andrew Langdon, Olivia's first cousin, who was about the same age as Twain.

3. Cataract House Hotel registry, August 4–5, 1869, at the Local History Department of the Niagara Falls, New York, Public Library. Mr. and Mrs. Brooks later were among the few to be present at the private wedding ceremony of Twain and Olivia in Elmira. Mrs. Brooks clasped pearls around Olivia's neck and draped her wedding veil at the ceremony. Still later, she sent a cradle to Buffalo as a gift for their infant son, Langdon. See Mary Boewe, "The Brooks Family: A Biographical Note," *Mark Twain Society Bulletin* 13, no. 2 (1990): 5. The Sayles family was also among the select company who attended the wedding.

4. SLC to Mary Mason and Abel W. Fairbanks, in Fischer and Frank, *MTL3*, p. 298.

5. In a curious historical footnote, Twain nearly missed bumping into landscape archi-tect Frederick Law Olmsted, architect Henry Hobson Richardson, and wealthy, politically con-nected Buffalo lawyer William Dorsheimer, all of whom signed in at the Cataract House on Saturday, August 7, 1869 (Twain and the Langdon party appear to have returned to Elmira on the sixth or early on the seventh). The three power brokers were meeting to explore ways to pre-serve the area around Niagara Falls as parkland. See Francis R. Kowsky, "In Defense of Niagara: Frederick Law Olmsted and the Niagara Reservation," SUNY College at Buffalo, Preservation Coalition of Erie County Board of Directors, originally published in "The Distinctive Charms of the Niagara Scenery: Frederick Law Olmsted and the Niagara Reservation," the catalog for the 1985 Niagara Reservation art exhibit, http://buffaloah.com/h/kowsky/nf/index.html (accessed June 20, 2012). It is also tantalizing to speculate whether at some point in his exploration of Falls tourist sites, Twain happened to walk past Lydia Thompson, Nellie Henderson, and Alexander Henderson of the Blondes Burlesque troupe. On Thursday, August 5, they crossed the pedestrian bridge to tour Goat Island, paid the twenty-five-cent fee at the tollbooth, and signed their names in the Goat Island Register. They were in Western New York for a week-long booking in Buffalo.

6. Once back in Elmira, in a statement titled "Expenses at Niagara," dated August 9, Charles Langdon totaled Twain's tab for the trip as $15.40—$10.50 for the Cataract bill and $4.90 for the train fare to Elmira. It is highly unlikely that the Langdons expected, much less received, payment (in Fischer and Frank, *MTL3*, p. 300).

7. "A Day at Niagara" concludes with an angry mob tossing Twain over the Falls. While swirling about in the whirlpool at the base of the Falls, he calls out for help to a man squatting on the shore holding a pipe. The man ignores his pleas and asks Twain instead if he has a match. The bad Samaritan is a coroner hoping to collect a cadaver. Thus began a running gag that Twain used in the *Express*, singling out the avarice of coroners who constantly drummed up business. One of Twain's favorite targets in the *Express* was Dr. John J. Burke, a coroner in Buffalo. Twain's mock feud with Burke was particularly intense in the spring of 1870 when Twain referred to Burke as "our pompous and officious coroner" and complained about Burke's "personal abuse of the City Editor of the Express" (City and Vicinity, *BME*, May 3, 1870). In the April 30 *Express*, Twain took aim at his greed: "The zeal of Dr. Burke outruns his wit." And in March, Twain also criticized the coroner profession in the *Express* (City and Vicinity, March 23, 1870). Again Twain had just used this bit of comic business in chapter 17 of *The Innocents Abroad* when he wrote of a predatory undertaker in San Francisco who eagerly sat at deathbeds with a watch in hand. Later on, Twain alludes to a greedy coroner in chapter 11 of *A Connecticut Yankee in King Arthur's Court* when Hank Morgan says listening to Sandy's tale was "as welcome as a corpse to a coroner."

8. Apparently, the traumatic effect on Twain of excessive signs dotting the Falls grounds was long lasting. Years later, in his charming story "The Earliest Authentic Mention of Niagara Falls: Extracts from Adam's Diary Translated from the Original MS.," Twain sets the Garden of Eden in Niagara Falls and describes Adam's complaint that with each new day Eve is "littering the

whole estate with . . . offensive signs: 'Keep Off the Grass;' 'This Way to the Whirlpool;' 'This Way to Goat Island;' 'Cave of the Winds This Way.'" See Twain's story in *The Niagara Book*, ed. Irving Underhill and Walter Nichols (Buffalo, NY: Underhill and Nichols: 1893).

9. Walter Blair's *Native American Humor, 1800–1900* (New York: HarperCollins College, 1960) is the seminal text on this subject.

10. Mark Twain, "Mark Twain and Niagara," *Niagara Gazette*, August 25, 1869. The author discovered this item in September of 1983 around two thirty in the morning after completing a copyediting shift. It was found while reading back issues of the *Gazette* on a microfilm reader in the cramped library off the second-floor editorial room in an effort to determine if indeed the Niagara Falls paper had acknowledged Twain's humorous *Buffalo Express* treatment of the Falls. However, Robert Hirst, the general editor of the Mark Twain Project, was not able to indisputably establish Twain's authorship. A case may be made, however, that if Twain did not write it himself, then it was submitted with Twain's heavy influence by his right-hand *Express* reporter, the intrepid and talented Earl Berry (thus the *B* initial as a byline). "Mark Twain and Niagara" was reprinted in the *Niagara Gazette*, October 16, 1983, but has never before been reprinted in book form.

11. Bruce R. McElderry Jr., *Contributions to the* Galaxy *1868–1871 by Mark Twain* (Delmar, NY: Scholars' Facsimiles and Reprints, 1977), p. 101.

12. Mark Twain's "In Trouble" (*BME*, August 27, 1869) has never been reprinted in book form. It has been reprinted in the following: Robert W. Bingham, "Buffalo's Mark Twain," *Buffalo Historical Society Museum Notes* 2, nos. 4–6 (August 1935); Lloyd Graham, "Blondin: The Hero of Niagara," *American Heritage* (August 1958): 107; Tom Reigstad, ed., "Mark Twain: The Buffalo Years," *Buffalo Courier-Express Sunday Magazine* series, June 27, 1982; and again in David Fears, ed., *Mark Twain Day by Day, Volume 1: 1835–1885* (Banks, OR: Horizon Micro Publishers, 2008), p. 292.

13. Pierre Berton, *Niagara: A History of the Falls* (Toronto: McClelland and Stewart, 1992), pp. 124–49.

14. "Big Thing for Jenkins," *Niagara Gazette*, September 1, 1869.

15. Mark Twain, "Mark Twain in a Fix," *BME*, September 9, 1869. This story has never been reprinted in book form and was reprinted only once before, in the *Buffalo Courier-Express Sunday Magazine* series, "Mark Twain: The Buffalo Years," June 27, 1982.

16. The six illustrations supplied by John Harrison Mills for Twain's Niagara feature stories (*BME*, August 21 and 28, 1869) and for the subsequent Saturday features called "Journalism in Tennessee" (*BME*, September 4, 1869) and "The Wild Man. Interviewed" (*BME*, September 18, 1869) have never been reprinted.

17. SLC to OL, in Fischer and Frank, *MTL3*, pp. 303, 349.

18. SLC to Whitelaw Reid, in ibid., pp. 342–43.

19. Earl Berry, "Mark Twain as a Newspaper Man," *Buffalo Express*, November 11, 1917, section 5, p. 40. In his reminiscence, Berry inaccurately named the police court judge as Ryan, apparently confusing Vanderpoel with a contemporary, Justice of the Peace James Ryan.

20. It is worth noting the possibility of an inside joke between Berry and Twain when their *Niagara Gazette* spoof, "Mark Twain and Niagara," mocks Twain as an incompetent newspaper scribbler barely talented enough to handle his customary lowly assignments, "reporting court cases and street-rows." Five years earlier, Twain had spent the summer at the *San Francisco Daily Morning Call* as a crime reporter, assigned to goings-on at San Francisco prisons and the police court. As such, Twain was familiar with the range of sensory experiences in police courts. In *The Innocents Abroad*, he described an exotic marketplace as smelling like a police court.

21. Earl D. Berry, "In the Fenian War. Earl D. Berry Writes of the *Express* in Those Stormy Days," *BME*, January 15, 1896, p. 2.

22. SLC to OL, in Fischer and Frank, *MTL3*, p. 345.

23. Quoted in the *BME* advertising supplement, October 9, 1869.

24. People and Things, *BME*, August 17, 1869.

25. People and Things, *BME*, August 23, 1869.

26. Although it began as an unsigned item in People and Things, Twain later republished this as "A Fine Old Man" in his 1875 collection *Sketches New and Old*. The book contained twenty additional stories originally published in the *Buffalo Express*.

27. People and Things, *BME*, September 9, 1869.

28. People and Things, *BME*, September 4, 1869.

29. SLC to OL, September 7, in Fischer and Frank, *MTL3*, p. 345.

30. Mark Twain, "The Legend of the Capitoline Venus," *BME*, October 23, 1869; and "A Ghost Story," *BME*, January 15, 1870.

31. People and Things, *BME*, August 21 and 24 (containing two Vanderbilt briefs) and September 24 and 25.

32. People and Things, *BME*, September 8, 1869: "The new order requiring the New York policemen to wear their uniforms on all occasions, is making trouble—they do not like to sleep with their clothes on." In chapter 31 of *The Innocents Abroad*, Twain honors a Roman guard who remained at his post despite the volcanic ash strewn by Mt. Vesuvius: "Let us remember that he was a soldier—not a policeman—and so praise him. Being a soldier, he stayed—because the warrior instinct forbade him to fly. Had he been a policeman, he would have stayed also—because he would have been asleep."

33. Mark Twain, "Only a Nigger," *BME*, August 26, 1869.

34. See appendix 4 for John Harrison Mills's drawing with the caption "That stove is utterly ruined."

35. See in appendix 4, image A4.6, "To dig up the Byron family!"

36. Mark Twain, "Rev. H. W. Beecher—His Private Habits," *BME*, September 25, 1869.

37. Mark Twain, "Arthur," *BME*, September 28, 1869. "Arthur" was reprinted once, in the *Buffalo Courier-Express Sunday Magazine* series, "Mark Twain in Buffalo," August 22, 1982, but never in book form. Twain's sarcasm about being happy never to see the prince again is ironic. In 1907, when Twain was awarded an honorary doctor of letters degree at Oxford University, Twain stood alongside Prince Arthur.

38. Josephus Larned, "From J.N. Larned," *BME*, January 15, 1896.

39. John Harrison Mills, "When Mark Twain Lived in Buffalo," *Buffalo Sunday News*, May 15, 1910.

3. THIS CARAVANSERY

1. Kate Burr, "Meet Mark Twain of Delaware Avenue," *BT*, April 12, 1931, magazine sec., p. 2.

2. Matthews, who came to Buffalo from Elmira, became a prominent developer of hydro-electric power facilities in Niagara Falls and a philanthropic multimillionaire in Buffalo.

3. Burr, "Meet Mark Twain of Delaware Avenue," p. 2.

4. Earl Berry, "Mark Twain as a Newspaper Man," *Buffalo Express*, November 11, 1917, p. 40.

5. John Harrison Mills, "When Mark Twain Lived in Buffalo," *Buffalo Sunday News*, May 15, 1910.

6. SLC to OL, September 7, 1869, in *MTL3*, ed. Victor Fischer and Michael Frank (Berkeley: University of California Press, 1992), p. 344.

7. SLC to Edward H. Paige, May 20, 1870, in *MTL4*, Victor Fischer and Michael Frank (Berkeley: University of California Press, 1995), p. 133.

8. According to Mills ("When Mark Twain Lived in Buffalo"), Twain also went swimming off the smooth, sandy stretches of a beach in the Buffalo River or Lake Erie with Larned and Gray.

9. Slee, Underhill, and McWilliams worked at Buffalo's Anthracite Coal Association office as part of a coal syndicate that included the J. Langdon and Company coal firm from Elmira, the Delaware, Lackawanna and Western Railroad Company, and the Pittston and Elmira Coal Company.

10. SLC and OLC to Jervis Langdon, March 2 and 3, 1870, in Fischer and Frank, *MTL4*, p. 81.

11. SLC to OL, September 1, 1869, in Fischer and Frank, *MTL3*, p. 325.

12. SLC to OL, February 27, 1869, in ibid., pp. 115–16.

13. "Change in the Express," *BDC*, September 1, 1869.

14. "A Liberal Gift to the General Hospital," *BME*, August 27, 1869, p. 4.

15. SLC to OLC, January 20, 1872, in *MLT5*, ed. Lin Salamo and Harriet Elinor Smith (Berkeley: University of California Press, 1997), p. 29.

16. *Mercersburg* 16, no. 3 (Spring 1989):19. The portrait now hangs in the library of the Mercersburg Academy in Pennsylvania.

17. "Popular Books," *BME*, August 5, 1870.

18. Kate Burr, "That Famous 'Nameless' with Its Thirteen," *BT*, November 4, 1928.

19. City and Vicinity, *BME*, March 15, 1870.

20. Mark Twain, *AMT*, ed. Harriet Elinor Smith (Berkeley: University of California Press, 2010), p. 375.

21. Stephen R. Powell, *Rushing the Growler: A History of Brewing in Buffalo* (Buffalo, NY: Digital Print Services, 1996).

22. SLC to OL, September 1, 1869, in Fischer and Frank, *MTL3*, p. 325.

23. J. D. F. Slee to SLC, December 27, 1869, in the Mark Twain Papers, ed. Robert H. Hirst (Berkeley: Bancroft Library, University of California).

24. Mills, "When Mark Twain Lived in Buffalo."

4. MY RASCALLY PILGRIMAGE

1. Fred W. Lorch, "Mark Twain's 'Sandwich Island' Lecture and the Failure at Jamestown, New York, in 1869," *American Literature* 25 (November 1953): 314–25. Also informative is Lorch's *The Trouble Begins at Eight: Mark Twain's Lecture Tours* (Ames: Iowa State University Press, 1966).

2. SLC to OL, September 3, 1869, in *MTL3*, ed. Victor Fischer and Michael Frank (Berkeley: University of California Press, 1992), p. 333.

3. Mark Twain, "Around the World: Letter No. 1," *BME*, October 16, 1869.

4. I am indebted to Herbert A. Wisbey Jr., former professor emeritus of Elmira College, and to the Elmira College Archives, for much of the biographical data on Ford.

5. SLC to OL, March 12, 1869, in Fischer and Frank, *MTL3*, p. 162.

6. Ibid., p. 350.

7. SLC to Elisha Bliss Jr., January 1870, in *MTL4*, ed. Victor Fischer and Michael Frank (Berkeley: University of California Press, 1995), p. 33.

8. SLC to Mary Fairbanks, September 26 and 27, 1869, in Fischer and Frank, *MTL3*, p. 359.

9. SLC and OLC to Jervis and Olivia Lewis Langdon, March 27, 1870, in Fischer and Frank, *MTL4*, p. 99.

10. Justin Kaplan, *Mr. Clemens and Mark Twain* (New York: Simon and Schuster, 1966), p. 76.

11. D. R. Ford to Col. H. M. Smith, March 22, 1870, Elmira College Archives.

12. Herbert A. Wisbey Jr., "Another Ford Letter Discovered," *Mark Twain Society Bulletin* 18, no. 1 (January 1995): 5–6.

13. *BME*, "Around the World Letter No. One," October 16, 1869.

14. "Prof. D. R. Ford, D.D., Died at Noon Yesterday," *Elmira Daily Advertiser*, November 26, 1904.

15. Mark Twain, "The Legend of the Capitoline Venus," *BME*, October 23, 1869.

16. Twain's imagination was so captured by the swindle that three months later, while off lecturing, he sent another story to the *Express* satirizing the materialistic success of the Cardiff Giant hoax, he titled it "A Ghost Story," and it appeared in the *BME* of January 15, 1870.

17. Fischer and Frank, *MTL4*, p. 6.

18. SLC to OL, December 15 and 16, 1869, in Fischer and Frank, *MTL3*, p. 427.

19. SLC to OL, November 15 and 16, 1869, in ibid., p. 395.

20. Ibid., p. 66. Quotes taken from Twain's report in the *San Francisco Alta California* of February 1867.

21. Anna Dickinson to Mary E. Dickinson, March 14, 1873, in Fischer and Frank, *MTL3*, p. 66.

22. Mark Twain, "Civilized Brutality," *BME*, November 20, 1869.

23. Mark Twain, "Hanging to Slow Music," *BME*, November 11, 1869.

24. Mark Twain, "The Paraguay Puzzle," *BME*, November 9, 1869.

25. Mark Twain, "The Richardson Murder," *BME*, December 3, 1869; Mark Twain, "The Law of Divorce," *BME*, December 4, 1869.

26. Mark Twain, "An Indignant Rebuke," *BME*, December 29, 1869; "The Hyenas," *BME*, December 30, 1869.

27. Mark Twain, "A Good Letter. Mark Twain's Idea of It," *BME*, November 10, 1869.

28. In "Browsing Around," *BME*, November 27 and December 4, 1869.

29. A few months later, Twain wrote humorously again about participating in a meet-and-greet reception line at President Grant's White House in "At the President's Reception," *BME*, October 1, 1870.

30. SLC to OL, December 14, 1869, in Fischer and Frank, *MTL3*, p. 424.

31. SLC to Elisha Bliss Jr., January 28, 1870, in Fischer and Frank, *MTL4*, p. 40.

32. SLC to OL, November 10 and 11, 1869, in Fischer and Frank, *MTL3*, p. 391.

33. SLC to OL, November 24 and 25, 1869, in ibid., p. 403.

34. Resa Willis, *Mark and Livy* (New York: MacMillan, 1992), p. 53.

35. Original property deed located in Erie County Clerk's office, Old Erie County Hall, Basement Record Room, 92 Franklin Street, Buffalo, New York.

36. Mary Lawton, *A Lifetime with Mark Twain* (New York: Brace, 1925), pp. 65–66.

37. John Harrison Mills, "When Mark Twain Lived in Buffalo," *Buffalo Sunday News*, May 15, 1910.

38. SLC to OL, September 3, 1869, in Fischer and Frank, *MTL3*, p. 429.

39. SLC to OL, January 10, 1870, in Fischer and Frank, *MTL4*, p. 17.

40. SLC to James Redpath, January 8, 1870, and SLC to OL, January 10, 1870, in ibid., pp. 10, 15.

41. Charles Webster, ed., *Mark Twain, Business Man* (Boston: Little, Brown, 1946), p. 109. Twain later includes this song in chapter 3 of *Life on the Mississippi* and in chapter 16 of *Adventures of Huckleberry Finn.*

42. Various sources have supplied bits of information on the wedding ceremony and train trip to Buffalo: Annie Moffett's recollections in Webster, *Mark Twain, Business Man*, pp. 109–10; "Personal," *BME*, February 3, 1870; Mary Fairbanks's article, "The Wedding of 'Mark Twain," in Fischer and Frank, *MTL4*, pp. 46–47; and in David Fears, ed., *Mark Twain Day by Day, Volume 1: 1835–1885* (Banks, OR: Horizon Micro Publishers, 2008), p. 309.

5. ALADDIN'S PALACE

1. For descriptions of director's cars, I found the following informative: John H. White Jr., *The American Railroad Passenger Car* (Baltimore: John Hopkins University Press, 1978); Edward T. Dunn, *A History of Railroads in Western New York*, 2nd ed. (Buffalo, NY: Canisius College Press, 2000).

2. Mark Twain, *AMT*, ed. Harriet Elinor Smith (Berkeley: University of California Press, 2010), p. 321.

3. "Twain and Cable," *BME*, December 11, 1884, p. 4.

4. According to Charles Dudley Warner in *The Courtship of Olivia Langdon and Mark Twain*, by Susan K. Harris (New York: Cambridge University Press, 1996), p. 136.

5. Mary Fairbanks, "The Wedding of 'Mark Twain,'" *Cleveland Herald*, February 7, 1870.

6. Annie Moffett's account in *MTL4*, ed. Victor Fischer and Michael Frank (Berkeley: University of California Press, 1995), pp. 45–46.

7. Robert Bingham, "Buffalo's Mark Twain," *Buffalo Historical Society Museum Notes 2*, nos. 4–6 (August 1935), p. 10.

8. "Sign on Mark Twain's Door Is Recalled by Old Timer," *Buffalo Courier-Express*, March 8, 1942. This news story recounts William J. Jamison's recollections of having a paper route for the *BME* on Twain's side of Delaware Street.

9. Francis R. Kowsky, "Delaware Avenue: Buffalo, New York," in *The Grand American Avenue 1850–1920*, ed. Jan Cigliano and Sarah Bradford Landau (San Francisco: Pomegranate Artbooks, 1994), p. 55.

10. City and Vicinity, *BME*, August 16, 1869.

11. Richard C. Brown and Bob Watson, *Buffalo: Lake City in Niagara Land* (Woodland Hills, CA: Windsor Publications, 1981), p. 215.

12. James Howard Kunstler, *The Geography of Nowhere* (New York: Touchstone, 1994), p. 52.

13. Kowsky, "Delaware Avenue," p. 44.

14. Edward T. Dunn, *Buffalo's Delaware Avenue Mansions and Families* (Buffalo, NY: Canisius College Press, 2003), p. 198.

15. Architectural historian Martin Wacledo suggests that, because much of Delaware Avenue's landscape has changed radically since Twain's time, twenty-first century visitors should stroll Buffalo's Franklin Street or Park Street, which is directly behind Twain's former house, to capture a more authentic feel of the 1870s neighborhood.

16. SLC and OLC to Jervis and Olivia Lewis Langdon, February 9, 1870, in Fischer and Frank, *MTL4*, p. 66.

17. SLC to Joel Benton, February 20, 1870, in ibid., p. 74.

18. Harriet Elinor Smith and Richard Bucci, eds., *Mark Twain's Letters, Volume 2: 1867–1868* (Berkeley: University of California Press, 1990), p. 311.

19. SLC to Mary Fairbanks, December 12, 1867, in ibid., p. 134.

20. SLC to OL, December 4, 1868, in ibid, p. 305.

21. March 11, 1870, in Fischer and Frank, *MTL4*, p. 91.

22. Suggestion made by Frank Kowsky, personal conversation with the author, autumn 2010.

23. James D. DiLapo Sr., interview with the author, May 11, 1989.

24. Mary Fairbanks, "The Wedding of 'Mark Twain,'" *Cleveland Herald*, February 7, 1870.

25. OLC to Alice Hooker Day, March 17, 1870, MTM, Hartford, CT.

26. Victor Fischer and Michael Frank, eds., *MTL3* (Berkeley: University of California Press, 1992), p. 150.

27. Alan Gribben, *Mark Twain's Library: A Reconstruction* (Boston: G. K. Hall, 1980), pp. 26, 274.

28. DiLapo, interview with the author.

29. Charles Neider, ed., *The Autobiography of Mark Twain* (New York: Harper and Row, 1959), p. 147. The billiards table was donated to the Chemung County Historical Society in 1986. My thanks to Timothy L. Decker, the historical society's curator, for sharing information about the table.

30. Roland R. Benzow, letter to author, March 20, 1989. Other first-hand recollections came from face-to-face exchanges, correspondence, and/or phone conversations in the 1980s, 1990s, and 2000s with James DiLapo, Carl R. Grever, Peter Maher, and Richard Scibilia, each of whom had visited, worked in, or owned the house before it was demolished.

31. SLC to John Fuller, February 8, 1870, in Fischer and Frank, *MTL4*, p. 64.

32. OLC to Langdons, February 12, 1870, in ibid., p. 68.

33. Ibid., p. 71.

34. Mark Twain, *The Innocents Abroad* (Hartford, CT: American Publishing Company, 1887), p. 95.

35. SLC and OLC to Jervis and Olivia Lewis Langdon, April 16 and 17, 1870, in Fischer and Frank, *MTL4*, p. 111.

36. SLC and OLC to Jervis and Olivia Lewis Langdon, in Fischer and Frank, *MTL4*, p. 110.

37. *Elmira Daily Advertiser*, April 11, 1870, in ibid., p. 112.

38. SLC and OLC to Jervis and Olivia Lewis Langdon, June 19, 1870, in ibid., p. 154.

39. Charles M. Underhill, "Recollections of Mark Twain" (unpublished manuscript, written between October 18, 1922, and December 18, 1924).

40. OLC to Mary Fairbanks, in Fischer and Frank, *MTL4*, p. 96.

41. OLC to Alice Hooker Day, March 17, 1870, MTM, Hartford, CT.

42. SLC and OLC to Langdons, March 27, 1870, in Fischer and Frank, *MTL4*, p. 100.

43. Charles A. Brady, *The First Hundred Years: Canisius College* (Buffalo, NY: Holling Press, 1969), p. 63.

44. Mabel Dodge Luhan, *Intimate Memories: Background* (London: Martin Secker, 1933), p. 13.

45. SLC to OL, February 28, 1869, in Fischer and Frank, *MTL3*, p. 126.

46. Ibid.

47. Ibid., p. 117.

48. SLC and OLC to Jervis and Olivia Lewis Langdon, March 27, 1870, in Fischer and Frank, *MTL4*, p. 98.

49. Earl Berry, "Mark Twain as a Newspaperman," *BME*, November 11, 1917.

50. SLC to Redpath, September 15, 1871, in Fischer and Frank, *MTL4*, p. 455.

51. Mark Twain, "Removal of the Capital," *BME*, August 17, 1869.

52. "Mark Twain's Wanderings at an End," *New York Times*, March 31, 1907.

53. SCL to OLC, December 18, 1871, in Fischer and Frank, *MTL4*, p. 517.

54. Ibid., p. 518.

55. Kate Burr, "Meet Mark Twain of Delaware Avenue," *BT*, April 12, 1931, magazine section, p. 2.

56. SLC to Langdons, March 26, 1870, in Fischer and Frank, *MTL4*, p. 99; Johnny Oldboy, "Col. Selkirk Bought Mark Twain's Stock," *BT*, October 11, 1928, p. 23. Ironically, a passerby pulled a fire alarm box at the same corner of Virginia and Delaware at 6:58 p.m. on Thursday, February 8, 1963, to report a fire at Twain's former residence. The building was unoccupied. The fire caused several thousand dollars' worth of damage and the charred remains of the house were soon demolished. See "Mark Twain House Saved from Flames," *Buffalo Courier-Express*, February 8, 1963.

57. Twain, *AMT*, p. 321.

58. SLC to Elisha Bliss Jr., March 3, 1870, in Fischer and Frank, *MTL4*, p. 85.

59. SLC to Jervis Langdon, May 22, 1870, in ibid., p. 138.

60. OLC and SLC to Susan L. Crane, April 16, 1870, in ibid., p. 108.

61. Louis Budd, *Our Mark Twain* (Philadelphia: University of Pennsylvania Press, 1983), p. 44.

62. Delancey Ferguson, *Mark Twain: Man and Legend* (New York: Bobbs-Merrill, 1943), p. 153.

63. Bingham, "Buffalo's Mark Twain," p. 5.

64. Joseph T. Goodman, "Letter to Paine, March 13, 1908," *Twainian* 15 (January–February 1956): 1.

65. SLC and OLC to Jervis and Olivia Lewis Langdon, April 1, 1870, in Fischer and Frank, *MTL4*, p. 104.

66. SLC and OLC to Jervis and Olivia Lewis Langdon, April 16 and 17, 1870, in ibid., p. 110.

67. Nathaniel Gorham, "Link with City's Past Faces Crisis," *Buffalo Courier-Express*, April 26, 1941.

68. OLC to Alice Hooker Day, March 17, 1870, MTM.

69. SLC to Fairbankses, February 13, 1870, in Fischer and Frank, *MTL4*, p. 70.

70. SLC to Langdons, February 20, 1870, in ibid., p. 75.

71. SLC to Howlands, March 6, 1870, in ibid., p. 87.

72. SCL to Langdons, February 9, 1870, in ibid., p. 66.

73. SCL to Langdons, February 9, 1870, in ibid., p. 67.

74. SLC to Langdons, April 16 and 17, 1870, in ibid., p. 110.

75. Jervis Langdon to SLC, March 2, 1870, in ibid., p. 83.

76. SLC and OLC to Olivia Lewis Langdon, February 20, 1870, in ibid., p. 75.

77. Luhan, *Intimate Memories*, pp. 15–16.

78. OLC to Langdons, May 13, 1870, in Fischer and Frank, *MTL4*, p. 129.

79. SLC to Langdons, March 2 and 3, 1870, in ibid., p. 81.

80. SLC to Langdons, June 19, 1870, in ibid., p. 154.

81. Henry Nash Smith, *Mark Twain: The Development of a Writer* (New York: Atheneum, 1967), p. 72.

82. SLC to OL, March 4, 1869, in Fischer and Frank, *MTL3*, pp. 134–35.

83. Mark Twain, *Mark Twain Papers*, holograph manuscript, microfilm edition of Mark Twain's literary manuscripts (Berkeley: Bancroft Library, University of California, 2001).

84. In chapter 51 of *Roughing It*, Twain wrote a parody, "The Aged Pilot Man," of a popular Erie Canal folk song called "The Raging Canal."

85. Bruce R. McElderry Jr., ed., *Contributions to the* Galaxy *1868–1871 by Mark Twain* (Delmar, NY: Scholars' Facsimiles and Reprints, 1977), p. 68.

6. WRITING FOR ENJOYMENT, AS WELL AS PROFIT

1. SLC to Langdons, February 9, 1870, in *MTL4*, ed. Victor Fischer and Michael Frank (Berkeley: University of California Press, 1995), p. 66.

2. SLC to Mary Fairbanks, in ibid., p. 70.

3. SLC to Elisha Bliss Jr., in ibid., p. 77.

4. SLC, "A Wail," sketch, March 1870, MTP.

5. SLC, "A Protest," March 1870, MTP.

6. Mark Twain, "Personal," *BME*, March 7, 1870.

7. "Amusements. Academy of Music," *BME*, August 17, 1869.

8. Kurt Ganzl, *Lydia Thompson: Queen of Burlesque* (New York: Routledge, 2002).

9. Mark Twain, "The Blondes," *BME*, February 28, 1870.

10. Mark Twain, note in *BME*, May 4, 1870.

11. SLC and OLC to Mary Fairbanks, March 22 and 24, 1870, in Fischer and Frank, *MTL4*, p. 95.

12. Mark Twain, "A Mysterious Visit," *BME*, March 19, 1870.

13. Mark Twain, "A Curious Dream. Containing a Moral," *BME*, May 7, 1870.

14. Robert Bingham, "Buffalo's Mark Twain," *Buffalo Historical Society Museum Notes 2*, nos. 4–6 (August 1935), p. 11.

15. Mark Twain, "Street Sprinkling," *BME*, May 27, 1870.

16. Jane Meade Welch, "Helping Mark Twain," *Our Record* 57, no. 6 (September 1925): 277–79.

17. "City Notes," *BME*, May 30, 1870.

18. City and Vicinity, *BME*, May 31, 1870.

19. "Fairy Tale House. One of Generation's Showplaces, Lord Home Recalls Famed Romance, Tales of Children," *BT*, January 1, 1937.

20. Earl Berry, "Mark Twain as a Newspaper Man," *Buffalo Express*, November 11, 1917, p. 11.

21. City and Vicinity, p. 3.

22. Donald K. Schmid, president of the Central Park Men's Club, conversation with the author, April 5, 2011. In May of 2008, Central Presbyterian Church of Buffalo closed its doors and consolidated with the First Presbyterian Church of Buffalo.

23. Mary Helen O'Connell, "Central Presbyterian Had Beginning in Log Cabin," *Buffalo Courier-Express*, May 9, 1943; "Livewire Buffalo Church," *Buffalo Courier-Express*, November 13, 1960.

24. BECHS, unpublished history of Central Presbyterian Church, from file box on John C. Lord.

25. Jane Meade Welch, "In the Library. Another Chapter upon the Treasures of the Late Dr. John C. Lord's Collection," *BDC*, October 4, 1885.

26. Robert A. Foster, "Largely Froth" (unpublished manuscript, January 11, 1982).

27. Mark Twain, "Buffalo Female Academy. Commencement Exercises Last Evening," *BME*, June 24, 1870. Twain's report was embedded in a larger story covering the entire evening's event.

28. Foster, "Largely Froth," p. 9.

29. Tom Reigstad, "Readin', Ritin' and Reformin': Mark Twain Judges Schoolgirl Essays," *The Write Word: Journal of the Western New York Writing Project* (2002–2003): 60–66.

30. SLC to Earl Berry, January 6 or 7, 1871, in Fischer and Frank, *MTL4*, p. 300.

31. "The Orphan's Homestead Concert," *BME*, January 13, 1871.

32. SLC to Elisha Bliss Jr., February 23, 1870, in Fischer and Frank, *MTL4*, p. 77.

33. SLC to Elisha Bliss Jr., March 11, 1870, in ibid., p. 90.

34. SLC to Mary Fairbanks, March 22 and 24, 1870, in ibid., p. 95.

35. SLC to Langdons, April 1, 1870, in ibid., p. 104.

36. SLC and OLC to Mary Fairbanks, May 29, 1870, in ibid., p. 145.

37. September 2, 1870, in ibid., p. 189.

38. SLC and OLC to Langdons, March 27, 1870, in ibid., p. 100.

39. SLC to Orion Clemens, March 11 and 13, 1871, in ibid., p. 349.

40. SLC to Jervis Langdon, May 13, 1870, in ibid., p. 130.

41. This story also was printed in the July *Galaxy*.

42. Earl Berry, "Mark Twain as a Buffalo Editor," *Globe*, April 1873, p. 7.

43. SLC to Elisha Bliss Jr., March 11, 1870, in Fischer and Frank, *MTL4*, p. 91.

44. Bill Loos, personal conversation with the author, June 5, 2012. The portrait is reputed to be the property of Mills's great-grandson living in the Chicago area.

45. SLC and OLC to Langdons, June 9, 1870, in Fischer and Frank, *MTL4*, p. 153.

46. Ibid.

47. Henry G. White, "Reminiscences of Buffalo since 1836," handwritten copy of speech to Buffalo Historical Society, March 29, 1869, from an unpublished manuscript, BECHS.

48. OLC to Langdons, June 19, 1870, in Fischer and Frank, *MTL4*, p. 154.

49. Jervis Langdon to Charley Langdon, May 30, 1870, in ibid., p. 140.

50. SLC to Ellen White, June 11, 1870, in ibid., p. 150.

51. SLC to Mary Fairbanks, June 25, 1870, in ibid., p. 157.

52. Mark Twain, *AMT*, ed. Harriet Elinor Smith (Berkeley: University of California Press, 2010), p. 361.

53. SLC to Elisha Bliss Jr., August 5, 1870, in Fischer and Frank, *MTL4*, p. 180.

54. SLC to Elisha Bliss Jr., August 11, 1870, in ibid., p. 183.

7. TOPPLING PYRAMIDS

1. "The Earthquake," *BDC*, October 21, 1870.

2. Mark Twain, "The Libel Suit," *BME*, October 21, 1870.

3. "The Earthquake in This City," *BDC*, October 24, 1870.

4. Mark Twain, *AMT*, ed. Harriet Elinor Smith (Berkeley: University of California Press, 2010), p. 360.

5. Ibid., p. 363.

6. Susan K. Harris, *The Courtship of Olivia Langdon and Mark Twain* (New York: Cambridge University Press, 1996), p. 138.

7. SLC to Mary Fairbanks, September 2, 1870, in *MTL4*, ed. Victor Fischer and Michael Frank (Berkeley: University of California Press, 1995), p. 189.

8. SLC to Elisha Bliss Jr., September 7, 1870, in ibid., p. 191.

9. SLC to Orion Clemens, September 9, 1870, in ibid., p. 193.

10. Herbert A. Wisbey Jr., "The Tragic Story of Emma Nye," *Mark Twain Society Bulletin* 16, no. 2 (July 1991): 3.

11. Ibid.

12. OLC and SLC to Alice Day Hooker, January 25, 1871, in Fischer and Frank, *MTL4*, p. 312.

13. SLC to Pamela A. Moffett and family per telegraph operator, September 8 and 29, 1870, in ibid., p. 192; Charles Webster, *Mark Twain, Business Man* (Boston: Little, Brown, 1946), pp. 49–50.

14. SLC to Franklin D. Locke, September 24, 1870, in Fischer and Frank, *MTL4*, p. 200.

15. Twain, *AMT*, p. 362.

16. Ibid., p. 363.

17. Kay Redfield Jamison, "Manic-Depressive Illness and Creativity," *Scientific American* (February 1995): 62–67.

18. Fischer and Frank, *MTL4*, p. 199. In February 1871 correspondent Donn Piatt recalled this conversation with Twain.

19. Mark Twain, "First Day. The European War!!!" *BME*, July 25, 1870.

20. David A. Gerber, *The Making of an American Pluralism: Buffalo, New York, 1825–1860* (Urbana: University of Illinois, 1989), p. 163.

21. *Niagara Gazette*, June 16, 1869.

22. A generation later, my maternal grandmother, Katherine Grassle, was one of them. She left the family farm in Germany at the age of sixteen, came to Buffalo, and was hired as a live-in cleaner and cook by a family who lived on the city's west side on Bedford Avenue, off Delaware Avenue.

23. OLC and SLC to Susan L. Crane, April 16, 1870, in Fischer and Frank, *MTL4*, p. 107.

24. Charles A. Brady, *The First Hundred Years: Canisius College 1870—1970* (Buffalo, NY: Holling Press, 1969), p. 54.

25. Mark Twain, "Another Prussian Victory," *BME*, September 7, 1870.

26. Albert Bigelow Paine, *Mark Twain: A Biography*, vol. 1 (New York: Harper and Brothers, 1912), p. 399; Irving Underhill, "Two Excessively Rare Clemens Items," from *First Editions and Autograph Letters and Manuscripts by Famous Modern Authors* (American Art Association Anderson Galleries, 1936) (this is a catalog of an auction sale held January 29–30).

27. "Mark Twain's Map," *BME*, September 24, 1870, p. 1.

28. Twain, *AMT*, pp. 362–63.

29. Mark Twain, "War and 'Wittles,'" *BME*, December 16, 1870.

30. Brady, *First Hundred Years*, p. 64.

31. Owner Samuel G. Cornell was the grandfather of Katharine Cornell, an actress born in Buffalo after Twain moved away, who became one of America's most famous stage performers.

32. "This Day in Buffalo History," *BT*, December 27, 1922; Buffalo City Directory of 1870, p. 164 (Buffalo, NY: Warren, Johnson, 1870).

33. "Somewhat Lengthy," *BDCA*, October 22, 1870.

34. Henry G. White, "Reminiscences of Buffalo since 1836," handwritten copy of speech to Buffalo Historical Society, March 29, 1869, from an unpublished manuscript, BECHS.

35. Jane Meade Welch, "Helping Mark Twain," *Our Record* 57, no. 6 (September 1925): 277–79.

36. James Howard Kunstler, *The Geography of Nowhere* (New York: Touchstone, 1994), p. 35.

37. SLC to Twichells, November 12, 1870, in Fischer and Frank, *MTL4*, p. 237.

38. Twain, *AMT*, p. 362.

39. SLC to Orion Clemens, November 11, 1870, in Fischer and Frank, *MTL4*, p. 230.

40. Alan Gribben, *Mark Twain's Library: A Reconstruction* (Boston: G. K. Hall, 1980), p. 767.

41. SLC to Eunice Ford, November 11, 1870, in Fischer and Frank, *MTL4*, p. 232.

42. Ibid., p. 227. Twain's friend and fellow humorous lecturer Josh Billings was known for an absurdly funny talk on "Milk and Natral Histry."

43. SLC to Joseph Twichell, December 19, 1870, in ibid., p. 275.

44. SLC to Whitelaw Reid, December 26, 1870, in ibid., p. 288.

45. SLC to Charles Henry Webb, November 26, 1870, in ibid., p. 247.

46. SLC to Warren Brigham, December 1, 1870, in ibid., p. 254.

47. "Magazines for March," *BME*, February 21, 1871.

48. Bruce R. McElderry Jr., *Contributions to The* Galaxy *1868–1871 by Mark Twain* (Delmar, NY: Scholars' Facsimiles and Reprints, 1977), p. 131.

49. SLC to Thomas Bailey Aldrich, January 22, 1871, in Fischer and Frank, *MTL4*, p. 305; Martin B. Fried, "The 'Hy Slocum' Controversy," *Buffalo Courier-Express*, May 18, 1969; Martin B. Fried, "Hy Slocum, Carl Byng, and Mark Twain," *Niagara Frontier* 17, no. 3 (Fall 1970): 79–82.

50. "Vicinity Correspondence. Mr. Frank Thorn," *BDC*, February 9, 1876, p. 2.

51. Mark Twain, "Dogberry in Washington," *BME*, December 10, 1870.

52. Evelyn Hawes, *Proud Vision: The History of the Buffalo General Hospital, The First Hundred Years* (New York: Thomas Y. Crowell, 1964), p. 15.

53. OLC to Alice Hooker Day, January 25, 1871, in Fischer and Frank, *MTL4*, p. 311.

54. Victor A. Doyno, "Samuel Clemens as Family Man and Father," in *Constructing Mark Twain*, ed. Laura E. Skandera Trombley and Michael J. Kiskis (Columbia: University of Missouri Press, 2001), pp. 28–49.

55. SLC to Joseph Twichell, December 19, 1870, in Fischer and Frank, *MTL4*, p. 275.

56. SLC to Susan L. Crane, March 14, 1871, in ibid., p. 358.

57. SLC to Joseph H. Twichell, in ibid., p. 275.

58. "Twain's Success Puzzle to His Old Office Boy," *Buffalo Courier-Express*, February 24, 1929.

59. "Fast Driving," *BME*, January 6, 1871.

60. SLC to Whitelaw Reid, February 22, 1871, in Fischer and Frank, *MTL4*, p. 336.

61. SLC to Susan L. Crane, March 14, 1871, in ibid., p. 358.

62. SLC to Elisha Bliss Jr., March 17, 1871, and SLC to Orion Clemens, March 15–18, 1871, in ibid., pp. 363–64.

63. SLC to Elisha Bliss Jr., March 17, 1871, in ibid., p. 366.

64. Twain, *AMT*, p. 363.

65. Bill Loos, phone conversation with the author, August 27, 1997; John H. Conlin, *The Buffalo Club, 1867–1997* (Tonawanda, NY: Sterling Sommer, 1997), p. 9.

66. Robert H. Hirst, presentation at the Buffalo and Erie County Public Library, September 25, 2010; SLC to John Hay, January 6, 1871, in Fischer and Frank, *MTL4*, pp. 299–300.

67. Robert Bingham, "Buffalo's Mark Twain," *Buffalo Historical Society Museum Notes 2*, nos. 4–6 (August 1935): 10.

68. David Fears, ed., *Mark Twain Day by Day, Volume 1, 1835–1885* (Banks, OR: Horizon Micro Publishers, 2008), p. 34.

69. SLC to Orion Clemens, March 4, 1871, in Fischer and Frank, *MTL4*, p. 341.

70. SLC to Elisha Bliss Jr., March 17, 1871, in ibid., p. 365.

71. SLC to John Henry Riley, March 3, 1871, in ibid., p. 337.

EPILOGUE: THIS RENEWAL OF THE OLD TIMES

1. "Twain No Financier," *BME*, July 14, 1895.

2. Charles M. Underhill, "Recollections of Mark Twain" (unpublished manuscript written between October 18, 1922 and December 18, 1924).

3. Irving Underhill, quoted in "The Crow's Nest," by Frederick B. Adams Jr., *Colophon* 1, no. 4 (Spring 1936): 632–36.

4. Underhill, untitled item, pp. 632–36.

5. "Social Topics," *BDC*, July 4, 1886.

6. Mark Twain, "Personal," *BME*, June 23, 1886.

7. Underhill, untitled item, pp. 632–36.

8. Ibid.

9. Charles S. Underhill, "Was the Garden of Eden at Niagara Falls? Mark Twain Said 'Yes,'" *Gleaner* 1, no. 8 (March 1928): 14–19.

10. Tom Reigstad, "Mark Twain and Buffalo in 1901," *Western New York Heritage* 4, no. 1 (Fall 2001): 20–21, 48.

11. Victor Doyno (unpublished manuscript, September 25, 2001).

12. "Mark Twain's Poem," *Buffalo Express*, December 11, 1880.

13. David H. Fears, *Mark Twain Day by Day, Volume 2, 1886–1896* (Banks, OR: Micro Publishers, 2009), pp. 260–63.

14. Alan Gribben, *Mark Twain's Library: A Reconstruction* (Boston: G. K. Hall, 1980), p. 273.

15. Mark Twain, *AMT*, ed. Harriet Elinor Smith (Berkeley: University of California Press, 2010), p. 375.

16. Paul Fatout, *Mark Twain on the Lecture Circuit* (Bloomington: Indiana University Press, 1966), p. 212.

17. "Mark Twain and Cable—Two Distinguished Literateurs at Music Hall," *BT*, December 11, 1884.

18. Ibid.

19. "The Thursday Club," *BDC*, December 14, 1884.

20. Ibid.

21. Arlin Turner, *Mark Twain and George W. Cable* (East Lansing: Michigan State University Press, 1960), p. 69.

22. SLC to OLC, December 12, 1884, MTP.

23. Ralph Dibble, "The Twain Did Meet, Eventually, and Thursday Club Story Began," *Buffalo Evening News*, December 6, 1973.

24. SLC to George Willard Benson, 1883, manuscript box of George W. Benson Collection, BECHS.

25. "The Gilded Age," *BME*, September 8, 1874.

26. SLC to J. N. Larned, November 1, 1900, MTP.

27. Gribben, *Mark Twain's Library*, p. 397.

28. Tom Reigstad, "Literary Treasures Legacy of 19th-Century Falls Man," *Niagara Falls Gazette*, July 23, 1984; James Fraser Gluck to SLC, November 7, 1885, and November 14, 1885, Grosvenor Room, Buffalo and Erie County Public Library.

29. SLC to Joseph J. Albright, July 17, 1874, in *MTL6*, ed. Michael Frank and Elinor Smith (Berkeley: University of California Press, 2002), p. 191.

30. Tom Reigstad, "Harriet Langdon Albright: Olivia Clemens's Buffalo Cousin," *Mark Twain Society Bulletin* 15, no. 1 (January 1992): 1–3.

31. George H. Brownell, "Some Remarks on the 'Letter from the Recording Angel,'" *Twainian* 5 (March–April 1945): 3; Paul Baender, ed., *The Works of Mark Twain: What Is Man?* (Berkeley: University of California Press, 1973), pp. 538–39.

32. SLC to Eunice Ford, November 11, 1870, in *MTL4*, ed. Victor Fischer and Michael Frank (Berkeley: University of California Press, 1995), p. 233.

33. Mark Twain, "Letter from the Recording Angel," in *Report from Paradise* (New York: Harper and Brothers, 1952), p. 94.

34. "Sixty Tons of Coal. The Courier Relief Supply. Most Liberally Aided," *Buffalo Courier*, January 26, 1894.

35. "John J. McWilliams Dies of Pneumonia," *Buffalo Evening News*, June 12, 1912.

36. "A Wonderful Telephone Feat," *Elmira Daily Advertiser*, January 12, 1891; "Put to a New Use. The Long-Distance Telephone for Churches," *Buffalo Express*, January 12 1891.

37. "Buffalo Pioneer Dead," *BT*, February 24, 1928.

38. Anne Emery, "George Urban, Jr., City's Grand Old Man, Observes His 75th Birthday Today," *Buffalo Sunday Times*, July 12, 1925.

39. "Two Related Works of Art?" *The Fence Painter* 7, no. 1 (Spring 1987): 1–4; Lin Salamo and Harriet Elinor Smith, eds., *MTL5* (Berkeley: University of California Press, 1997), p. 99; the

Arnot Art Museum in Elmira, New York, owns Graves's painted plaster bust of Langdon and a bronze-cast version made by the museum with the permission of the Langdon family in the 1960s.

40. Carl Wall, "'The Lilacs,' Gen. Graves' Huge Home, Set an All-Time Record for Hospitality," *BT*, July 8, 1931.

41. Sean Peter Kirst, "Mark Twain and Fredonia, New York," *Mark Twain Society Bulletin* 5, no. 2 (June 1982): 1, 3–5; Elizabeth L. Crocker, "Mark Twain and Fredonia," Yesterdays . . . in and around Pomfret, NY, *Fredonia Censor*, 1963.

42. Original property deed located in Erie County Clerk's office, Old Erie County Hall, Basement Record Room, 92 Franklin Street, Buffalo, New York.

43. Charles J. Langdon to SLC, October 9, 1905, MTP, microfilm collection, Center for Mark Twain Studies, Elmira College.

BIBLIOGRAPHY

"Amusements. Academy of Music." *BME*, August 17, 1869.

"Another Prussian Victory." *BME*, September 7, 1870.

"The Blondes." *BME*, February 28, 1870.

City and Vicinity. *BME*, May 31, 1870.

"City Notes." *BME*, May 30, 1870.

Baender, Paul, ed. *The Works of Mark Twain: What Is Man?* Berkeley: University of California Press, 1973.

Bennett, A. Gordon, *Buffalo Newspapers since 1870*. Buffalo, NY: BECHS, 1974.

Bergengren, Ralph. "The Annals of Our Age-Worn World." *Boston Evening Transcript*, October 25, 1924.

Berry, Earl D. "The Fenian War. Earl D. Berry Writes of the Express in Those Stormy Days." *BME*, January 15, 1896.

———. "Mark Twain as a Buffalo Editor." *Globe: A Magazine of Literary Record and Criticism* 1, no. 1 (April 1873): 6–7.

———. "Mark Twain as a Newspaper Man." *Buffalo Express*, November 11, 1917, sec. 5, p. 40.

Berton, Pierre. *Niagara: A History of the Falls*. Toronto: McClelland and Stewart, 1992.

"Big Thing for Jenkins." *Niagara Gazette*, September 1, 1869.

Bingham, Robert. "Buffalo's Mark Twain." *Buffalo Historical Society Museum Notes* 2, nos. 4–6 (August 1935): 3–15.

Blair, Walter. *Native American Humor, 1800–1900*. New York: HarperCollins College, 1960.

Boewe, Mary. "The Brooks Family: A Biographical Note." *Mark Twain Society Bulletin* 13, no. 2 (July 1990): 5.

Brady, Charles A. *The First Hundred Years: Canisius College 1870–1970*. Buffalo, NY: Holling Press, 1969.

Brown, Richard C., and Bob Watson. *Buffalo: Lake City in Niagara Land*. Buffalo, NY: Windsor Publications, 1981.

Brownell, George H. "Some Remarks on the 'Letter from the Recording Angel.'" *Twainian* 5 (March–April 1945): 3.

Budd, Louis. *Our Mark Twain*. Philadelphia: University of Pennsylvania Press, 1983.

Buffalo City Directory of 1870. Buffalo, NY: Warren, Johnson, 1870.

"Buffalo Female Academy. Commencement Exercises Last Evening." *BME*, June 24, 1870.

"Buffalo Pioneer Dead." *BT*, February 24, 1928.

"Buffalo's Grand Old Man." *Buffalo Courier*, January 25, 1925.

Burr, Kate. "Meet Mark Twain of Delaware Avenue." *BT*, April 12, 1931.

———. "That Famous 'Nameless' with Its Thirteen." *BT*, November 4, 1928.

Burrill, Samuel Potter. "Yesterday, Today, Tomorrow: Twain in Buffalo." *Buffalo Courier-Express*,
    November 11, 1928, sec. 9, pp. 2, 7.

"Change in the Express." *BDC*, September 1, 1869.

"Col. Selkirk, Grand Old Man of Buffalo, Is Still Young Despite 90 Active Years." *Buffalo Courier*,
    January 25, 1925.

"Colonel Selkirk." *BME*, May 19, 1925.

Conlin, John H. *The Buffalo Club, 1867–1997* (Tonawanda, NY: Sterling Sommer, 1997).

Cornwell, E. L., ed. "A Letter from Mark Twain." *Globe* 1, no. 2 (May 1873): 28–29.

Crandall, Francis A. "Voice from Washington." *Buffalo Express*, January 15, 1896, p. 4.

Crocker, Elizabeth L. "Mark Twain and Fredonia." *Fredonia Censor*, 1963.

Dibble, Ralph. "The Twain Did Meet, Eventually, and Thursday Club Story Began." *Buffalo
    Evening News*, December 6, 1973.

Doyno, Victor A. "Samuel Clemens as Family Man and Father." In *Constructing Mark Twain*.
    Edited by Laura E. Skandera and Michael J. Kiskis, pp. 28–49. Columbia: University of
    Missouri Press, 2001.

———. Unpublished manuscript, September 25, 2001.

Dunn, Edward T. *Buffalo's Delaware Avenue: Mansions and Families*. Buffalo, NY: Canisius
    College Press, 2003.

———. *A History of Railroads in Western New York*. Buffalo, NY: Canisius College Press, 2000.

"Earl D. Berry Is Dead." *New York Times*, December 23, 1919, p. 9.

"An Early City Editor: Some of the Experiences of Thomas Kennett." *Buffalo Express*, January 15, 1896.

"The Earthquake." *BDCA*, October 21, 1870.

"The Earthquake in This City." *BDC*, October 24, 1870.

Emery, Anne. "George Urban Jr., City's Grand Old Man, Observes His 75th Birthday Today."
    Buffalo Courier, July 12, 1925.

"Fairy Tale House. One of Generation's Showplaces, Lord Home Recalls Famed Romance, Tales
    of Children." *BT*, January 1, 1937.

"Fast Driving." *BME*, January 6, 1871.

Fatout, Paul. *Mark Twain on the Lecture Circuit*. Bloomington: Indiana University Press, 1966.

Fears, David H. *Mark Twain Day by Day, Volume I: 1835–1885*. Banks, OR: Horizon Micro
    Publishers, 2008.

———. *Mark Twain Day by Day, Volume II: 1886–1896*. Banks, OR: Horizon Micro Publishers,
    2009.

Ferguson, Delancey. *Mark Twain: Man and Legend*. New York: Bobbs-Merrill, 1943.

Fischer, Victor, and Michael Frank, eds. *MTL3*. Berkeley: University of California Press, 1992.

———. *MTL4*. Berkeley: University of California Press, 1995.

Foster, Robert A. "Largely Froth." Unpublished manuscript, January 11, 1982.

"Four Streets Remind Buffalo of Elam R. Jewett." *Buffalo Courier-Express*, June 22, 1941.

Frank, Michael B., and Harriet Elinor Smith., eds. *MTL6*. Berkeley: University of California Press, 2002.

Fried, Martin B. "Hy Slocum, Carl Byng and Mark Twain." *Niagara Frontier* 17 (Autumn 1970): 79–82.

———. "The Hy Slocum Controversy." *Buffalo Courier-Express Magazine*, May 18, 1969, pp. 6–8.

Ganzl, Kurt. *Lydia Thompson: Queen of Burlesque*. New York: Routledge, 2002.

Gerber, David A. *The Making of an American Pluralism: Buffalo, New York, 1825–1860*. Urbana: University of Illinois Press, 1989.

"The Gilded Age." *BME*, September 8, 1874.

Goodman, Joseph T. "Letter to Paine, March 13, 1908." *Twainian* 15 (January–February 1956): 1.

Gorham, Nathaniel. "Link with City's Past Faces Crisis." *Buffalo Courier-Express*, April 26, 1941.

———. "100th Anniversary of Mark Twain's Birth Stirs Memories among Buffalonians Who Knew Him Here." *Buffalo Courier-Express*, December 1, 1935, sec. 7, pp. 1, 5.

Graham, Lloyd. "Blondin: The Hero of Niagara." *American Heritage* (August 1958): 107.

Gribben, Alan. *Mark Twain's Library: A Reconstruction*. Boston: G. K. Hall, 1980.

Harris, Susan K. *The Courtship of Olivia Langdon and Mark Twain*. New York: Cambridge University Press, 1996.

Hawes, Evelyn. *Proud Vision: The History of the Buffalo General Hospital, The First Hundred Years*. New York: Thomas Y. Crowell, 1964.

"It Vanished Like a Dream." *BME*, February 2, 1870.

Jamison, Kay Redfield. "Manic-Depressive Illness and Creativity." *Scientific American* 272, no. 2 (February 1995): 62–67.

"Jewett Homestead." *Buffalo Evening News*, June 12, 1925.

"John J. McWilliams Dies of Pneumonia." *Buffalo Evening News*, June 12, 1912.

Kaplan, Fred. *The Singular Mark Twain: A Biography*. New York: Doubleday, 2003.

Kaplan, Justin. *Mr. Clemens and Mark Twain: A Biography*. New York: Simon and Schuster, 1966.

Kirst, Sean Peter. "Mark Twain and Fredonia, New York." *Mark Twain Society Bulletin* 5, no. 2 (June 1982): 1, 3–8.

Kowsky, Francis. R. "Delaware Avenue: Buffalo, New York." In *The Grand American Avenue 1850–1920*. Edited by Jan Cigliano and Sarah Bradford Landau, pp. 35–63. San Francisco: Pomegranate Books, 1994.

Kunstler, James Howard. *The Geography of Nowhere*. New York: Simon and Schuster, 1993.

Larned, Josephus Nelson. "From J. N. Larned." *BME*, January 15, 1896, p. 1.

———. *Larned's History of the World*. New York: World Syndicate, 1915.

————. *Letters, Poems and Selected Prose Writings of David Gray*. Buffalo, NY: The Courier Company, 1888.

Lawton, Mary. *A Lifetime with Mark Twain*. New York: Brace, 1925.

"A Liberal Gift to the General Hospital." *BME*, August 27, 1869, p. 4.

"Livewire Buffalo Church." *Buffalo Courier-Express*, November 13, 1960.

Long, E. Hudson. *The Mark Twain Handbook*. New York: Hendricks House, 1957.

Lorch, Fred W. "Mark Twain's 'Sandwich Island' Lecture and the Failure at Jamestown, New York, in 1869." *American Literature* 25 (November 1953): 314–25.

————. *The Trouble Begins at Eight: Mark Twain's Lecture Tours*. Ames: Iowa State University Press, 1966.

Loving, Jerome. *Mark Twain: The Adventures of Samuel L. Clemens*. Berkeley: University of California Press, 2010.

Luhan, Mabel Dodge. *Intimate Memories: Background*. London: Martin Secker, 1933.

"Magazines for March." *BME*, February 21, 1871.

"Mark Twain and Cable—Two Distinguished Literateurs at Music Hall." *BT*, December 11, 1884.

"Mark Twain and Niagara." *Niagara Gazette*, August 25, 1869.

"Mark Twain House Saved from Flames." *Buffalo Courier-Express*, February 8, 1963.

"Mark Twain's Map." *BME*, September 24, 1870, p. 1.

"Mark Twain's Poem." *Buffalo Express*, December 11, 1880.

"Mark Twain's Wanderings at an End." *New York Times*, March 31, 1907.

"Mark Twain Years Ago." *New York Times*, April 18, 1909.

McElderry, Bruce R. *Contributions to the* Galaxy *1868–1871 by Mark Twain*. Delmar, NY: Scholars' Facsimiles and Reprints, 1977.

Mills, John Harrison. "When Mark Twain Lived in Buffalo." *Buffalo Sunday Morning News*, May 15, 1910, pp. 13–20.

Munson, Almira Hutchinson. "Details of Langdon-Clemens Wedding Described in Diary." *Mark Twain Society Bulletin* 13, no. 1 (January 1990): 4–5.

Neider, Charles, ed. *The Autobiography of Mark Twain*. New York: Harper and Row, 1959.

"New Year's Presentations." *Buffalo Express*, January 3, 1870.

O'Connell, Mary Helen. "Central Presbyterian Had Beginning in Log Cabin." *Buffalo Courier-Express*, May 9, 1943.

Oldboy, Johnny. "Col. Selkirk Bought Mark Twain's Stock." *BT*, October 11, 1928.

Olmsted, John B. "Josephus Nelson Larned." *Buffalo Historical Society Publications* 19 (1915): 3–33.

O'Neill, Marty. "Mark Twain, Buffalo Editor Who Wielded a Biting Pen." *Buffalo Evening News*, November 29, 1947.

"The Orphan's Homestead Concert." *BME*, January 13, 1871.

Paine, Albert Bigelow. *Mark Twain: A Biography*. Vol. 1. New York: Harper and Brothers, 1912.

Powell, Stephen R. *Rushing the Growler: A History of Brewing in Buffalo*. Buffalo, NY: Digital Print Services, 1996.

"Power Pioneer Dead." *BT*, February 26, 1928.

Powers, Ron. *Mark Twain: A Life*. New York: Free Press, 2005.

"Put to a New Use. The Long-Distance Telephone for Churches." *Buffalo Express*, January 12, 1891.

Reigstad, Tom. "Harriet Langdon Albright: Olivia Clemens's Buffalo Cousin." *Mark Twain Society Bulletin* 15, no. 1 (January 1992): 1–3.

———. "Literary Treasures Legacy of 19th Century Falls Man." *Niagara Falls Gazette*, July 23, 1984.

———. "Mark Twain and Buffalo in 1901." *Western New York Heritage* 4, no. 1 (Fall 2001): 20–21, 48.

———. "Readin', Ritin' and Reformin': Mark Twain Judges Schoolgirl Essays." *The Write Word, 2002–2003*, 60–66.

Salamo, Lin, and Harriet Elinor Smith, eds. *MTL5*. Berkeley: University of California Press, 1997.

Scott, Arthur. *Mark Twain at Large*. Chicago: Henry Regenery, 1969.

"Sixty Tons of Coal. The Courier Relief Supply. Most Liberally Aided." *Buffalo Courier*, January 26, 1894.

Skandera-Trombley, Laura E. *Mark Twain in the Company of Women*. Philadelphia: University of Pennsylvania Press, 1994.

Smith, Henry Nash. *Mark Twain: The Development of a Writer*. New York: Atheneum, 1967.

"Social Topics." *Buffalo Daily Courier*, July 4, 1886.

"Somewhat Lengthy." *BDCA*, October 22, 1870.

"This Day in Buffalo History." *BT*, December 27, 1922.

"The Thursday Club." *BDC*, December 14, 1884.

Turner, Arlin. *Mark Twain and George W. Cable*. East Lansing: Michigan State University Press, 1960.

Twain, Mark. "Around the World: Letter No. 1." *BME*, October 16, 1869.

———. "Arthur." *BME*, September 28, 1869.

———. "At the President's Reception." *BME*, October 1, 1870.

———. *AMT*. Edited by Harriet Elinor Smith. Berkeley: University of California Press, 2010.

———. "Browsing Around." *BME*, November 27 and December 4, 1869.

———. "Civilized Brutality." *BME*, November 20, 1869.

———. "A Curious Dream." *BME*, May 7, 1870.

———. "Dogberry in Washington." *BME*, December 10, 1870.

———. "The Earliest Authentic Mention of Niagara Falls: Extracts from Adam's Diary Translated from the Original MS." In *The Niagara Book*. Edited by Irving Underhill and Walter Nichols. Buffalo, NY: Underhill and Nichols, 1893.

———. "First Day. The European War!!!" *BME*, July 25, 1870.

———. "A Ghost Story." *BME*, January 15, 1870.

———. "A Good Letter. Mark Twain's Idea of It." *BME*, November 10, 1869.

———. "Hanging to Slow Music." *BME*, November 11, 1869.

———. "The Hyenas." *BME*, December 30, 1869.

———. "An Indignant Rebuke." *BME*, December 29, 1869.

———. *The Innocents Abroad*. Hartford, CT: American Publishing, 1887.

———. "The Law of Divorce." *BME*, December 4, 1869.

———. "The Legend of the Capitoline Venus." *BME*, October 23, 1869.

———. "Letter from the Recording Angel." In *Report from Paradise*. New York: Harper and Brothers, 1952.

———. "The Libel Suit." *BME*, October 21, 1870.

———. "Mark Twain in a Fix." *BME*, September 9, 1869.

———. "A Mysterious Visit." *BME*, March 19, 1870.

———. "Only a Nigger." *BME*, August 26, 1869.

———. "The Paraguay Puzzle." *BME*, November 9, 1869.

———. "Personal." *BME*, March 7, 1870.

———. "Removal of the Capital." *BME*, August 17, 1869.

———. "Rev. H. W. Beecher—His Private Habits." *BME*, September 25, 1869.

———. "The Richardson Murder." *BME*, December 3, 1869.

———. "Salutatory." *BME*, August 21, 1869.

———. "Street Sprinkling." *BME*, May 27, 1870.

———. "War and 'Wittles.'" *BME*, December 16, 1870.

"Twain and Cable." *BME*, December 11, 1884.

"Twain No Financier." *BME*, July 14, 1895.

"Twain's Success Puzzle to His Old Office Boy." *Buffalo Courier-Express*, February 24, 1929.

"Two Related Works of Art?" *The Fence Painter* 7, no. 1 (Spring 1987): 1–4.

Underhill, Charles M. "Recollections of Mark Twain." Unpublished manuscript, written between October 18, 1922, and December 18, 1924.

Underhill, Charles S. "Was the Garden of Eden at Niagara Falls? Mark Twain Said 'Yes.'" *Gleaner* 1, no. 8 (March 1928): 14–19.

Underhill, Irving. "Two Excessively Rare Clemens Items." In *First Editions and Autograph Letters and Manuscripts by Famous Modern Authors*, January 29–30, 1936.

———. Untitled item. *Colophon* 1, no. 4 (Spring 1936): 632–36.

United States Government Printing office. *Statistical Abstracts of the United States, 1910* (Washington, DC: US Government Printing Office, 1911).

"Vicinity Correspondence. Mr. Frank Thorn." *BDC*, February 9, 1876, p. 2.

Wall, Carl. "The Lilacs. Gen. Graves' Huge Home, Set an All-Time Record for Hospitality." *BT*, July 8, 1931.

Webster, Samuel Charles. *Mark Twain, Business Man*. Boston: Little, Brown, 1946.

Welch, Jane Meade. "Helping Mark Twain." *Our Record* 57, no. 6 (September 1925): 277–79.

———. "In the Library. Another Chapter upon the Treasures of the Late Dr. John C. Lord's Collection." *BDC*, October 4, 1885.

Welch, Sam. "Sam Welch, Reporter." *Buffalo Express*, January 15, 1896.

"When Mark Twain Was Editor of a Buffalo Newspaper." *New York Times*, June 30, 1912.

White, Henry. "Reminiscences of Buffalo since 1836." Manuscript in BECHS, March 29, 1869.

White, John H. *The American Railroad Passenger Car*. Baltimore: Johns Hopkins University Press, 1978.

Willis, Resa. *Mark and Livy*. New York: Atheneum, 1992.

Wisbey, Herbert A., Jr. "Another Ford Letter Discovered." *Mark Twain Society Bulletin* 18, no. 1 (January 1995): 5–6.

———. "The Tragic Story of Emma Nye." *Mark Twain Society Bulletin* 14, no. 2 (July 1991): 1–4.

"A Wonderful Telephone Feat." *Elmira Daily Advertiser*, January 12, 1891.

INDEX

Academy of Music, 35, 93, 151, 197, 303

Adams and Meldrum, 143

Adventures of Huckleberry Finn (Twain), 15, 77, 145, 189, 195, 199, 292, 299

Adventures of Tom Sawyer, The (Twain), 131, 145, 189, 292

Adirondack Mountains
proposed trip by SLC and OLC, 166

Albany Argus, 103

Albright, Charlotte Spaulding, 26, 190

Albright, Harriet M. Langdon, 18, 26, 190, 200, 309

Albright, John J., 18, 200

Albright, Joseph J., 199, 309

Albright-Knox Art Gallery, 200

Albright, Langdon, 190

Aldrich, Thomas Bailey, 183, 307

Allison, George M., 120

American Publishing Company, 104. *See also* Bliss, Elisa, Jr.

"Another Prussian Victory" (Twain), 306

Anthracite Coal Association, 85, 87, 111, 113, 297

Arabian Nights, The, 120

"Around the World" series (Twain), 95–100, 165, 285

"Arthur" (Twain), 57, 74, 77–78, 297

"At the President's Reception" (Twain), 299

Baender, Paul, 309

Ball, A. M., 114

Barber, Julia Langdon, 200

Barker, Joanna, 108

Barker, Prelate, 108

Barnum, Phineas T., 199

Bazaar Bulletin, 195

"Beautiful Snow," 135

Beckett, Harry, 151

Beecher, Thomas K., 108, 110, 114, 116, 131–32, 172, 201

Bennett, David S., 171

Bennett, Joseph L., 146

Benson, George W., 197, 309

Benton, Joel, 139, 300

Benzow, Roland, 301

Bergtold Bros., 136–37

Berry, Clinton, 51

Berry, Earl D., 10, 16, 43, 51, 53, 54, 64, 65, 70, 71, 78, 82, 104, 105, 151, 163, 166, 290, 291–93, 295–97, 302, 305

Berton, Pierre, 295

Besser, Otto, 53

Billings, Josh, 75, 241, 307

Bills Insider, 22

Bingham, Robert W., 295, 300, 302, 304, 308

Bishop, Coleman E., 134

Blair, Walter, 295

Blake, Amanda, 15

Blanchard, Arthur, 81

Blanchard, Mrs. Kitty, 81

Bliss, Elisha, 36, 38, 48, 139, 150, 163, 165, 169, 181, 185, 187, 302, 304, 305, 307, 308

Blocher Family Memorial, 190

"Blondes, The" (Twain), 150–53, 291, 303

Blondin (Jean Francois Gravelet), 68, 103, 295

Boas, Samuel, 39

Boewe, Mary, 293

Boston Lyceum Bureau, 94, 101

Boston, MA, 103, 107, 231, 235, 257

Bowen, Dennis, 17, 37, 160, 174, 291

Bowen, William, 139, 145–46

Bowen, Mollie, 139

Bowen and Rogers, 17, 37, 160, 174, 291

Brady, Charles A., 26, 301, 306

Brady, Mathew, 167, 185–86

Braun Brothers, 128

Brennan, James, 53, 185

Brigham, Warren L., 182, 292, 307

British Blondes, 35, 63, 74, 150–53, 171, 244, 291, 294, 303

Brooks, Fidele, 60, 293

Brooks, Remsen, 60

Brooks, Henry, 60, 293

Brown, Anna Marsh, 134

Brown, Mrs., 180

"Browsing Around" (Twain), 299

Brush, Alexander, 177

Budd, Louis, 140, 302

Buffalo and Erie County Public Library, 15, 76, 89, 121, 125, 127, 137, 308, 309

Buffalo Business First, 22, 28

Buffalo, NY
 boardinghouse residence of SLC (1869), 81–90
 Delaware Street house
  domestic servants, 116–17, 142–43
  exterior, 114–15, 120–21
  friends and neighbors, 129–43
  interior, 108, 114–16, 122–29
  purchase, 108
  sale, 187
 departure of SLC and OLC, 188
 lecture by SLC, 135–36
Buffalo Club, 18, 188, 307
Buffalo coroner, 159, 183, 294

Buffalo Courier-Express, 21, 25, 28, 295, 296

Buffalo Daily Commercial Advertiser, 35, 36, 39, 78, 105, 171

Buffalo Daily Courier, 35, 39, 51–52, 78, 87, 103, 162, 172, 185, 187, 190, 199

Buffalo Evening News, 21, 128, 290

Buffalo Express
  building, exterior and interior, 30–31, 39–42
  contributions by SLC, 44, 55–79
  history and publication, 37–39
  political stance, 37, 57–58
  publicizes SLC's works, 44
  SLC as editor of
    antipathy for newspaper, 79
    changes made to newspaper, 43–44
    enthusiasm for newspaper, 42–43, 70
  SLC as owner of
    purchase, 31–32, 37, 85, 143
    sale, 49, 187
  staff, 44–45

Buffalo Female Academy, 155, 160–61, 304

"Buffalo Female Academy. Commencement Exercises Last Evening" (Twain), 161–62, 304

Buffalo General Hospital, 87, 184–85, 297, 307

Buffalo Library, 88, 190, 198, 199

Buffalo Normal School, 177

Buffalo Postmaster, 183

Buffalo Public Library, 198

Buffalo street commissioner, 155–57, 183, 185

Buffalo Union Iron Works, 133

Bull, Alexander T., 46, 51, 83

Burke, John J., 157, 294

Burr, Kate, 292, 297, 302

Byng, Carl, 182–83, 307

Byron, George Gordon, 13, 75, 77, 94, 103, 150, 219, 244–45, 247, 250, 251, 252, 254, 261, 267, 269, 271, 296

Cable, George Washington, 196–98, 300, 309

Cahill, J. W., 151

Canisius College, 26, 27, 176–77, 301

Cardiff Giant, 74, 101, 298

Cataract House, 60–61, 191, 193, 293, 294

Celebrated Jumping Frog of Calaveras County, and Other Sketches, 136, 181, 290

Central Presbyterian Church, 47, 83, 159–60, 161, 304

Central Wharf, 117–18, 291

Chemung County Historical Society, 301

Chester, Albert T., 160

Chicago Times, 152

Christian Advocate, 35

Church, Francis P., 163, 165

Church, William, 163, 165

Church and Sons, 30

Cincinnati Red Stockings, 75, 247, 261

"Civilized Brutality" (Twain), 103

Clemens, Clara (SLC's daughter), 190

Clemens, Jane (SLC's mother), 139, 203

Clemens, Langdon (SLC's son)
    birth, 179, 200, 293
    health, 180, 181, 183, 186, 187, 202

Clemens, Olivia Langdon "Livy" (SLC's wife). See Langdon, Olivia

Clemens, Orion (SLC's brother), 48, 165, 180, 185, 188, 305, 307, 308

Clemens, Pamela, 103, 114, 129, 139, 145, 179, 203, 306. See also Moffett, Pamela

Clemens, Samuel (Mark Twain)
    and diamond rush book idea, 182
    and Niagara Falls, 59–70
    and recreation, 84, 86
    and Western New York weather, 136–38
    anti-French feelings of, 174–77
    as property owner in Western New York, 203–205
    boardinghouse life, 81–90
    fatherhood, 179–80, 187
    financial affairs, 187–88
    hardships of lecture circuit, 101–102, 108

Livy's typhoid fever, 184
    marriage, 107–10
    religion
        church and ministerial friendships, 130–31, 133, 157, 159
        turning point as writer, 163–66, 182–83

Cleveland, Grover, 10, 42, 71, 88, 141, 177, 201, 290

Cleveland Herald, 31, 32, 176, 236

Colfax, Schuyler, 106

Commercial Report and Market Review, 35

Concert Hall, 196

Conlin, John H., 27, 308

Connecticut Yankee in King Arthur's Court, A (Twain), 189, 191, 294

Cook, Elihu, 83

Cooper, James Fenimore, 64

Cooper Marble Works, 177

Cornell, Katherine, 306

Cornell, Samuel G., 306

Cornell White Lead Works, 177–78

Cottier and Denton's, 151

Crandall, F. A., 292

Crane, Susan L., 107, 139, 140, 169, 181, 302, 306, 307

Crane, Theodore, 167

Crocker, Elizabeth L., 310

"Curious Dream, A" (Twain), 154, 196, 304

Curtis, George William, 58, 267

"Cuteness," 105

Daily Alta California, 31

"Danger of Lying in Bed, The" (Twain), 183

Daniels, Rodney W., 290

Dart, Joseph, 291

Day, Alice Hooker, 123, 133, 142, 184, 306

"Day at Niagara, A" (Twain), 44, 64, 66, 69, 214, 215, 294

Decker, Timothy L., 301

Delaware, Lackawanna and Western Coal Co., 297

Delaware Park, 16–18, 36, 177

Delaware Street, 9, 12, 16, 17, 18, 20, 78, 108, 113, 114, 116–20, 128, 132, 134, 138, 142, 145–48, 149, 153–55, 157, 160, 171, 172, 175, 177, 178, 179, 180, 184, 185, 187, 188, 300

Demokrat, 35

Dibble, Ralph, 309

Dickens, Charles, 62, 105, 107, 262, 282, 292

Dickie, James, 81

Dickinson, Anna, 10, 102, 131, 244, 266, 299

Dickinson, Leon T., 19

DiLapo, James, Jr., 26, 301

Divin, Alexander, 144

Divin, Amanda, 144

"Dogberry in Washington" (Twain), 183, 307

"Dombrowski," 191, 193

Dorsheimer, William, 117, 171, 294

Douglass, Frederick, 103

Doyno, Victor, 27, 307, 308

Dunkirk, NY, 107, 139, 202

Dunn, Edward T., 300

Ebbitt House, Washington, DC, 185

Edison, Thomas, 201

Ellicott, Joseph, 39

Elmira, NY
    Langdon mansion, 108, 169, 188
    Quarry Farm, 26, 28, 188

Elmira College Center for Mark Twain Studies, 26

Elmira Daily Advertiser, 100, 132, 301, 309

Elmira Female College, 95, 98

Elmira Opera House, 132, 172

Elmira Water Cure, 109, 184

Emerson, Ralph Waldo, 88, 232

"English Festivities. And Minor Matters" (Twain), 66, 68, 69, 216, 217

Erie Canal, 71, 86, 147, 176, 203, 291, 303

Erie Railway, 167, 168

Evening Post, 35

"Experience of the McWilliamses with Membranous Croup" (Twain), 201

"Extracts from Adam's Diary Translated from the Original MS" (Twain), 191, 294

"Facts in the Case of George Fisher, Deceased, The" (Twain), 183

"Facts in the Great Landslide Case, The" (Twain), 165

Fairbanks, Abel, 294

Fairbanks, Mary Mason
    attends SLC's wedding, 109, 114–16, 299
    mentor, "Mother," 96–97, 119, 133, 149, 164, 168, 173, 301–302, 304–305
    visits SLC and OLC, 180

Fargo, William G., 15, 18, 78, 140, 188

Farrar, Chelion M., 118, 196–98

Fears, David, 295, 299, 308

Ferguson, Delancey, 20, 289, 302

Fillmore, Millard, 10, 17, 37, 42, 47, 78, 136, 157, 276–77, 290, 291

"First Authentic Mention of Niagara Falls" (Twain), 193

"First Day, The European War!" (Twain), 306

Fitzsimmons, Bob, 290

Flint and Kent, 143

Ford, Darius R., 94, 95, 98, 167, 298

Ford, Eunice, 109, 181, 183, 307, 309

Forest Lawn Cemetery, 9, 16–18, 27, 28, 111, 154, 157, 190, 205, 289

"Fortifications of Paris, The" (Twain), 174–76

Forty-Ninth Regiment of New York Volunteers, 47

Foster, Robert A., 304

Foster, William E., 81

Franco-Prussian War, 176

Fredonia, NY, 28, 129, 139, 145, 174, 202–203, 310

Freie Press, 35

French, Tom, 138

Fried, Martin B., 25, 307

Fuller, John, 301

Galaxy, 65, 120, 147, 163–65, 176, 182, 183, 305

Ganzl, Kurt, 303

Gatchell, William, 53

Genesee College, 111

Gerber, Charles, 140

Gerber, David A., 306

"Ghost Story, A" (Twain) 296, 298

Gilded Age, The (Twain), 197–98, 309

Gildersleeve, Mrs. C. H., 53

Gillespie, George W., 155, 157

Gillig, Henry, 39

Gleason, Rachel, 109, 184

Globe, 51

Gluck, James Fraser, 199, 309

"Good Letter. Mark Twain's Idea of It, A" (Twain), 103

Goodman, Joseph T., 140

Gordon, Archie, 152

Gorham, Nathaniel, 302

Graham, Lloyd, 295

Grand Army of the Republic (GAR) lecture, 135, 136, 195, 198

Graves, Augusta C. M., 16, 27, 202, 309–10

Graves, John C., 159, 202, 310

Gray, David, 9, 18, 19, 25–26, 28, 51–53, 54, 78, 79, 83, 86, 88–89, 90, 134, 135, 140, 142, 160–62, 166, 172, 185–86, 188, 190, 191, 195–96, 201, 202, 293, 297
Gray, David, Jr., 195, 202
Gray, Martha "Mattie," 18, 53, 89, 134, 135, 136, 140, 142, 166, 172, 191, 195
Greeley, Horace, 75, 123, 241, 242, 251
Greene, McMillan, and Gluck, 199
Grever, Carl R., 301
Gribben, Alan, 301, 307, 308, 309
Guthrie, Ebenezer, 117
Gwinn, J. Morris, 138

Hall, John J., 43, 53
Hall, Nathan, 291
"Hanging to Slow Music" (Twain), 103
Hannibal, MO, 54, 115, 145–46, 173
Harris, Susan K., 300, 305
Harte, Bret, 182
Hartford Courant, 31
Hartford Post, 236
Haven, Solomon G., 291
Hawes, Evelyn, 307
Hay, John, 182, 188, 195, 308
Hawkins, Laura, 145
Hazard and Guthrie, 117
Hazen, John C., 117
Heacock, Grosvenor, 16, 130–33, 159, 163

Henderson, Alexander, 63, 152, 294
Hirst, Robert H., 27, 295, 298, 308
Holliday, Melicent S., 173
Holmes, Oliver Wendell, 42, 123
Hospital of the Sisters of Charity, 184
House, Edward H., 139
"Housekeeping" sketches, unpublished (Twain), 146
Howard and Bunting, 30
Howells, James S., 16, 117
Howells, William Dean, 103, 137, 194
Howland, Louise, 139, 142, 303
Howland, Robert, 139, 142, 303
"Hyenas, The" (Twain), 299

"In Trouble" (Twain), 68, 209–10, 295
"Indignant Rebuke, An" (Twain), 299
"Innocence at Home; Or Hunting a Hero in Washington" (Twain), 105, 281–84
Innocents Abroad, The (Twain), 9, 11, 13, 19, 20, 31, 33, 37, 44, 49, 59, 64, 65, 66, 68, 75, 88, 100, 101, 103, 104, 105–107, 120, 130, 131, 132, 136, 142, 143, 153, 157, 191, 281, 290, 294, 296, 301
Irving, Washington, 197

James, Rick, 15
Jamestown Journal, 93, 134
Jamestown, NY, 93, 102, 108, 134
Jamison, Kay Redfield, 306
Jamison, William, 300
Janes, Henry, 117

Jenkins, Prof. J. F., 62, 68–70, 209, 211–12

Jewett, Elam R., 35–37, 291

J. Langdon and Company, 18, 26, 60–61, 86, 87, 111, 167, 190, 200, 204–205, 297

Johnson, Andrew, 62

Johnston, James N., 16, 53

Johnston, William H., 45–47

Jones, Amanda, 53

"Journalism in Tennessee" (Twain), 77, 147, 150, 218, 295

Kaplan, Fred, 20

Kaplan, Justin, 20, 290, 298

Kavanagh, Patrick B., 27, 289

Kean, Tom, 53

Kelsey, Lillie, 162

Kennett, Thomas, 16, 31–32, 39, 85, 87, 291

Kennett, William, 39

Kibbee, George R., 153

King, Francis, 117

Kinne, Henry M., 120

Kirst, Sean Peter, 310

Kowsky, Frank, 26, 294, 300, 301

Kuhn and Co., 196

Kunstler, James Howard, 116, 300, 307

L. Enos and Company, 81

Lafayette Presbyterian Church, 16, 83, 130–31, 159

Lake Shore and Michigan Southern Railway, 202

Landsittel, W., 53

Langdon, Charles Jervis, 31, 96, 98, 144, 167, 180, 203–204, 294, 305, 310

Langdon, Jervis, 10, 11, 12, 14, 31–32, 37, 60, 84, 85, 87, 98, 99, 107–109, 113–14, 128, 139, 143, 144, 148, 165, 166, 167–69, 172, 173, 178, 200, 203

Langdon, Olivia, 9, 10, 11, 12, 16, 17, 18, 20, 23, 31, 34, 37, 46, 47, 58, 59, 60, 62, 70, 72, 83, 86, 87, 90, 95–96, 101, 102, 103, 106, 107, 108–109, 113–19, 122–26, 128, 129, 130–31, 132–34, 135, 138–43, 144–45, 146, 152, 166, 167–69, 172–73, 174, 175, 178, 179–80, 184–85, 187–88, 190, 191, 192, 195, 197, 200, 201, 202, 203, 290, 291, 292, 293.

Langdon, Olivia Lewis (Olivia's mother), 108, 114, 126, 172, 179, 180, 201

Larned, Frances, 17, 46, 89,

Larned, Josephus N., 10, 17, 45–46, 47, 49, 51–52, 54, 57, 58, 71, 78, 82, 83, 87, 88, 109, 151, 157, 160, 168, 176, 185, 190, 195, 198–99, 292, 297, 309

"Last Words of Great Men, The" (Twain), 73–74

"Latest Novelty—Mental Photographs, The" (Twain), 94

"Law of Divorce, The" (Twain), 299

Lawton, Mary, 299

Leader, George, 53

Lee, Mrs. Andrew, 81

Lee, Philip, 11, 14, 47, 54

"Legend of the Capitolene Venus, The" (Twain), 101, 296, 298

Letchworth, William Pryor, 18, 53

"Letter From the Recording Angel" (Twain), 33, 200, 309

"Lilacs, The," 310

"Little Red Riding Hood," 105–106, 284

Locke, David Ross, 42, 43, 134, 149. *See also* Nasby, Petroleum V.

Locke, Franklin D., 174, 306

Lockport, NY, 72, 134, 135, 145, 146, 151, 159, 223

Long, E. Hudson, 289

Long and Carpenter's Oysters, 30

Loos, Bill, 27, 305, 308

Lorch, Fred W., 293, 298

Lord, John Chase, 18, 47, 157, 159–61, 202, 304

Lord, Mary Elizabeth Johnson, 18, 157–59

Loving, Jerome, 20, 289

Luhan, Mabel Dodge, 134, 143, 302

Lydia Thompson's Burlesque Troupe, 35, 63, 74, 150–53, 171, 244, 291, 294

Lyon and Baker Erie Land Office, 117

Lyon, James S., 88, 117–18

Maher, Peter, 301

Marine Bank, 138

Markham, Pauline, 152

"Mark Twain and Niagara" (Twain), 64–66, 207, 295, 296

"Mark Twain. His Greeting to the California Pioneers of 1849" (Twain), 100

"Mark Twain in a Fix" (Twain), 69, 211

Mark Twain's (Burlesque) Autobiography and First Romance, 181

Martin, George A., 53

Massey, Rose, 151

Mathews, George B., 17, 81, 202, 234, 297

Matthews, James N., 171, 234

Maurois, Andre, 116

McAleer, Patrick, 115, 116, 130, 138–39, 168

McArthur's, 136

McClelland, George, 62

McCoole, Mike, 35, 265

McElderry, Bruce R., Jr., 295, 303, 307

McFarland, Daniel, 103

McKinley, William, 201

McWilliams, Esther, 10, 19, 84, 85–86, 201

McWilliams, John J., 10, 19, 22, 27, 84–86, 88, 90, 113–14, 200–201, 297, 309

"McWilliamses and the Burglar Alarm, The" (Twain), 201

"Memoranda" (Twain), 163–64, 182

Mercantile Library Association, 93

Mercersburg Academy, 297

Mills, John Harrison, 10, 49–50, 52, 54, 69, 74, 77, 83, 166, 213–19, 290, 292, 293, 295, 296, 297, 298, 299, 305

Moffett, Annie, 103, 109, 114, 129, 299, 300

Moffett, Pamela Clemens (SLC's sister), 103, 109, 114, 129, 139, 203, 306

Moffett, Sammy, 139

"'Monopoly' Speaks, The" (Twain), 87

"More Distinction" (Twain), 159

"More Texans," 104

"Mrs. McWilliams and the Lightning" (Twain), 201

"My Watch—An Instructive Little Tale" (Twain), 183

"Mysterious Visit, A" (Twain), 153

Nameless Club, 10, 16, 18, 46, 48, 52–53, 88–90, 135, 188, 297

"Napoleon and Abdul" (Twain), 44

Nasby, Petroleum V., 42, 43, 134, 149

Neider, Charles, 301

Newman, William C., 117

"New Year's Presentations," 104, 292

New York Central Railroad, 109, 203

New York City, 36, 60, 86, 101, 102, 107, 108, 120, 123, 181, 184, 190, 195, 197, 202

New York Sun, 199, 256

New York Times, 51, 190

New York Tribune, 31, 242, 182

Niagara and Plimpton elevator, 77

Niagara Book, The, 193–95, 295

Niagara Falls Gazette, 22, 62, 64, 66, 69, 87, 174, 207, 295–96, 306

Niagara Falls Public Library, 23

Niagara Lithograph Company, 201

Noe, J., 39

North Street Cemetery, 154–55, 196

Norwood stables, 190

Nye, Emma, 172–74, 305

"Oakwood," 157, 159

O'Baldwin, Ned, 35

O'Connell, Mary Helen, 304

Olmsted, Frederick Law, 16, 36, 172, 294

O'Neill, Marty, 289, 290

"Only a Nigger" (Twain), 77, 296

Opera House, 35, 132, 172

Orchard Park, NY, 183

Paige, Edward H., 84, 297

Paine, Albert Bigelow, 9, 19–20, 289, 292, 293, 306

"Paraguay Puzzle, The" (Twain), 103

Park Church, Elmira, NY (Independent Congregational Church), 88, 201

Parke, Mrs. J. B., 195

Patti, Adelina, 266–67, 290

Peabody, William, 117

Pennsylvania Northern Central Railroad, 109

"People and Things" (Twain), 44, 57, 60, 71–75, 150, 151, 153, 231–73, 296

Pierce and Company Lumber, 290

Pierce and Polley Livery Stable, 83

Pike County Ballads, 182

Pittsburgh, PA, 93, 101

Pittston and Elmira Coal Company, 297

Plogsted, Louis H., 291

Polhemus, Mrs. Josephine, 60

"Police Court," 44, 70–71, 75, 221–29, 233, 295, 296

"Political Economy" (Twain), 147–48

Post and Viergiver, 30

Powell, Lillie W., 161

Power, Bessie, 151

Prince and the Pauper, The (Twain), 189, 195

"Protest, A" (Twain), 151

Quaker City, 31, 96, 106, 132

Quarry Farm, 26, 28, 188

Randall, Mrs. J. C., 11, 81–84, 90, 146

Raymond, John, 42, 197

Red Jacket, 64

Redpath, James, 94, 198, 234, 299, 302

Reid, Whitelaw, 182, 295, 307

Reigstad, Lucas, 198

Reigstad, Maryanne, 5, 18, 292

Reigstad, Tom, 9, 11, 13, 14, 295, 304, 308, 309

"Removal of the Capital" (Twain), 136, 151

Revenue Record, 154

Richardson, Albert, 103

Richardson, Henry Hobson, 118, 294

"Richardson Murder, The" (Twain), 103, 299

Riley, John Henry, 181–82, 188, 308

Rochester, NY, 13, 65, 66, 111, 254, 272

Rogers, Henry, 136

Rogers, Henry Huttleson, 201

Rogers, Sherman S., 17, 37, 160, 174, 291

Root, Adrian R., 153

Roughing It (Twain), 9, 10, 13, 14, 53, 74, 99, 165, 174, 181, 189, 195, 303

"Running for Governor" (Twain), 183

Salisbury, Guy H., 89

"Salutatory" (Twain), 44, 58–59

Samson, Azuba, 99

Sayles, Emma, 60, 139, 167, 293

Sayles, Henry, 60, 167, 293

Schmid, Donald K., 304

Scibilia, Richard, 301

Scott, Arthur L., 20

Sears, S. Burrell, 117

Second Battle of Bull Run, 49

Selkirk, Charles, 86

Selkirk, Emily, 17, 33, 48, 133

Selkirk, George H., 10, 17, 47–49, 52, 53, 54, 78, 86, 88, 89, 101, 103, 159–60, 165, 187, 190, 202, 292, 302

Selkirk, John H., 47, 86

Sheldon, Grace Carew, 293
Simson, Andrew, 16, 84
"1601" (Twain), 195
Skandera Trombley, Laura E., 54, 307
Sketches New and Old (Twain), 154, 296
Slee, Emma, 18, 28, 107, 111, 129, 133
Slee, Jay, 88
Slee, John De La Fletcher, 18, 84–85,
    86–88, 90, 94, 197, 108, 110,
    111–14, 129, 133, 144–45, 167,
    172, 191, 297, 298
Slocum, Hy, 183, 269, 273, 307
Slote, Daniel, 106
Smith, Col. H. M., 99
Smith, Henry Nash, 303
Smith, Mary L., 187
Smith, William Sooy, 89
Spaulding, Alice, 95, 96, 139, 173
Spaulding, Clara, 95, 96, 139, 173
Spaulding, Samuel S., 190
St. Gaudens, Augustus, 49, 202
St. James Hall, 10, 48, 88, 102, 135
St. John's Episcopal Church, 30, 83
St. Nicholas Hotel, 86, 107
Stambach, Peter C., 117
Stanton, Edwin, 103
Sternberg, Charles F., 118, 120
Stillson, Jerome, 53
Storey, Wilbur, 30, 39, 152
Stowe, Harriet Beecher, 13, 75, 77,
    103, 149, 150, 244, 249, 252, 254,
    267, 271
"Street Sprinkling" (Twain), 155–57,
    183, 304

Sullivan, John L., 290
SUNY at Buffalo, 15
SUNY College at Buffalo, 22, 23, 25,
    27, 234

"Tale: For Struggling Young Poets,
    A," (Twain), 195
Thompson, Lydia, 35, 63, 151–52,
    291, 294
Thorn, Frank M., 183, 307
"Those Texas Steers," 104
"Three Aces," 182–83
Thursday Club, 196–98, 309
"Ticket—Explanation, The" (Twain),
    58
Tillinghast, James, 109
Tiphaine, Victor L., 17, 39, 89–90
Tifft, George, 290
Tifft House, 32–33, 77–78, 113–14,
    116, 158, 276, 290
Toledo Blade, 43
Townsend, George Alfred, 185–86
Turner, Arlin, 309
Tyler, Hattie Marsh, 134
Twain, Mark. *See* Clemens, Samuel.
Twenty-First New York Volunteer
    Regiment, 49
Twichell, Joe H., 108, 119, 129–30,
    133, 142, 179, 181, 307

Underground Railroad, 37, 133
Underhill, Anna, 18, 111, 129, 190,
    192
Underhill, Charles M., 18, 84, 111–

14, 129, 190–93, 195, 293, 297, 301, 308
Underhill, Charles S., 25, 308
Underhill, Irving, 18, 191, 193–95, 295, 306, 308
Urban, George, Jr., 201–202, 309

Van Buren Point, 203
Vanderbilt, Cornelius, 62, 74, 237, 244, 245, 261, 267, 270, 296
Vanderpoel, Isaac V., 44, 70–71, 221, 222–23, 224–25, 226–28, 295
Virginia City Territorial Enterprise, 55, 165

Wadsworth, Mrs. Charles, 133
Wadsworth, Emily Marshall, 18, 133
Wadsworth, George, 18, 133
"Wail, A" (Twain), 151
Wall, Carl, 310
"War and Wittles" (Twain), 29
Wardell, Francis, 53
Warner, Charles Dudley, 197, 300
Warren, James D., 171
Washington Baptist Church, 83
Washington, DC, 166, 167, 168
Watson, John Whitaker, 135
Wayland, John, 53
Weathersby, Eliza, 151
Webb, Charles Henry, 181, 290, 307
Weber and Fields, 290
Webster, Charles, 306
Welch, Jane Meade, 18, 154–55, 161, 178, 304, 306

Welch, Tom, 156
Wells, Henry, 159
Western New York Poultry Society, 158
Western New York Press Club, 36
Westminster Presbyterian Church, 132
W. H. Glenny, Son and Company, 143
Wheeler, George W., 196
White, Ellen, 116, 123, 134, 143, 168, 305
White, Erskine N., 132
White, Henry G., 166, 178, 305–306
White, John H., Jr., 300
White, Mrs. Henry G., 166
Whittier, John Greenleaf, 180
Wilcox, Chester A., 53
Wilcox, Horace, 53
"Wild Cattle," 104
"Wild Man Interviewed, The" (Twain), 77, 150, 295
William E. Storey's Liquors and Bitters, 30, 39
Willis, Resa, 299
"Willow Lawn," 36–37
Wilson, Peter, 89
Wisbey, Herbert A., Jr., 25, 298, 305
Wright, Andrew R., 17, 173, 179, 181, 184
Wyckoff, Cornelius Cox, 17, 117, 119, 184

Young, Brigham, 13, 74, 176, 247, 267

Young Men's Association, 45, 46, 88–89, 188, 198, 199

Young's Hotel, 103

Ziegele, Albert, 174